Kotlin for Java Developers

Confidently transition from Java to Kotlin through hands-on examples and idiomatic Kotlin practices

José Dimas Luján Castillo
Ron Veen

<packt>

Kotlin for Java Developers

Portfolio Director: Kunal Chaudhary
Relationship Lead: Rithika Shetty
Project Manager: Ashwin Dinesh Kharwa
Content Engineer: Sujata Tripathi
Technical Editor: Irfa Ansari
Copy Editor: Safis Editing
Indexer: Rekha Nair
Proofreader: Sujata Tripathi
Production Designer: Ponraj Dhandhapani
Growth Lead: Vinishka Kalra

First published: October 2025

Production reference: 1171025

Published by Packt Publishing Ltd.
Grosvenor House
11 St Paul's Square
Birmingham
B3 1RB, UK.

ISBN 978-1-83588-482-9

www.packtpub.com

To my wife and daughter, who have been an essential part of this journey and a constant source of joy, your love and support make every challenge worthwhile.

To my parents, for their unwavering belief in the value of education and for investing in the learning of their children – your dedication has shaped my path.

And to my grandmother, who was still with us when I started writing this book but is no longer here to see it completed. A warm embrace to her memory.

– José Dimas Luján Castillo

To Wendy and Penny for being as amazing as they are!!

– Ron Veen

Contributors

About the authors

José Dimas Luján Castillo is a software developer with 20 years of experience in backend and mobile development. He has worked both as an engineer and a manager, leading teams on projects ranging from small apps to enterprise systems. His career spans multiple American companies, where he has contributed both as a developer and a technical leader.

His main interests include optimizing software development with best practices and emerging technologies such as blockchain and artificial intelligence. He specializes in Java, Kotlin, and Rust.

Beyond coding, he is passionate about mentorship, guiding students on their learning journeys. He values these interactions, as they allow him to give back to the community while continuing to grow as a developer.

I want to thank the people who have been close to me, especially my wife, my daughter, and my parents.

Ron Veen is a seasoned software engineer with extensive experience ranging from microservices to mainframes. His passion for software engineering and architecture has been his guiding force throughout his career. With over 20 years of expertise in the JVM and the Java ecosystem, Ron is an **Oracle Certified Java Programmer** (**OCP**) and a certified **Sun Business Component Developer** (**SCBCD/OCPBCD**). A dedicated Java enthusiast, Ron also has a keen interest in alternative JVM languages, particularly Kotlin. At Team Rockstars IT, he serves as a special agent and lead developer, frequently speaking at international conferences. Ron is the author of books on Java Cloud-native migrations with Jakarta EE and on virtual threads, structured concurrency, and scoped values.

About the reviewers

Mikhail Stepanov is a staff software engineer at RingCentral Spain, recognized for his expertise in building and scaling high-load distributed systems. He began actively using Kotlin even before version 1.0 and has been at the forefront of modern JVM development.

With over 15 years of experience, Mikhail has designed, developed, and optimized full-cycle technical solutions across diverse domains, including blockchain, machine learning, AI, and distributed systems using Java, Kotlin, and Spring technologies. He is an active speaker at corporate meetups and technical conferences.

Mikhail thrives on staying at the cutting edge of technology, actively exploring innovations not only within the Java ecosystem but beyond it, to adopt best practices and sharpen his skills. He applies these new capabilities through his own start-ups.

You can follow Mikhail's career and creative journey on LinkedIn at *stepanovmixail*.

I want to thank my wife for her support and faith in me. I also want to thank my daughter for her smiles, which warmed my heart and gave me the strength to continue my work.

Venkata C. Thota is a U.S. Bank enterprise solution architect and an Azure Certified Solutions Architect with a passion for artificial intelligence, machine learning, and GraphQL technologies. He holds a postgraduate diploma in AI/ML from Austin University and is recognized as a GraphQL **Subject Matter Expert** (**SME**).

He is an experienced mentor and judge at global recognition programs such as the Stevie Awards and Globee Awards. He is also an active contributor to the GraphQL community, having published numerous articles focused on modern API architectures and schema design practices. With over 25 years of experience as a technical architect and technology leader, Venkata has a proven track record of proposing scalable technical designs, reviewing enterprise-grade solutions, and leading complex digital transformations across both cloud and on-premises environments.

His expertise spans enterprise integration, API management, cloud strategy, and solution governance, with a strong focus on aligning technology initiatives to business strategy. Known for his leadership and mentorship, Venkata effectively guides teams in implementing enhancements, resolving technical challenges, and ensuring adherence to industry standards and best practices.

Table of Contents

Chapter 9: Lambda 217

Chapter 10: Collections and Sequences 247

Part IV: Coroutines, Testing and DSLs 277

Chapter 11: Coroutines 279

Chapter 12: Synchronous and Asynchronous Programming 301

Preface

Hello there! Kotlin has rapidly become one of the most powerful and versatile programming languages in the modern development landscape. Originally designed to be fully interoperable with Java, Kotlin brings expressive syntax, enhanced safety features, and functional programming capabilities that significantly improve the development experience. Whether you're working with Android, backend services, or even multi-platform applications, Kotlin offers a more concise and efficient way to write code while maintaining compatibility with existing Java projects.

There are three key aspects that make Kotlin a compelling choice for Java developers:

- **Interoperability and seamless transition**: Kotlin allows developers to use existing Java code without friction, ensuring an easy adoption process.
- **Conciseness and expressiveness**: It reduces boilerplate and enhances readability, making code more maintainable.
- **Advanced features and modern paradigms**: It introduces functional programming capabilities, coroutines for concurrency, and enhanced type safety mechanisms.

Many resources introduce Kotlin from scratch, but this book takes a different approach. It is specifically crafted for Java developers who want to leverage their existing knowledge to master Kotlin efficiently. Instead of simply listing syntax differences, this book highlights key areas where Kotlin improves upon Java, offering practical insights on how to transition, optimize, and modernize your development practices.

This book will take you through this journey using two main sources of knowledge:

- Our extensive experience in Java and Kotlin development, along with years of teaching both languages to developers.
- Best practices and industry insights, ensuring that you not only learn Kotlin but also understand how to use it effectively in real-world scenarios.

According to industry trends, Kotlin adoption continues to grow across multiple domains, particularly in Android development and server-side applications. Companies are increasingly migrating from Java to Kotlin due to its advantages in safety, conciseness, and performance. This transition creates a high demand for Kotlin-skilled developers who can bridge the gap between legacy Java systems and modern Kotlin implementations.

If you are a Java developer looking to elevate your coding experience, write cleaner and more expressive code, and expand your career opportunities, this book is your ultimate guide. We hope to help you discover a new level of development potential as we embark on this exciting journey into Kotlin together!

Who this book is for

Kotlin is a powerful and modern language designed to enhance Java development by making code more concise, safe, and expressive. This book is intended for Java developers who want to transition to Kotlin efficiently while leveraging their existing Java knowledge. Instead of starting from scratch, this book helps readers map their Java skills to Kotlin and adopt best practices for writing idiomatic Kotlin code.

The three primary audiences for this book are as follows:

- **Java developers**: Experienced Java programmers who want to explore Kotlin without having to discard their existing knowledge. This book provides a structured way to compare Java and Kotlin features, enabling a smooth transition.
- **Android developers with Java experience**: Developers working with Java in Android applications who need to adopt Kotlin, following best practices and maximizing code efficiency.
- **Backend developers working with Java frameworks**: Engineers who use Spring, Jakarta EE, or other Java-based frameworks and want to integrate Kotlin into their projects for more readable and maintainable code.

This book aims to equip you with practical knowledge to write idiomatic Kotlin code, understand key differences from Java, and improve productivity using Kotlin's modern features. Whether you are looking to modernize your Java applications or fully transition to Kotlin, this book serves as a comprehensive guide tailored specifically for Java developers.

What this book covers

Chapter 1, An *Introduction to Kotlin and Its Basic Types*, introduces Kotlin as a modern programming language and highlights its key advantages over Java. It covers the fundamental types in Kotlin, explains type inference, and discusses how Kotlin handles primitive types differently from Java. The chapter sets the foundation for understanding the language while maintaining a Java-friendly perspective.

Chapter 2, *Interoperability, Gradle, and Maven*, covers interoperability with Java, which is one of Kotlin's most significant strengths. It explains how Kotlin and Java coexist, including calling Java code from Kotlin, and vice versa. It also covers how Kotlin integrates with build tools such as Gradle and Maven, ensuring a smooth transition for Java developers working with existing projects.

Chapter 3, Null and Non-Nullable Types, discusses one of the biggest improvements Kotlin introduces: its null safety mechanism. It dives into how Kotlin eliminates `NullPointerException` risks through nullable and non-nullable types. It also covers safe calls, the Elvis operator, and other null-handling techniques, helping Java developers understand how to avoid common pitfalls.

Chapter 4, Extension Functions and the Apply Function, explains the ways in which Kotlin allows developers to extend the functionality of existing classes without modifying them. It explores extension functions, companion object extensions, and how to use the `apply` function to improve code readability and conciseness.

Chapter 5, Object-Oriented Programming Basics, covers OOP principles in Kotlin, explaining how classes, interfaces, and visibility modifiers work compared to Java. It also introduces constructors, properties, and getter/setter methods, showing how Kotlin simplifies common OOP patterns.

Chapter 6, Generics and Variance, explores generics, which are crucial for writing reusable and type-safe code. This chapter explains generic classes, functions, and reified types, while also addressing variance modifiers (`in` and `out`) and how they compare to Java's wildcard types.

Chapter 7, Data and Sealed Classes, talks about the data classes that Kotlin introduces to reduce boilerplate code for modeling immutable data structures. It explains their benefits, along with sealed classes, which provide a more expressive alternative to enums for handling restricted hierarchies.

Chapter 8, Basics of Functional Programming, explains how functional programming is a core feature of Kotlin. It covers higher-order functions, inline functions, and includes their translation into Java bytecode.

Chapter 9, Lambda, covers Kotlin's lambda expressions and function types, which enhance code flexibility. It explains how to use lambdas, anonymous functions, and function receivers to simplify operations on collections and improve code readability.

Chapter 10, Collections and Sequences, discusses collections in Kotlin, which introduce significant improvements over Java's Collections framework. It covers lists, sets, maps, functional transformations (`map`, `filter`, and `reduce`), and the use of sequences for lazy evaluation, optimizing performance in large datasets.

Chapter 11, Coroutines, explores Kotlin's coroutines, which provide a structured way to write asynchronous code without callbacks. It explains coroutines, dispatchers, scopes, and structured concurrency, making it easier for Java developers to transition from traditional threading models.

Chapter 12, Synchronous and Asynchronous Programming, explains how synchronous and asynchronous programming is different from each other in detail. This chapter will also cover exception handling in the asynchronous context, a critical aspect that significantly differentiates it from traditional error handling.

Chapter 13, Kotlin Testing, explains how testing is crucial in software development. It introduces unit testing and integration testing, and provides a quick overview of test frameworks such as JUnit and Kotest.

Chapter 14, Domain-Specific Languages in Kotlin, introduces **domain-specific languages** (**DSLs**) and shows how Kotlin's features, such as lambdas with receivers and extension functions, make it ideal for building internal DSLs. Using a `Book` model, we explore how to design a type-safe DSL, enhance it with optional features, and discuss its benefits and trade-offs.

To get the most out of this book

To fully benefit from this book, you should have a basic understanding of Java programming and familiarity with its core principles, such as object-oriented programming, collections, and exception handling. While you don't need to be an expert, having hands-on experience with Java will make it easier to understand the concepts presented in Kotlin and how they relate to Java's features.

Additionally, familiarity with build tools such as Gradle or Maven and a general understanding of modern software development practices, such as testing and version control, will enhance your experience as you explore Kotlin's unique capabilities. If you're transitioning from Java, this book is designed to help you map your existing knowledge to Kotlin, guiding you every step of the way.

Software/hardware covered in the book	OS requirements
Kotlin Compiler	Windows, Mac OS X, and Linux (any)
IntelliJ IDEA	Windows, Mac OS X, and Linux (any)
Gradle	Windows, Mac OS X, and Linux (any)
Java Development Kit (JDK)	Windows, Mac OS X, and Linux (any)

While Kotlin 2.0 is not mandatory, it is highly recommended to use the latest version to take full advantage of Kotlin's modern features and improvements. This ensures compatibility with new tools, libraries, and enhanced language capabilities that may be referenced in this book.

Download the example code files

The code bundle for the book is hosted on GitHub at `https://github.com/PacktPublishing/Kotlin-for-Java-Developers`. We also have other code bundles from our rich catalog of books and videos available at `https://github.com/PacktPublishing`. Check them out!

Download the color images

We also provide a PDF file that has color images of the screenshots/diagrams used in this book. You can download it here: `https://packt.link/gbp/9781835884829`.

Conventions used

There are a number of text conventions used throughout this book.

`CodeInText`: Indicates code words in text, database table names, folder names, filenames, file extensions, pathnames, dummy URLs, user input, and X/Twitter handles. For example: "Say we want to know whether a certain `String` value is a palindrome."

A block of code is set as follows:

```
fun String.isPalindrome() =  this.reversed().equals(this, true)

fun main() {
    println("Hello, world!!!".isPalindrome())
    println("Anna".isPalindrome())

}
```

When we wish to draw your attention to a particular part of a code block, the relevant lines or items are set in bold:

```
class MyClass {

    fun printString(){
        println("Just a new String")
    }
}
```

Any command-line input or output is written as follows:

```
Just a new String
```

Warnings or important notes appear like this.

Tips and tricks appear like this.

Get in touch

Feedback from our readers is always welcome.

General feedback: If you have questions about any aspect of this book or have any general feedback, please email us at `customercare@packt.com` and mention the book's title in the subject of your message.

Errata: Although we have taken every care to ensure the accuracy of our content, mistakes do happen. If you have found a mistake in this book, we would be grateful if you reported this to us. Please visit `http://www.packt.com/submit-errata`, click **Submit Errata**, and fill in the form.

Piracy: If you come across any illegal copies of our works in any form on the internet, we would be grateful if you would provide us with the location address or website name. Please contact us at `copyright@packt.com` with a link to the material.

If you are interested in becoming an author: If there is a topic that you have expertise in and you are interested in either writing or contributing to a book, please visit `http://authors.packt.com/`.

Share your thoughts

Once you've read *Kotlin for Java Developers*, we'd love to hear your thoughts! Scan the QR code below to go straight to the Amazon review page for this book and share your feedback.

`https://packt.link/r/1835884830`

Your review is important to us and the tech community and will help us make sure we're delivering excellent quality content.

Join us on Discord!

Read this book alongside other users, developers, experts, and the author himself.

Ask questions, provide solutions to other readers, chat with the authors via Ask Me Anything sessions, and much more. Scan the QR or visit the link to join the community.

`https://packt.link/deep-engineering-java`

Part 1

Getting Started with Kotlin

In this part, you will be introduced to the fundamental aspects of Kotlin, from its core syntax and basic types to its seamless interoperability with Java and the essential tools for managing Kotlin projects. You will explore how Kotlin enhances type safety with its nullability system, effectively eliminating `NullPointerException` issues through nullable and non-nullable types, safe calls, and the Elvis operator. Additionally, you will learn about extension functions, a powerful feature that allows you to add functionality to existing classes without modifying their source code, and the `apply` function, which simplifies object configuration and enhances code readability. By the end of this part, you will have a strong foundation in Kotlin's key features, allowing you to write more concise, expressive, and maintainable code.

This part has the following chapters:

- *Chapter 1*, An *Introduction to Kotlin and Its Basic Types*
- *Chapter 2*, *Interoperability, Gradle, and Maven*
- *Chapter 3*, *Null and Non-Nullable Types*
- *Chapter 4*, *Extension Functions and the Apply Function*

1

An Introduction to Kotlin and Its Basic Types

In this chapter, we will look at the relationship between **Kotlin** and **Java**. We will study the basic elements of Kotlin, such as some types, and we will go through some recommendations to consider if you are starting with this language, and leverage your previous experience with Java to help you master Kotlin.

Before delving into the technical content, this chapter will highlight the strong points of Kotlin. We will explain why references to general elements of Java are necessary, covering not just new or old versions, but also providing a comprehensive view. The book will maintain a neutral tone, avoiding negative comparisons between languages. Our focus will be on the technical elements of both languages to optimize your prior knowledge of Java. We aim to introduce you to the world of Kotlin in a pleasant and engaging manner, explaining the dynamics of the book and studying the types available in Kotlin.

Kotlin offers several advantages over Java, including enhanced readability, reduced boilerplate code, and more powerful features such as null safety, extension functions, and coroutines for asynchronous programming. These features not only make Kotlin a more modern and expressive language but also improve developer productivity and code quality.

By the end of this chapter, you will have a solid understanding of why Kotlin is an exciting and powerful language worth learning. You will see how your Java skills can be directly applied to Kotlin and begin to appreciate the enhancements that Kotlin offers. This foundation will prepare you for the more advanced topics covered in subsequent chapters, ensuring a smooth and enjoyable learning journey.

As we dive into the basics of Kotlin, we will cover essential types to consider when starting with this language. By understanding these fundamentals, you will be able to seamlessly transition from Java to Kotlin and harness its full potential. This chapter aims to provide a solid foundation.

In this chapter, we're going to cover the following main topics:

- Looking at the origin
- Relationship between Java and Kotlin
- Types available in Kotlin

Getting the most out of this book – get to know your free benefits

Unlock exclusive **free** benefits that come with your purchase, thoughtfully crafted to supercharge your learning journey and help you learn without limits.

Here's a quick overview of what you get with this book:

Next-gen reader

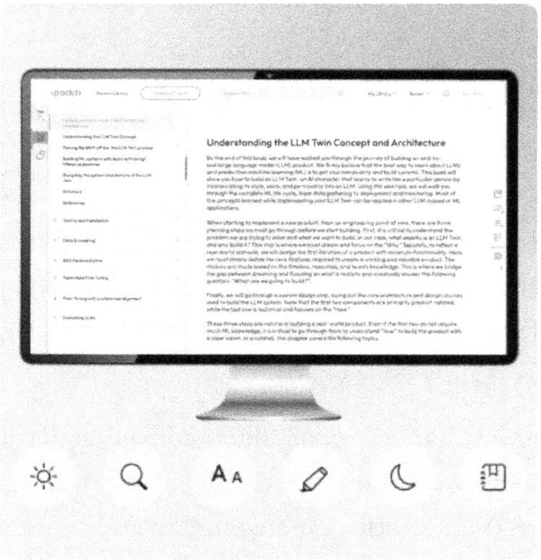

Figure 1.1 – Illustration of the next-gen Packt Reader's features

Our web-based reader, designed to help you learn effectively, comes with the following features:

Multi-device progress sync: Learn from any device with seamless progress sync.

Highlighting and notetaking: Turn your reading into lasting knowledge.

Bookmarking: Revisit your most important learnings anytime.

Dark mode: Focus with minimal eye strain by switching to dark or sepia mode.

Interactive AI assistant (beta)

Figure 1.2 – Illustration of Packt's AI assistant

Our interactive AI assistant has been trained on the content of this book, to maximize your learning experience. It comes with the following features:

- ✦ Summarize it: Summarize key sections or an entire chapter.
- ✦ AI code explainers: In the next-gen Packt Reader, click the Explain button above each code block for AI-powered code explanations.

Note: The AI assistant is part of next-gen Packt Reader and is still in beta.

DRM-free PDF or ePub version

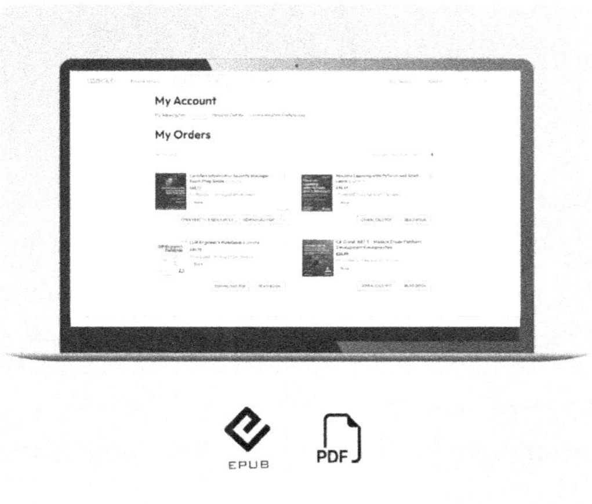

Figure 1.3 – Free PDF and ePub

Learn without limits with the following perks included with your purchase:

- Learn from anywhere with a DRM-free PDF copy of this book.
- Use your favorite e-reader to learn using a DRM-free ePub version of this book.

Technical requirements

To begin, you can use any text editor or **integrated development environment** (**IDE**) of your choice with the Java language. We recommend the IntelliJ IDEA **Community Edition** (**CE**) IDE. This tool already comes with everything you need to work with both Java and Kotlin.

The following software is required (with version) for this chapter:

- Java JDK 17 or higher
- IntelliJ IDEA CE
- Kotlin 1.x or 2.x

The code used in the chapters can be found in the book's accompanying GitHub repository:

`https://github.com/PacktPublishing/Kotlin-for-Java-Developers`.

Looking at the origin

Kotlin is a language that has taken a relevant role in the world of software development in recent years. It has been linked to the Java programming language since its inception, and this is because the developers who created it used Java as a starting point. They used the concepts of Java, Groovy, C#, and Scala. Kotlin uses many features that can be found in modern programming languages.

Kotlin was created by JetBrains, but it is also closely associated with Google, and this is because of Google's decision to make it its main language for the development of Android applications a few years ago.

The reality is that Kotlin was born within JetBrains, the company behind development tools such as IntelliJ IDEA, under the direction of Andrey Breslav. They decided to create a language that was completely interoperable with Java, but also, as we already mentioned, contained many modern language features. With the creation of Kotlin, they created a language that avoids being ambiguous, eliminates repetitive code, and increases the speed of coding while avoiding verbosity.

Kotlin was conceived in 2010 by JetBrains as a project to address the shortcomings of other languages used in its development tools, especially Java. The name *Kotlin* comes from the island of Kotlin, located near St. Petersburg.

In 2011, Kotlin was announced to the public. JetBrains decided to develop Kotlin openly from its initial stages, publishing its code on GitHub.

In 2016, Kotlin 1.0 was officially released, marking the first stable version of the language. This meant that JetBrains guaranteed forward compatibility, indicating that future versions would maintain compatibility with code written in Kotlin 1.0.

In 2017, Kotlin was introduced and mentioned for the first time at an official Google event – in this case, it was at Google I/O. This was done with a series of events around the world to present the advantages associated with Kotlin. But specifically, it was associated with the development of mobile applications on Android.

In 2019, two years later, Google shared it directly, pointing out that Kotlin would not only become an option within mobile development but would also become the primary option for Android application developers. This meant that the majority of tools, libraries, and other future elements that were going to be built for Android were considering Kotlin as the main language and thus being prepared in the best way to connect it to the projects.

Currently, mobile development is not Kotlin's only major focus. We find the possibility of using Kotlin in different departments of the software industry, such as the backend and some relatively new ones, such as blockchain. For example, in the case of the backend, it is increasingly common to find positions where the use of Kotlin with Spring is requested. This trend is growing, and in a short time, we will likely see other positions constantly requesting Kotlin as a default skill.

There is also **Kotlin Multiplatform**, allowing for the development of code that can be reused across different platforms.

In the well-known surveys that are done annually, such as the one on `www.stackoverflow.com`, we can see that Kotlin continues to grow and is one of the languages with the greatest acceptance, and that it has maintained this growth for a couple of years now.

A quick review of Kotlin's popular features

Let's take a quick look of the main or most popular features that might be why Java developers decide to give the Kotlin programming language a chance:

- **Null safety**: Kotlin introduces a type system that distinguishes between references that can be null and those that cannot. This helps avoid `NullPointerException` errors, one of the most common errors in Java.

- **Type inference**: Kotlin has a strong type inference that reduces the need to explicitly specify the type of each variable, making the code cleaner and easier to read.
- **Extension functions**: Extension functions allow you to add new functionality to existing classes without having to modify them or use patterns such as the decorator. This makes it easier to write cleaner, more maintainable code.
- **Lambda expressions**: Kotlin enhances functional capabilities with lambda expressions with receivers, making it easier to create **domain-specific languages (DSLs)** and improve the functional use of the language.
- **Coroutines**: Kotlin handles asynchronous programming and callbacks in a cleaner and less error-prone way by using coroutines, which allows asynchronous code to be written sequentially.
- **Data classes**: Kotlin introduces data classes, which are very useful for classes that only serve to hold data. Data classes automatically derive methods such as `equals()`, `hashCode()`, and `toString()`.
- **Delegated properties**: Delegated properties allow you to delegate the logic of a property to a different object, facilitating certain design patterns and helping to reduce boilerplate code.
- **Smart casts**: The Kotlin compiler can use smart casts, reducing the need for explicit casts in the code.
- **Improved flow control**: Kotlin offers improved control flow structures, such as `when` and `try-catch` expressions that can return values.
- **100% interoperability with Java**: Kotlin is fully interoperable with Java, allowing developers to use all existing Java libraries and frameworks in their Kotlin applications without problems.
- **Support for cross-platform development**: With Kotlin Multiplatform, it is possible to write the logical core of applications and compile it for various platforms, such as iOS, Android, web, and servers, helping to share code and reduce development time. The main idea is to share business logic and other common components across different platforms while writing platform-specific code only when necessary.

As we have just seen, the list of popular features in Kotlin is extensive and will attract any developer interested in getting the most out of Kotlin. In our day-to-day projects, it is not necessary to master every single one of these features; in fact, it is not necessary to use them all. The reality is that the most important thing is simply to be aware of their existence so that when we face a challenge, we know which path to take or which options to consider to solve the problem.

Kotlin programming paradigms

The programming paradigm that is used most often when we work with Kotlin is **object-oriented programming**, similar to Java. But we can also use the structured or functional programming paradigm. More paradigms and elements will be added in the future since Kotlin is a language that is constantly evolving at a very fast rate. Just by observing the progress from its beginnings to now, we can notice the great speed of its evolution.

Kotlin supports the following programming paradigms:

- Object-oriented programming
- Functional programming
- Data-oriented programming
- Imperative programming
- Structured programming
- Declarative programming
- Concurrent programming
- Reflective programming

At the time of writing this book, **functional programming** in Kotlin is currently a hot topic, especially when we are working as Android application developers in the following areas:

- State management
- Declarative interfaces
- Event handling

These cases are causing us to have to implement a combination of object-oriented programming, functional programming, and other paradigms within the development of modern applications.

Nowadays, it is inevitable that a Kotlin developer, regardless of whether they are focused on mobile development or not, uses more than one paradigm. So, sooner or later, the developer will have to develop the ability to work with several programming paradigms in the same project.

The fact that Kotlin is a multi-paradigm language shows us how flexible it is. If we decide to use it, in the medium and long term, this can lead to us writing more efficient code, and code readability is another important element that we should consider.

Code reuse becomes evident through support for the object-oriented paradigm and by separating the code into smaller pieces or modules. This not only improves the quality of our project at the code level, but also boosts our productivity. It is simply a matter of reusing some element previously created by us and other developers.

Cross-platform mobile development with Kotlin

In recent years, Kotlin has become much more appealing due to the possibility of cross-platform development, which means that you can work on a base project and, from this, create two versions of the app, for example, a version for Android and a version for iOS.

Projects are currently being added that include these two operating systems. Small attempts are also being made to develop web or desktop applications for other operating systems.

This has been a new reason for more developers to join this world of development, with Kotlin offering a pleasant, simple, and flexible first experience.

In recent years, the emergence of Kotlin Multiplatform has become a welcome reality and has been widely adopted by a part of the community. To them, it is a great option to develop on modern mobile operating systems, such as Android and iOS, and on desktop and other devices.

Nowadays, the role of a native Android application developer, who usually must know Java and Kotlin, is increasingly mentioned. However, you should also keep an eye on cross-platform Kotlin, as this path is proving to be a solid and improved option. Kotlin continues to offer developers the ability to develop a code base for different platforms quickly and easily, with many advantages and improvements.

Open source availability

Another important point about Kotlin is that it is an open source project.

In essence, this means that the source code of the language is freely available for anyone to examine, modify, and distribute. This transparency fosters collaboration among developers worldwide, who can contribute ideas, fix bugs, and continuously improve the language's capabilities.

Kotlin is evolving at a rapid pace. The current Kotlin version is 2. Developers can freely experiment with new ideas and implement them quickly, allowing the language to adapt to the ever-changing needs of the software world. Being open to public scrutiny, Kotlin's code undergoes a rigorous review and testing process. This leads to a higher level of trust among developers who use it and confidence that the language is stable and secure.

The community can propose and implement new elements or properties and make changes that will allow it to stay a versatile language. In our 15 years of experience, we can say that we have only seen 2 or 3 languages evolve as quickly as Kotlin has, and if it continues like this, very soon it will be the fastest-evolving programming language.

Kotlin backend

When we understand that Kotlin is 100% interoperable with Java, the first question on our mind is whether we can include it in our Java projects. The short answer is yes. Many developers doubt, at first, whether this is possible since, as mentioned at the beginning of the chapter, the main idea was to use it for the development of native applications on Android. But if we have the possibility of using it with Java, or since we already use Java, we can use it in one of the ways in which Java is currently most used – the backend.

We have many tools and an extensive ecosystem that works with Java, so we could take advantage of it without problems.

If we used Kotlin in the backend, we would have the advantages of the learning curve. For example, Java is known for being a verbose programming language; in Kotlin, this learning curve is much shorter. On the other hand, there is also the issue of improvements in the code regarding the issue of null handling, which, as many Java developers know, is one of the main problems when we are working with Java.

Some of the main backend tools that you will find available to work with Kotlin are **Spring** and **Ktor**. Spring is one of the most famous Java frameworks, and you can find many projects and developers that already use it with Kotlin today. On the other hand, Ktor, which is a framework designed for Kotlin itself, is beginning to gain strength to work directly on the web with Kotlin as a backend language. Let's just remember that almost any tool that has current support and is used for Java could start using elements or parts of code completely in Kotlin.

Kotlin/JS

Kotlin/JavaScript (Kotlin/JS) is a compiler that allows you to write web applications and server services using the Kotlin programming language. This means that using Kotlin, we can write the base code and then compile it to JavaScript. This feature is especially valuable for web developers who prefer a statically typed language, such as Kotlin, over JavaScript, which is dynamically typed.

> **Note**
>
> 1. **Static typing:** Data types are defined in the code and checked at compile time
> 2. **Dynamic typing:** Data types are determined at runtime

Let's briefly explain how it works. Kotlin/JS takes the Kotlin source code and compiles it into pure JavaScript. This resulting JavaScript can run in any modern browser or in environments such as Node.js for server-side applications or tooling development.

Kotlin/JS offers complete interoperability with JavaScript libraries and frameworks. This is something that has surprised the community since you can call JavaScript code from Kotlin, and vice versa. This is made possible by **type definitions** that allow Kotlin to understand how to interact with JavaScript libraries.

Another of the main questions that JavaScript developers ask is whether Kotlin/JS supports a dynamic function that allows any part of the code to be treated as dynamic JavaScript, facilitating integration with JavaScript libraries that may not have well-defined types. The answer is yes.

Let's talk about some advantages of using Kotlin for this:

- **Type safety:** Kotlin offers compile-time type safety, which can help prevent many common errors in JavaScript related to data type, such as undefined properties.
- **Modern Kotlin features:** Kotlin/JS allows developers to use all modern Kotlin features and coroutines.

We can give more details, but in reality, those are the two most important advantages, speaking specifically for the web. There are other advantages too, but they are more general and could apply to any development environment or application ecosystem.

Kotlin for data analysis

Something that is not so well known is that we can use Kotlin for data analysis. This is not so well-known because other languages and tools have been around longer and are more popular, but Kotlin is starting to gain attention in this area.

Some tools are beginning to appear that are adding value so that more developers use Kotlin in this part of the industry, for example, Kotlin Notebook and Kandy.

Kotlin Notebook is very similar to what is already used with other technologies (such as Python). It is like Jupyter Notebook. In fact, we could, through some configurations, make them share the same project.

If we want to start on this topic, it would be recommended to read a little more about **Kotlin Kernel for Jupyter** (you may visit `https://kotlinlang.org/docs/get-started-with-kotlin-notebooks.html` for more information). This is an open source project that will allow us to run Kotlin within Jupyter. Some of the advantages of using Kotlin are a bit obvious since we can take advantage of null safety to avoid many errors that normally occur when we use other technologies. In addition, we have a much simpler syntax compared to many technologies. Finally, let's remember that Kotlin and Java are 100% interoperable, which means we can use many of the tools that were originally built to work with Java.

Jupyter is an open source tool that lets you create and share documents containing live code, visualizations, and narrative text. It's especially useful for data analysis workflows where quick feedback, experimentation, and visualization are key.

Jupyter notebooks are widely used in the data science world because they combine code execution and rich documentation in a single, interactive environment. While Python is the most common language used in Jupyter, Kotlin can also run in this environment, thanks to tools such as Kotlin Kernel for Jupyter, making it a powerful option for Kotlin developers who want to explore data analysis interactively.

Kandy is an open source library that allows us to use a DSL for plotting charts. One thing that makes it very attractive is that we can combine it with several tools that we have already mentioned or will mention. The same goes for many tools that are used for data analysis within the Kotlin ecosystem.

Another tool to work with data is **Kotlin DataFrame**. This is a library that allows us to manipulate data structures in Kotlin projects. We can work with different formats, including the most commonly used formats in data, such as JSON, CSV, and XLS.

Kotlin WASM

WebAssembly (**WASM**) is an open standard that defines a binary code format and a way to execute it. In simple words, WASM allows us, as developers, to create code in what is known as **high-level languages**, such as Rust, Java, and Kotlin, and compile it into a format that can be executed in the browser, such as JavaScript.

Kotlin is currently starting to take this step by providing support for us to compile Kotlin code into native machine code.

This opens doors for developers since it means Kotlin can be used in the frontend as well. In addition, WASM is also interoperable with JavaScript, so these technologies will be able to work together smoothly and take advantage of the strengths of both languages. Although WASM is currently seen as experimental, it has attracted a lot of interest from the development community since it will be useful in expanding the use and possibilities of programming languages.

How to use Kotlin

To finish this first part of the chapter, we are going to see how we can use Kotlin to put into practice what we will be learning in this book.

To begin, we don't do much more than use one of these two IDE options: IntelliJ IDEA or Android Studio. The main difference between the two is that Android Studio is based on IntelliJ IDEA and is optimized, as its name suggests, for the development of Android applications. In fact, it is very common for Android developers and developers who use Flutter technology to use it. Both are Google technologies. So, the initial recommendation for Kotlin would be IntelliJ IDEA since many things in the second option are not necessary, and thus, we can focus better on Kotlin. But if you already know Android Studio, you can follow everything that we are going to explore in this book without any major setbacks. Simply downloading the IDE is enough.

Within the official `jetbrains.com` site, simply select the **Developer Tools** section and look for the **IntelliJ IDEA** option. As already mentioned, we recommend using the CE.

Once we have the IDE on our computer, all we have to do is open it, create a new empty project, and select **Kotlin** as the project's programming language.

The other way to use Kotlin, without having to install it on our computers, is by going to the website: `https://play.kotlinlang.org/`.

This site is a type of playground where we can write our code in Kotlin and see the result of it. Initially, it can be a good idea since it is not necessary to add things or packages to our computer; just write the address in the URL, and we are ready. However, it may not be the best option for the detail required in some examples or complex exercises found later in the book.

For now, we can say that in the first chapters, we will not notice a difference between using the playground or Kotlin in an editor installed on our computer.

As we conclude our introduction to Kotlin, let's take a moment to reflect on what we've covered and why it's important. We've learned about the origins and evolution of Kotlin, from its creation by JetBrains to its adoption by Google as the preferred language for Android development. This background gives us a solid understanding of why Kotlin has become such a relevant and powerful tool in the software development world.

Understanding Kotlin's history and its association with Java helps us appreciate the language's design principles and improvements, which aim to enhance productivity and code quality. This context is crucial as it highlights the rationale behind Kotlin's features and the benefits it offers to developers. This will help you understand how to leverage Kotlin's capabilities to write cleaner, more efficient code. So, let's now move on to explore the key relationship between Java and Kotlin in the next section.

Relationship between Java and Kotlin

In this section, we will look at the similarities and differences between Java and Kotlin. We will emphasize very particular parts to share at which points the similarities might arise, and what the differences are between the two. The main objective is for this to be the starting point to understand simple differences, but also to know that we will explain the differences that are more complex and that deserve explanation in detail in later chapters.

Kotlin and the Java Virtual Machine

Kotlin is a programming language that works on the **Java Virtual Machine** (**JVM**). In other words, this means that Kotlin needs a JVM installed on the device where we want our code to work. It is very common that when we start, we have many doubts about this, but later in this book, we will address the topic in detail.

Although Java is usually the language that is considered the one that had the most influence on the creation of Kotlin, there are also others, such as Scala, Groovy, and C#.

Kotlin is not the only programming language that uses the JVM. Although at present it may be the most popular, there are programming languages that have been doing it much longer, as shown here:

- Groovy
- Scala
- Clojure
- Jython

- Fantom
- JRuby

The concept is as simple as it is smart. A compiler compiles source code in any of these languages into a format called **bytecode**. The JVM then takes the bytecode and transforms it into machine-specific instructions.

As the bytecode is platform- and CPU-independent, this allows it to run on any platform where a JVM is available. This was called **WORA** back in the day, which stands for **write once, run anywhere**.

Knowing that Kotlin needs the JVM to function, we can say that the discussion around Kotlin being a language that wants to end Java loses a bit of meaning. On the contrary, we, as developers who work in such a fast and flexible industry, must learn to be open to changes but always respect technologies and languages, be attentive to true contributions, and not get carried away by sensationalist comments.

The portability that the JVM offers to all the languages that can work with it is a great advantage since you can use this to grow quickly, and you also do not have to rewrite the code for it to work on different platforms.

Another crucial point is the ecosystem that we just mentioned. There are already many libraries and tools available for the challenges that have had to be solved in recent years, and as developers, we only have to investigate what we already have available to add and use it in our project. The new ecosystem tools that are focusing on these challenges include handling asynchronous programming, managing dependencies, ensuring code quality, and facilitating testing and debugging. For instance, frameworks such as Ktor for web development, coroutines for managing asynchronous tasks, and Koin for dependency injection are just a few examples of the robust tools available. As developers, we only need to explore and utilize these existing resources to enhance our projects, thereby saving time and effort while leveraging tried-and-tested solutions.

Access modifiers

Java and Kotlin **access modifiers** are similar, but we must pay attention to some details. Access modifiers help us have control over the visibility of, and how to access, variables, classes, or methods. Depending on the needs of our programs, we can define the level of encapsulation and thus be able to ensure secure access to the data, both for reading and modifications.

As we already know, the Java modifiers are as follows:

- **public**: The member is accessible from any other class.
- **private**: The member is accessible only within the class in which it is declared.
- **protected**: The member is accessible within its own class, by derived classes, and by other classes (same package).
- **default**: The member is accessible only within classes of the same package.

In Kotlin, we have the following access modifiers:

- **public**: The member is accessible from anywhere (as in Java).
- **private**: The member is accessible only within the class or file in which it is declared (as in Java).
- **internal**: The member is visible within the same module.
- **protected**: This does not allow access from other classes in the same package, unlike Java, restricting it to subclasses only.

Another difference is that Kotlin does not have an equivalent of the `default` modifier. We could also say that Kotlin's `internal` access modifier is like Java's `protected` access modifier, but only accessible from the same class, child classes, and classes from the same module. The biggest difference between Java and Kotlin access modifiers lies in the scope of Kotlin's `internal` modifier, which provides module-level access control. This is in contrast to Java modifiers, which are limited to package, class, and subclass. This gives Kotlin greater flexibility in organizing and encapsulating code in multi-module applications.

A **module** is a set of Kotlin files that are compiled together. A module can contain source code, resources, and other files needed to build a part of the project. In other words, a module is a fundamental unit of organization and dependency management within a project. It encapsulates a set of related code, resources, and dependencies, promoting modularity and scalability for large projects.

Here is an example code in Kotlin applying the available access modifiers:

```
class Student(val name: String) {
    private val id = "AL0013670"

    internal fun printName() {
        println("Name: $name")
    }
```

```
    protected fun showId() {
        println("Id: $id")
    }
}
```

The following is an explanation of the code, focusing on the access modifiers:

- The `name` property is a constructor parameter that is immutable by the word `val`, meaning that by assigning a value to `name`, we can no longer change it.
- The `id` property is set to `private`, which means that it can only be accessed from within the `Student` class. The value with which we initialize it is `"AL0013670"`.
- The `printName` function is a function that is set as `internal`; this means that it will only be accessed within the same module in which this class resides. The function prints or displays the student's name.
- The `showId` function is a `protected` function; this means that it can only be accessed within the same class or by classes that inherit from `Student`. This function is just used to print or display only the student ID.

Important note

If we read the code carefully, we can see that we appear to be missing the `public` modifier. In Kotlin, if the access modifier is not placed, as is the case with `name`, then it is considered as the `public` modifier. So, this allows `name` to be accessed from anywhere.

Next, let us look at one of the most important features: null safety.

Null safety

Since the creation of Kotlin, one of the most important characteristics that has been important is **null safety**. This means that there is a certain security for null types, as we have mentioned previously, and any Java developer can confirm that most of the errors that are found in programs written in this language have to do with nulls. So, the creators of Kotlin put special emphasis from the beginning on reducing the possibility of this error appearing by simply eliminating the possibility that it could be null.

By default, objects cannot be null. In simple words, the possibility of objects being null is disabled by default.

On the other hand, we must remember that interoperability was a priority between Java and Kotlin. So, if we find code for Java, at some point, there will surely be the possibility of finding nulls somewhere; that is why we must then allow null handling, but not by default. This is what they did in Kotlin, so the developer will be able to find errors related to nullability faster. This will be addressed in detail and with more extensive examples later in this book. For now, this explanation is basic as we are only seeking to show an introductory overview.

For example, this code would generate a compilation error in Kotlin:

```
var name: String = "Viena"
name = null
```

The error would be as follows:

```
Null can not be a value of a non-null type String
```

This means that we do not have the option of making it null. But, let's see what happens if we make a change by adding a question mark (?) when we define the type, as follows:

```
var name: String? = "Viena"
name = null
```

We will see that we no longer get an error, since with this change, we are allowing the variable of this type to be null as well. As mentioned, later, we will go deeper into this concept with more elaborate examples.

For now, let us explore the types of variables in Kotlin.

Types available in Kotlin

In this section, we are going to touch on the topics related to the variables and the types that are available. In this section, we will focus on the different types available in Kotlin, including their characteristics, behaviors, and how they contribute to safer and more expressive code. Understanding Kotlin's type system is essential to writing robust applications, and this section will provide a clear overview of how types work and how to use them effectively.

Variables

As Kotlin is a technology that works with the JVM, we will find many similarities between Kotlin and Java. The topic of **variables** is no exception.

The general concept of variables is the same in both Java and Kotlin. These are elements that serve to store information. At a technical level, we can say that they are memory spaces that are reserved to store some type of data. Different types of data are available to help us adjust certain characteristics that we may need in our programs. For example, it is easier to tell whether a number is bigger or smaller than another if we treat it as a `number` type. Similarly, it is easier to know the size of a text string in characters if we use the `string` type.

When we are studying variables, we must talk about two options: `var` and `val`.

We use `var` when we want a variable that can be modified during the execution of the program. We normally use it if we know that data is going to change its value. Here is an example:

```
var name: String = " "
name = "Dimas"
```

We use `val` when we want to declare what we would know as an immutable variable, that is, a variable that, when it has a value assigned, this value will not change. If we come from the Java world, we associate this with the reserved word `final`. Here is an example:

```
val name: String = " "
name = "Dimas"// Error: Val cannot be reassigned
```

As we can see in the last line of the preceding code, we will see an error, and this is simply due to the change we made from using `var` to now using `val`, as this does not allow the variable to change its value.

Since we now understand two reserved words (`val` and `var`) in Kotlin, we can mention the base structure for declaring variables in Kotlin. It would be something like this:

```
// Example of variable declaration structure
#type name = value
var age = 38
```

Here is a brief explanation of the preceding code:

- In `type`, we specify either `val` or `var` to tell Kotlin whether the variable should be immutable (`val`) or mutable (`var`). This defines whether the value can be changed after it is assigned. Next, we are going to indicate a `name` value that can be whatever we want. We must remember that we cannot use words reserved by the Kotlin language, such as `var` or `val`, that already have a default use.
- `value` means that we are going to set a value to the variable.

If you create a variable and forget to place `var` or `val`, you will automatically receive feedback from the IDE that there is an error.

Type inference

Kotlin supports **type inference**, meaning the compiler can help us assign a type to a variable, considering its initial value (that is, it *infers* the type we need). This helps us avoid having to specify the data type of the variable in some cases where initially there is a possibility that we do not know exactly what we are going to have, receive, or save.

This feature has existed since the beginning of the Kotlin language, so people who learned to program with Kotlin find it a natural feature. On the other hand, Java developers have worked without this feature for many years.

Starting with the Java 10 version, type inference is allowed. This is due to the introduction of the word `var`, and this instruction is what began to allow Java to also work with type inference.

This is how you define a variable in Kotlin with its type:

```
var name: String = "Noemi"
```

We can see that we are indicating that the type is `String`. If we want Kotlin to infer the type, we remove the type that we explicitly placed:

```
var name = "Noemi"
```

Both instructions do the same thing, creating a `String` type. In the first instruction, we are explicitly indicating that the variable will be of the `String` type, and in the second, we are letting Kotlin infer the type. The result in both is the same: we create a variable, `name`, that is a string.

In Java, starting with version 10, which we already mentioned, you can use `var` and infer the type. The Java code is very similar to that of Kotlin:

```
var name = "Viena"
```

Something that we must highlight is that Java inference is mentioned as a limited inference. Type inference in Java is mostly limited to local variables and simple method parameters. In more complex cases, such as anonymous expressions or generics, explicit declarations are required. Kotlin offers a more powerful type inference that can handle instance variables, anonymous expressions, generics, lambdas, and more complex contexts, reducing the need for explicit declarations. In Java 10, some limitations of inference were presented. With the new versions, some features have been improved, but it is still known that Kotlin type inference is much more flexible. It can be considered a bit more precise if we compare it with Java.

Talking about inference in terms of the number of types, we can say that they have very similar basic elements. Kotlin treats Java's primitive types as objects; this makes it much simpler to work with the language.

Kotlin's type system is more flexible than Java's, not only because of type inference, but also due to its built-in support for nullable types and functional programming constructs. While Java relies on more explicit typing and primitive types, Kotlin allows developers to write more concise and expressive code. This may change with later versions of Java, but for now, this remains the case.

Variable types

We already mentioned that Java and Kotlin are very similar when it comes to the types of variables available. Now, we will look at this in more detail.

In Kotlin, the following are handled as basic types:

- Numbers
- Booleans
- Characters
- Strings
- Arrays

Number

The `Number` type allows our variables to work with numeric values. Within `Number`, we have the following types:

- **`Byte`**: The range of values that can be stored in a `Byte` type is from `-128` to `127`. The size is 8 bits.
- **`Short`**: The range of values that can be stored in a `Short` type is from `-32768` to `32767`. The size is 16 bits.
- **`Int`**: The range of values that can be stored in an `Int` type is from `-2147483648` to `2147483647`. The size is 32 bits.
- **`Long`**: The range of values that can be stored in a `Long` type is from `-9223372036854775808` to `9223372036854775807`. The size is 64 bits.
- **`Float`**: The range of values that can be stored in a `Float` type is from `1.4E-45` to `3.4028235E+38`. The size is 32 bits.
- **`Double` (64-bit)**: The range of values that can be stored in a `Double` type is from `4.9E-324` to `1.7976931348623157E+308`. The size is 64 bits.

This is an example code of how to use the types that we have mentioned:

```
var byte: Byte = 10
var short: Short = 100
var integer: Int = 1000
var long: Long = 10000
var float: Float = 10000F
var double: Double = 1000000.0
```

In Kotlin, Java primitive types (all of them) are treated specially to maintain compatibility and efficiency. Kotlin does not explicitly distinguish between primitive types and their corresponding wrapper classes as in Java (e.g., `Int` vs. `Integer`). Unlike Java, which has separate primitive types and wrapper classes, Kotlin treats all data as objects. This simplifies code but raises a question: how does Kotlin maintain efficiency when targeting the JVM?

To answer this, Kotlin provides a simpler and more efficient way to work with data types. You write your code using objects, and the compiler intelligently handles the underlying representation (primitive or wrapper) for optimal performance and seamless JVM integration. This frees you from manual type management and allows you to focus on writing expressive and efficient Kotlin code.

To conclude, when we program in Kotlin, we don't need to worry about choosing between primitive types and wrapper objects like in Java, as Kotlin handles this transparently for us.

Booleans

This is a type of data that is represented by two possible values: `false` or `true`. Here is the example code:

```
val validated: Boolean = true
```

Character

Although in Java and Kotlin, `Char` can be used to represent numbers, remember this is not its main objective. There are some important things that we must mention. First is that `Char` in Kotlin, like other types in Kotlin, is a class; Kotlin makes sure that it works without problems, considering this difference with Java. Besides this, in Kotlin, we cannot directly treat `Char` as just a number. Kotlin will not allow us to use direct arithmetic operations without a conversion. This is in principle, since for security reasons, it is avoided to perform this type of operation without the programmer explicitly indicating it in some way. We can see this limitation to encourage less error-prone code:

```
var c: Char = 'a'
```

String

The `String` type is also very similar between Java and Kotlin, but we have some differences.

In both languages, it is used to contain a string of characters and in both languages, and it is immutable.

One of the most obvious differences is that Kotlin uses **Unicode Transformation Format (UTF)** 8 for `String` types, but another that is not so obvious is what we know as template literals. **Template literals** are string literals that enable the use of embedded expressions. With them, it is possible to use character strings of more than one line and character string interpolation functionalities.

We will discuss this in detail in *Chapter 3* in the *Nullability* section.

In the case of strings, it is important to mention that many Java developers know that null and strings cause many errors in their programs. In Kotlin, strings are non-null by default to prevent these errors. Here is an example of how to work with `String`:

```
var name: String = "Viena"
```

Arrays

Like strings, **arrays** are one of the most popular elements in programming languages, but we must point out some similarities and differences. Arrays are used to store elements that belong to the same type, such as an array of integers, an array of strings, and so on – whatever type we want or need.

Now, let's start talking about the differences. In Kotlin, we have the possibility of having specific type arrays for primitive arrays, for example, `IntArray`, `CharArray`, and so on. This is so we can be more efficient in our code. These specialized arrays are designed to be more efficient because they store elements directly as primitives, without the overhead of boxing them into their wrapper classes. This leads to better performance in terms of both memory usage and processing speed, as the data is stored and accessed in its most compact form. By using these specific type arrays, Kotlin allows developers to write more efficient and performant code, especially in scenarios where large arrays of primitive data are involved.

We could say that in Kotlin, arrays are a bit more flexible, but this flexibility can sometimes lead to performance issues. In Java, arrays of primitive types, such as `int[]`, are extremely fast because they store raw values with no boxing. Kotlin achieves similar performance by providing specialized array classes such as `IntArray`, `CharArray`, and so on, which also avoid boxing. So, if we want the same performance in Kotlin, we should use these specialized classes instead of the generic `Array<T>`. Here is an example of how to work with arrays:

```
val days = arrayOf("Monday","Tuesday","Wednesday","Thursday","Friday",
"Saturday","Sunday")
```

If we need to create an empty array, the code is this:

```
val emptyDays = emptyArray<String>()
```

Now, let's explore how Kotlin allows us to perform type checks with the `is` and `!is` operators, enabling us to determine an object's type safely and efficiently at runtime.

Type checks (is and !is)

Kotlin, being a statically typed language, ensures type safety during development. This means that the compiler checks variable types at compile time to avoid errors at runtime. But there are situations where you may need to check or convert the type of an object. This is where type checking and conversions are used.

To verify, we have two instructions: `is and !is.`

This is an implementation example:

```
val name = "Noemi"
if(name is String){
print("String")
}
```

If we execute this code, we will see the word `"String"` as a result because `name` is a string, and then the condition is true. We could also make an example with what would be a similar instruction, but with the ! operator. This would be the code:

```
val name = "Noemi"
if(name !is String){
print("String")
}
```

The difference is that, in this case, the condition is not met and, therefore, we will not execute the code found within the `if` condition. As we can see, this is a quick way to check the type of an object at runtime.

Smart cast

Smart cast in Kotlin is a feature that will help us greatly reduce the code we place in the conversations we need. It is a way to automate or accelerate a cast safely. Something that Java has been criticized for for a long time is the verbosity it adds to its code. Sometimes it seems that we are saying something, and we must repeat it in the same sentence simply because the structure and semantics of Java require it.

Now, let's see how the smart cast, in conjunction with some rules, can verify what we need and allow us to use it if necessary.

Let's see an example:

```
fun testSmartCast(x:Any){
if(x is String){
println(x.length)
}
if(x is Int){
println(x.inc())
}
}
testSmartCast("Jose")
testSmartCast(9)
```

As we can see in the previous code, we have a function that we call `testSmartCast`. This function can receive `x`, which is of the `Any` type. Similar to `Object` in Java, `Any` is the superclass of all non-nullable types in Kotlin. This means every class and data type, except special types such as `Unit`, inherits from `Any`. So, we could be receiving different types of values. But within the function, what we do is have two conditions (we could do this in a better way, but for now, we want to make the code as clear as possible). We see that the first `if` condition prints the size of the string if `x` is of the `String` type:

```
if(x is String){
println(x.length)
}
```

The second `if` condition increments the value of `x` if it is of the `Int` type:

```
if(x is Int){
println(x.inc())
}
```

We are sure that the smart cast is being done in the first case, since upon entering the block, the compiler performs a smart cast from `x(Any)` to `String`, allowing you to directly access the `length` property of `String` without the need for an explicit cast.

In the second `if` condition, when it is verified that `x` is of the `Int` type, and that block is entered, a smart cast is applied to `Int`. This allows you to use the `inc()` method, which is specific to integers (`Int`) in Kotlin, and increments the value by one.

The smart cast is effective here for the following reasons:

- The `x` variable is evaluated directly within the `if` blocks and is used immediately afterward in a safe context.
- `x` is a local variable and not mutable (although, here, `x` is passed as a parameter to the function; the context in each function call is independent, and `x` does not change within each call.

This approach is safe and does not require explicit casting because the compiler can guarantee that the type of `x` does not change between type checking and its use within each `if` block. However, if `x` were a global variable or shared between multiple threads, then the smart cast might not be applied due to the potential for the value or type of `x` to change in concurrent environments or between checks and uses.

Using smart cast simplifies code and improves readability, allowing you to write clearer and more concise code without the need for repetitive explicit casting.

Unsafe cast operator and safe cast operator

When we talk about the *unsafe conversion operator* in Kotlin, we are talking about the `as` operator. This operator tries to explicitly convert a variable to a type that we indicate. If the conversion is not possible (since, as we know, some types are not compatible with each other), an exception will be thrown.

It is called *unsafe* since the operator, when making the conversion, does not verify whether the object can really be converted to the type that we have indicated. This ultimately generates an error, as we just mentioned, so the use of the word *unsafe* indicates the possibility of having an exception within our code. Here is an example:

```
var name: Any = 100
val lastname: String = name as String
```

This code in the editor will not show any errors, so as developers, we might be sure that it will work, but the reality is that it will not. If we execute this code, it will show us an exception that complies with what was mentioned previously. This cast is insecure due to the possibility of having an error, although at first glance, it seems that everything is fine with our code.

Here, we can make the code a little interesting by playing with the question mark, which, as we already mentioned, is used to work with nulls:

```
var name: Any = 100
val lastname: String? = name as? String
```

We have made the change so that the variable can now be a `String` type that has the possibility of accepting `null`:

```
val lastname: String?
```

In addition, the `as` operator now also has the question mark, and thus we are protecting our code adequately against the failure of the conversion, which is why it is known as the *safe cast operator*. Here is an example:

```
name as? String
```

If we execute the code, we'll see that it is working; the code will compile, but at runtime, the `as?` operator will fall because `100` cannot be converted to `String`. The value assigned to `lastname` will be `null`.

If we print `lastname` in this case, we will see that the result of printing it will be `null`. This is because when the cast is attempted and it is not possible, the value of `null` is assumed for that element.

In conclusion, we can say that the `as` operator is a great Kotlin tool if we understand what is happening in the code and the value. The recommendation is that if we don't know the type of value, we can use `as?` to avoid exceptions and make our code more secure.

Summary

In this chapter, we explored the foundations of Kotlin and its significance in the world of software development. We learned about Kotlin's origins, its association with Java, and its rise in popularity, particularly due to Google's adoption of Kotlin for Android development. We also discussed Kotlin's robust ecosystem, including various libraries and tools designed to tackle common development challenges, such as asynchronous programming, dependency management, and code quality improvement. Additionally, we introduced Kotlin's key features, including null safety, type inference, and full interoperability with Java.

Understanding these foundational aspects is crucial as it highlights why Kotlin is such a powerful and versatile language, helping developers write cleaner, more efficient code while leveraging their existing Java knowledge. The insights gained in this chapter prepare us for more advanced topics, enabling us to appreciate and effectively use Kotlin's capabilities in real-world applications.

In the next chapter, we will explore Kotlin's interoperability with Gradle and Maven. This will provide you with a solid understanding of Kotlin's core, setting the stage for more complex and practical programming techniques.

2

Interoperability, Gradle, and Maven

Transitioning from Java to Kotlin is not just a change in syntax but an evolution towards more modern and efficient programming. In this chapter, we will focus on three fundamental pillars for developers who want to integrate Kotlin into their existing projects or start new projects leveraging the Java ecosystem: interoperability, Gradle, and Maven.

One of Kotlin's greatest advantages is its seamless integration with existing Java code. This interoperability between Kotlin and Java is a game-changer for developers, enabling them to leverage the extensive ecosystem of Java libraries, frameworks, and tools without disruption. The interoperability feature allows for a hybrid code base where Kotlin and Java can coexist, interact, and complement each other efficiently. This capability ensures that developers can call methods, instantiate classes, and use Java libraries directly from Kotlin code, thereby preserving their established workflows and investments in Java infrastructure.

In the world of Kotlin/Java development, Gradle and Maven are indispensable tools for project management and dependency management. These build systems have been the backbone of Kotlin/Java projects, providing structured and automated ways to compile code, manage dependencies, and package applications. The good news for developers adopting Kotlin is that both Gradle and Maven are fully compatible with Kotlin, allowing for seamless integration into existing workflows and providing robust support for new Kotlin projects.

Gradle is a flexible and powerful build automation tool that has gained widespread adoption due to its performance and versatility. It uses a **domain-specific language** (**DSL**) based on Groovy or Kotlin to describe builds, offering a rich and expressive way to manage project configurations.

Maven is another popular build automation tool that focuses on simplicity and convention over configuration. It uses an XML-based **Project Object Model** (**POM**) file to manage project configurations, dependencies, and the build lifecycle. For Kotlin/Java developers, Maven provides robust support through dedicated plugins and seamless integration with Java projects. In this chapter, we ′re going to cover the following main topics:

- Java Virtual Machine
- Kotlin and Java working together
- Calling Java code
- Gradle and Maven

Technical requirements

To begin, you can use any text editor or **Integrated Development Environment** (**IDE**) of your choice with the Java language, but it is certain that some extra configurations will have to be done. That is why IntelliJ IDEA **Community Edition** (**CE**) is recommended. This tool already comes with everything you need to work with both Java and Kotlin. The list of requirements for this chapter is as follows:

- Java JDK 17 or higher
- IntelliJ IDEA CE
- Kotlin 1.x or 2.x

The code used in the chapters can be found in the book's accompanying GitHub repository: `https://github.com/PacktPublishing/Kotlin-for-Java-Developers`.

Java Virtual Machine

The **Java Virtual Machine** (**JVM**) is a crucial component of the **Java Runtime Environment** (**JRE**) that enables Java applications to run on any device or operating system without modification. It abstracts away the underlying hardware and operating system, providing a uniform platform for Java bytecode execution.

To understand the importance of the JVM, we have to understand the concept of abstraction. This is key.

Abstraction allows developers to write code once and run it on any device or operating system that has a supported JVM, without requiring platform-specific modifications.

A simple example would be this: you are writing a Java application that needs to read and write files and modify directories in the file system. In a non-abstraction environment, you would have to worry about differences between operating systems, such as Windows, Linux, or macOS-specific commands for handling files.

The file system is different, and we would have a project in which we would have to change the instructions, the file writing methods, and the deleting methods, and all the instructions we use would have to be changed depending on the operating system. This would mean writing different code for each operating system. In short, we would have one problem in which we would have to program three solutions or variants of the code so that it adapts to the operating system where it will be executed.

This is where abstraction comes in. Thanks to abstraction, we don't have to worry about this.

The JVM is what provides this abstraction; we can use the same classes and methods of the standard Java API, and other instructions without worrying about the differences between the operating systems. The JVM is responsible for translating our calls to these methods into the specific operations of the underlying operating system.

Benefits of abstraction

Let us now explore the advantages associated with abstraction:

- **Portability**: By abstracting hardware and operating system details, the JVM allows the same Java code to run on any platform that has a compatible JVM. This eliminates the need to rewrite or adjust code for different environments, which is a significant advantage for developers. The portability provided by the JVM means that applications can be developed on one platform and deployed on multiple platforms without any changes. This reduces development time and costs associated with creating and maintaining different versions of the same application for various operating systems. Additionally, it ensures consistency in application behavior across different environments, enhancing reliability and user experience.
- **Simplification**: Developers can focus on writing business logic and application functionality without worrying about the complexities of the underlying systems. The JVM handles the intricacies of interacting with the hardware and operating system, allowing developers to work at a higher level of abstraction. This simplification leads to cleaner, more understandable code, as developers do not need to include platform-specific hacks or workarounds. Furthermore, it reduces the margin of error by eliminating the need for developers to manage low-level details, which are often error-prone and can lead to bugs that are difficult to diagnose and fix.

- **Maintenance**: Abstraction makes code maintenance easier, as changes to the hardware or operating system do not require modifications to the Java code. The JVM is responsible for handling these differences internally, which means that updates or changes to the underlying platform do not affect the application code. This separation of concerns allows developers to focus on improving and extending the functionality of their applications rather than spending time on platform-specific adjustments. It also means that when new hardware or operating system versions are released, the JVM is updated to support them, ensuring that existing Java applications continue to run smoothly without requiring any code changes.
- **Development efficiency**: By providing a uniform platform, the JVM allows developers to reuse existing libraries and tools, speeding up development and improving efficiency. This uniformity means that developers can rely on a consistent set of APIs and tools across different projects, which reduces the learning curve and improves productivity. Additionally, the vast ecosystem of Java libraries and frameworks can be leveraged across various projects, enabling developers to build on proven solutions rather than reinventing the wheel. This reusability extends to development tools as well, such as IDEs, build systems, and testing frameworks, which all work seamlessly with the JVM. The result is a more streamlined and efficient development process, allowing developers to deliver high-quality software faster and with fewer resources.

The abstraction provided by the JVM offers numerous benefits that significantly enhance the development, deployment, and maintenance of Java applications. By ensuring portability, simplifying development, easing maintenance, and improving development efficiency, the JVM allows developers to create robust, high-performing applications that can run on a wide variety of platforms. This powerful abstraction layer is one of the key factors that has contributed to Java's enduring popularity and success in the software development industry.

How the JVM achieves abstraction

The secret of the JVM is how it achieves abstraction through several sophisticated techniques, allowing it to provide a consistent execution environment on various hardware and operating systems for programmers. All these techniques ensure that Java applications can run smoothly on any platform if a compatible JVM is installed. Next, we'll delve a little more into the details of how the JVM achieves this.

Just-in-time interpretation and compilation

The JVM interprets and/or compiles Java bytecode into system-specific machine code at runtime. This double approach guarantees flexibility and performance. Many times, programming languages in general are classified by languages that are interpreted or languages that are compiled. The languages that use the JVM have the characteristic that they can be interpreted and compiled:

- **Interpretation**: Initially, the JVM interprets the bytecode and executes it instruction by instruction. This allows immediate execution without the need for pre-compilation into machine code. Interpretation is especially useful for code that runs infrequently.
- **Just-in-time compilation**: For code that runs frequently, the JVM employs **Just-in-time (JIT)** compilation. The JIT compiler translates bytecode into native machine code at runtime, optimizing the code for specific hardware. This native code is then executed directly by the CPU, significantly improving performance. The JVM monitors which parts of the code are used most frequently and applies more aggressive optimizations to these *hot spots*.

Standard Java API libraries

Standard Java API libraries play a crucial role in abstracting system-specific details. These libraries provide uniform interfaces for common tasks such as input/output operations, file manipulation, and networking:

- **Consistent interfaces**: Java API libraries provide consistent interfaces for developers, regardless of the underlying platform – for example, classes for file management, network connections, database connectors, and others. If we talk, for example, about the first case we mentioned of file management, then we are provided with methods for file operations that work in the same way on Windows, Linux, macOS, and other platforms. This would be the same for the other classes we mentioned.
- **Platform-specific implementations**: At its core, the JVM includes platform-specific implementations of these libraries. When a Java application calls a method from the standard API, the JVM routes this call to the appropriate native implementation. This ensures that the same Java code can take advantage of the full capabilities of the underlying system without modification. We are not going to see this with the naked eye, but it happens.

Resource management

Effective resource management is another key aspect of the JVM's abstraction capabilities. The JVM handles the allocation and release of resources such as memory and processes, optimizing these operations for any platform:

- **Memory management**: The JVM includes an automatic GC (we will explain it in the next section) that manages memory allocation and reclaiming. This GC runs in the background, identifying and freeing memory that is no longer in use. Different garbage collection algorithms are available (e.g., serial, parallel, CMS, G1, ZGC), each optimized for different use cases and system configurations.
- **Process and thread management**: The JVM abstracts the complexities of process and thread management. Java's threading model provides a high-level API for creating and managing threads, while the JVM maps these high-level threads to native operating system threads. This abstraction allows Java applications to take advantage of multicore processors and concurrent processing without having to deal with platform-specific threading complexities.

The Java garbage collector

The **garbage collector** (**GC**) is a critical component of the JVM that automatically handles memory management for Java applications. Its main objective is to identify and free memory that is no longer being used by the program, preventing memory leaks, and optimizing resource use. Next, we will see details of how the GC works in Java, its different algorithms, and its impact on application performance.

The main goal of the GC is to manage memory efficiently to ensure that unused memory is reclaimed and that applications do not run out of memory. This is achieved by the following:

- **Identification of unreachable objects**: The GC tracks objects that no longer have active references in the program. These objects are considered unreachable, and their memory can be recycled, meaning it can be used for other elements.
- **Automatic memory release**: Once unreachable objects are identified, the GC frees the memory they occupied, making it available for new allocations.

Components of the GC

Memory management in Java is organized into several memory areas called **generations**, each optimized for different object types and usage patterns. The fundamental areas are as follows:

- **Young Generation (on the heap)**: Stores young objects – those that have been created recently. Most of these objects are short-lived and are quickly collected by the GC. The Young Generation is further subdivided into the following:
    - **Eden Space (on the heap)**: Where new objects are initially created.
    - **Survivor Spaces (on the heap)**: Two spaces where objects that survive the first collection in Eden are copied and evaluated again in future collections.
- **Old Generation (Tenured Generation) (on the heap)**: Stores long-lived items that have survived multiple collections in the Young Generation. These items are rarer and are collected less often.
- **Permanent Generation (PermGen) (on the heap, up to Java 7)**: Stores metadata of classes and structures related to the JDK, such as class and method constants. In Java 8, this area has been replaced by **Metaspace (outside the heap)**, which more efficiently manages this metadata outside of the main heap.

Garbage collection algorithms

The JVM provides several garbage collection algorithms, each optimized for different usage scenarios and performance characteristics:

- **Serial GC**: Uses a single thread to perform garbage collection. It is simple and suitable for applications with small amounts of memory and fewer CPU cores.
- **Parallel GC**: Uses multiple threads to perform collection in the Young Generation, improving performance in multi-core applications. It is efficient in systems with more processing capacity.
- **Concurrent Mark-Sweep (CMS) GC (Removed since Java 14)**: Performs most of its work concurrently with the application thread, reducing collection pauses. It is suitable for applications that require low latency, although it may be less efficient in terms of CPU usage.
- **Garbage-First (G1) GC**: Designed for large applications. It divides the heap into regions and collects the ones that contain the most garbage first, providing a balance between performance and collection pauses. G1 is suitable for large server applications and has become the default GC in many recent versions of Java.
- **Z Garbage Collector (ZGC) (Introduced in Java 11)**: ZGC is a low-latency GC designed to handle very large heaps, with minimal pause times. It's ideal for application responsiveness and tolerating minor trade-offs.

- **Shenandoah GC (Introduced in Java 12)**: Low-latency GC, similar to ZGC, but focuses on concurrent collection. Reduces pause times regardless of the heap size by collecting garbage in parallel with the execution of application threads.

The garbage collection process usually goes through several essential phases to ensure efficient memory management in the JVM. These phases allow for identifying and freeing unused memory and optimizing memory organization for optimal performance. These phases are detailed next.

Marking

The **marking** phase is the first stage in the garbage collection process. During this phase, the GC identifies all accessible (reachable) objects from the GC roots (such as local variables, stack registers, and static references). This process involves traversing the object graph, starting from these roots and marking each object that can be reached directly or indirectly. Objects that are marked are considered alive and in use. The objective is to determine which objects are still in use and, therefore, should not be collected. The collector uses a traversal algorithm to follow references and mark reachable objects. This phase can be expensive in terms of CPU time, especially in applications with large object graphs. Dial pauses can also affect application latency.

Unmarking

Although it is not a formally recognized phase in all GC algorithms, **umarking** can be considered part of the post-collection cleanup process. In this phase, objects that are no longer in use (unreachable) are identified and unmarked. In some algorithms, this step involves preparing the memory occupied by these objects for reuse. The objective is to prepare unreachable objects to be collected and memory to be reused. The memory occupied by unchecked objects is put into a free memory list or directly recycled for new allocations. Ensure that all unreachable objects are correctly identified and unmarked without affecting live objects.

Compaction

The **compaction** phase is essential to reduce memory fragmentation and create contiguous blocks of free memory. During this phase, objects in use move to occupy contiguous areas of memory, consolidating free space into one large block rather than many small chunks. This improves the efficiency of future memory allocations and can reduce the need for frequent garbage collection. The objects are moved to new locations, and all references to these objects are updated to reflect their new positions. This process can be complex, as it requires maintaining consistency of references during movement. Compaction can be a time-intensive process, especially in applications with enormous amounts of memory and many objects. Additionally, it requires longer pauses, which can affect application latency.

During garbage collection, pauses refer to the periods of time when the JVM stops the execution of application threads to perform memory cleanup tasks. These pauses are often referred to as stop-the-world events. Pauses can vary in duration depending on the garbage collection algorithm used and the size of the memory heap.

The GC is a crucial part of the JVM, although in reality, we could describe garbage collection as a process that works without us, and many developers know of its existence but not the details, as we have just explained. Now that we are analyzing how interoperability is crucial between Java and Kotlin, and we know that this is thanks to the JVM, it is good to know the details, and one of the most important and key elements is the GC.

The garbage collection process in Java is a series of phases meticulously designed to efficiently manage memory. From identifying and marking objects in use to memory compaction, each phase plays a crucial role in maintaining the performance and stability of Java applications. Understanding these phases allows developers to tune and optimize GC settings to meet the specific needs of their applications, balancing memory efficiency and overall system performance.

In the next section, we will gain insight into how Kotlin and Java can work together.

Working together

This section will explore interoperability in action – we will see how Kotlin and Java can work together at a technical or code level.

Let's create a project using our IDE. The project doesn't need anything special; you just need to select Kotlin as the primary or default language. Here are the details to create the project.

- **Name**: `Interoperability`
- **Location**: The default location
- **Language**: Kotlin
- **Build system**: Gradle
- **Java Development Kit**: Java Corretto 17
- **Gradle Domain Specific Language**: Kotlin

All the parameters are optional and can be modified, but the recommendation is to use the same ones to avoid different results.

Now that we have the project created, let's create our first file with Kotlin. Inside the `src/main/kotlin` directory, we will create a file that will be our first Kotlin file. To easily recognize it, we will name the file `Main`, and its extension will be `.kt`.

The file will be empty at first, but now we will create a function called `main`. Just like in Java, we will specify that it receives the `args` parameter, which will be a `String` array.

```
fun main(args: Array<String>){
    println("Hello world!")
}
```

This `main` function simply receives `args`, which is an array of `String`, in case parameters are needed, and prints a line that says, `"Hello world!"` This is the classic `"Hello world"` print statement.

For now, our project is 100% Kotlin, meaning that all the code we have, even though it is minimal, is written in the Kotlin programming language. Now, we will explain how we can add Java to the project. If we want this project to also have Java code, we will create another file written in the Java programming language.

When we create the file, there will be one difference: in the Kotlin folder or directory, we will have files written using the Kotlin programming language, which we can recognize because the files end with the `.kt` extension. However, when we create programming files with the Java programming language, we need to create a directory at the same level as the Kotlin directory. This way, we can have two primary directories, each containing files of their respective programming languages, with Java files having the `.java` extension.

We will name this file `MyJFile`, indicating that it is our Java file, with the *J* standing for Java.

The name is just a suggestion – you can give the file any name as long as it is not a reserved word.

Now we also have our empty class. It is just a Java class named as mentioned, but inside it has no instructions, just the class definition. This is the code:

```
public class MyJFile{
}
```

Let's add a simple instruction, which is a method that prints `"Hello world"` but includes the word Java. This is the code:

```
public class MyJFile {
    public void hiJava(){
        System.out.println("Hello World Java!");
```

```
    }
}
```

These lines are easy to read. The first line is the file name, the second line is the name of the method we named `hiJava`, and within that function, we have an instruction that prints `"Hello world"` with the addition of the word `Java`.

Recapping so far, we have two files: `Main.kt` and `MyJFile.java`. The first file contains a print statement for `"Hello world"` and is written using Kotlin. The second file is written in the Java programming language and has a method that simply prints `"Hello world"`, but in this case, it also includes the word `Java` in the greeting.

Let's go back to the Kotlin file and use the Java code. We will add two lines for this. Here is the code:

```
fun main(args: Array<String>){
    println("Hello World Kotlin!")
    val javaGreeting = MyJFile()
    javaGreeting.hiJava()
}
```

In Java, a class is required (such as `MyJFile`) to encapsulate the entry point of the program due to its object-oriented structure. In Kotlin, this is not necessary because it allows functions to be declared at the file level, simplifying the code and removing the need for a class to run the application.

The first two lines are familiar; they are just the definition of `main`, which we use to execute the code we want. We will place within it what we want to execute.

The second line is the print statement we initially added for a simple `"Hello world"`. In this case, we add the word Kotlin.

The third line is the definition of a variable named `javaGreeting`, which we use to refer to the `MyJFile` Java file, which is written in the Java programming language.

The fourth line invokes the method where we use the variable to access the method. The method is `hiJava`, which will produce a greeting. If we run the code, we will see the following output:

```
Hello World Kotlin!
Hello World Java!
```

This is evidence that Kotlin and Java can work together on the same project. We need to understand that files always have an extension, and the extension tells the compiler or development environment how to handle and work with that file. Therefore, Kotlin files will use `.kt` and Java files will use `.java`.

That is why we previously explained certain key aspects that allow interoperability between Java and Kotlin. Although this is a basic example, it shows that we don't need to configure anything special or do anything different; we just need to ensure that both Kotlin and Java are supported by our development environment. Most of the integration work is handled automatically. In this section of the book, we wrote Kotlin and Java code side by side, and we demonstrated how Kotlin can directly call Java code. This showcases one of Kotlin's greatest strengths: the ability to reuse existing Java code, be it libraries, frameworks, or a full application, seamlessly and efficiently.

We are going to increase the complexity of this example by adding other elements to the code. This is the new Java code:

```
public class MyJFile {
    public void hiJava(String name){
        System.out.println("Hello World Java!" + name);
    }
}
```

The difference between this code and the first version of the `"Hello world"` code is that we define a parameter and print it within the `"Hello world"` message. We can see that we have a `name` variable, and this variable is a string. In the print instruction, we concatenate it to display it on the screen, and that is it.

```
fun main(args: Array<String>){
    println("Hello world Kotlin!")
    val javaGreeting = MyJFile()
    javaGreeting.hiJava("jose")
}
```

The only change, in this case, is the last line of code, where, using the `hiJava` method, we are adding a lowercase string with the name `"jose"` between the parentheses.

In this case, we are showing this example for two reasons. First, we can see that the existence of the parameter is defined in the Java file, meaning that the method we have defined in the Java file requires the parameter to execute properly.

Second, although Kotlin can interoperate seamlessly with Java, there is an important difference to note: Kotlin supports named parameters, while Java does not. When calling Java methods from Kotlin, we cannot use named parameters. This means that the order of parameters matters, and you must pass arguments in the exact order expected by the Java method. In our example, we are passing the string `"jose"` to satisfy the requirement of the `hiJava` method from the Java file.

This demonstrates how both languages can work together, but with limitations such as the lack of named parameters when interacting with Java code.

Now let's add a property to the class. The property will be named, but in a different way. Here is the code:

```
public class MyJFile {
    private String name;
    public void setName(String name) {
        this.name name;
    }
    public String getName() {
        return name;
    }
    public void hiJava() {
        System.out.println("Hello World Java! " + this.name);
    }
}
```

The first line is the class definition, which we are already familiar with. The next instruction defines the name property as a `String` and sets it to `private`. Access modifiers have differences between Java and Kotlin, but we will study these details carefully later. For now, any Java developer knows that we are limiting access to this property, and that is why we are using it for this example, as access modifiers are also considered interoperability. So, to summarize, we are protecting this property by setting it as `private`.

The `hiJava` method prints the `"Hello world"` greeting with the word Java and the instance property. So, from this method, we are accessing the `name` property of the object.

Now let's go to the Kotlin file and see what changed in the code.

```
fun main(args: Array<String>){
    println("Hello world Kotlin!")
    val javaGreeting = MyJFile()
    javaGreeting.name = "jose"
    javaGreeting.hiJava()
}
```

The first three lines are the same as what we did and reviewed earlier. First, we define the `main` function, then we print the `"Hello world"` message from Kotlin and define `javaGreeting`, referencing the `MyJFile` class instance. This has already been explained.

In line 4, which contains instructions, we can see that we access the `name` property and assign it the value `jose`. After this line, what can be considered the last line with instructions contains a call to the `hiJava` method. If we then run this code, we get the following result:

```
Hello world Kotlin!
Hello World Java!jose
```

As we can see, the difference from the previous code, where we did not use the property, is that now, from Kotlin, we are making more use of the code in Java. We need to consider access to the property and the access modifier to assign a value to the `name` property from Kotlin.

The important part here is that we do not need to call getters or setters in Java from Kotlin. This is done under the hood.

In summary, in this example, we interacted more with the Java code in different ways, addressing the challenges that arise from interacting between the languages. However, as we mentioned when presenting the JVM, we will not see these complexities while programming because they are resolved behind the scenes. If we define everything correctly and follow the general language rules, we will not encounter any problems, and the interaction will occur smoothly.

Calling Java code

Previously, we saw what interoperability in code is like; we looked at it in a tangible way. We have a file that contains Kotlin code and another file that contains Java code. From the Kotlin file, we call the class or any element that is defined in a Java file without problems.

Now, as an exercise and to clarify some points, we are going to share how this happens oppositely, that is, how a Java file uses the code of a Kotlin file.

We are going to create a Java file as we normally do in Java by default:

> **Note**
>
> Remember that the Java code goes into the Java directory and the Kotlin code goes into the Kotlin directory.

Let's start by creating a basic Java file:

```
public class Main {
    public static void main(String[] args){
```

```
    }
}
```

We are doing a literal translation of the Java code to Kotlin, but as we will see later, this would be much better written in a different way in Kotlin – it is much simpler and has fewer lines of code. If we wanted to do it in the best way, taking advantage of Kotlin 100%, we would use the `Data` class, but we will explain this topic later, in *Chapter 7*. For now, as we already mentioned, it is a translation of the literal code from Java to Kotlin:

```
class MyKFile {
    private var name: String? = null
    fun setName(name:String){
        this.name = name
    }

    fun getName(): String? {
        return name
    }

    fun hiKotlin(){
        println("Hello World Kotlin! ${this.name}")
    }
}
```

We create a new file in the Kotlin directory. Let's explain line by line.

```
class MyKFile {
```

The name is `MyKFile.kt`, and the first line is the instruction to create the class with the name:

```
private var name: String? = null
```

The second instruction is the definition of the variable named `name`. We can see we are using `null` and a question mark "?". For now, we don't need more details, but we are using the question mark because we need to be prepared for the possibility of receiving a null string (remember, Java can receive `null` at any moment). In the next chapter, we will see all the details about `null` and `nullable`.

```
fun setName(name:String){
        this.name = name
    }
```

```
    fun getName(): String? {
        return name
    }
```

`setName` and `getName` are two methods of this class. `setName` assigns a value that is received as a parameter and is assigned to the `name` variable.

`getName` is the method to return the value of the `name` variable:

```
fun hiKotlin(){
        println("Hello World Kotlin! ${this.name}")
    }
```

The last method is called `hiKotlin`, and the instruction is just a print instruction to type `Hello World Kotlin` and add the `name` variable value.

If we compare it with the last Java file where we created a class, it's very similar. The main difference is we are using Kotlin now.

Sometimes we need to use the ? mark again because it is a way to let the variable have a null value.

Let's go back to the Java `Main` class file. We need to add code to use the new Kotlin file. The code is as follows:

```
public class Main {
    public static void main(String[] args){
        MyKFile myKFile = new MyKFile();
        myKFile.setName("My Kotlin file");
        myKFile.hiKotlin();
        System.out.println("Hello World Java!");
    }
}
```

Let's explain the code line by line:

```
public class Main {
    public static void main(String[] args)
```

We already know the first two – they are the definition of the class and the function that allows executing code in Java.

```
MyKFile myKFile = new MyKFile();
```

Notice that the `new` keyword is required here because we are creating a Kotlin object from Java. However, when calling Java code from Kotlin, `new` is not used – Kotlin handles object instantiation without it. This is one of the syntax differences to keep in mind when working across both languages.

We create a new instance that will be called `myKFile`, and it will be of type `MyKFile` class, which is the Kotlin class that we defined:

```
myKFile.setName("My Kotlin file");
```

In this instruction, we assign a value to the `name` property. We use the text string `"My Kotlin file"`:

```
myKFile.hiKotlin();
```

Now, we are going to use the `hiKotlin()` method, which, as we already saw where we defined it, prints a line:

```
System.out.println("Hello World Java!");
```

Our last instruction then is a printout of `hello world` that references Java. The goal is that we can see that the first `hello world` is displayed from the Kotlin file and the second one from this Java file.

The result of running this code is as follows:

```
Hello World Kotlin! My Kotlin file
Hello World Java!
```

As we can see in a general and quick way, Kotlin can use elements that are in Java, and Java can use elements written in Kotlin, so we can say that interoperability looks friendly and quite practical from what we have been able to observe.

Of course, there are elements of one or the other language that we must pay attention to, but we will be able to find those details as we advance in the book. As we have yet to do on the subject of nulls, Kotlin, being different, has to adapt some things to the properties of Java itself, but that does not imply that we have a drastic change in the logic of the program.

Gradle and Maven

In today's software development world, we can see that tools appear every day to make programmers' lives easier. Many of them do not survive and simply become a fad for a year or a couple of years, if they are lucky, and then fade away.

In the world of software development with Java, we can say that the same thing happens in all languages. But some tools play an important role within the language, and the industry, and sometimes they stay for much longer. We can say that Gradle and Maven are examples of tools that have remained in the Java ecosystem for years and are probably the most used and well-known tools within the Java ecosystem.

Both tools have the main objective of being tools for project management. This can include tasks such as dependency management, as well as the automation of project construction or configuration.

There are more tools available, but these stand out due to their wide adoption. While they are often compared, they take different approaches to solving similar problems. Neither is inherently superior, and the choice depends on the specific situation and requirements.

We must remember that interoperability allows Kotlin to use many or most of the tools that are already being used in Java, which is why it is very common to find that the Kotlin market adopts the same tools or some slight variations.

Maven

Out of the two options we have mentioned, Maven is the tool that has been on the market the longest, since it began to be used in 2004 and is now widely recognized. Being on the market for longer, it is clear that it has more information, more help, more forums, and a large community. It is also known for being a very well-documented and robust technology. With the time it has existed, implementations, and projects, we can say that the developer community also considers it to be very reliable.

Maven uses an XML-based approach to work. Its name is **Project Object Model (POM)**. This is an XML file that defines the project model, which includes dependencies as well. This is a declarative structure.

There is a very popular principle in Maven, which is the *convention over configuration* principle. This means that a default structure is assumed and thus reduces the problem of having to configure the project.

Stability, as we mentioned, is not a problem for Maven, with the time it has been on the market, plus the community, it has a very clear focus and path to follow.

Finally, Maven integrates with what is known as a robust central repository, which facilitates dependency management.

To add Maven or Gradle to a project, it is best to do so during project creation. Typically, when creating a project, options for the project name, Java version, programming language, and the choice between Gradle or Maven are provided. This process is automated when using a wizard from the IDE. However, if you create the project manually, you will need to configure everything yourself. It is common practice to specify which build tool (Gradle or Maven) you will use at the start of the project.

There are more tools, but Maven and Gradle are the ones that dominate widely and stand out for the wide adoption they already have. Curiously, they are often compared, but the reality is that both have different approaches. They can solve the same or very similar problems, but they solve them in different ways. So, we cannot say that either is superior to the other. Depending on the situation, we can use either Maven or Gradle.

This would be the default code that is created when we select a Kotlin + Maven project:

```
<?xml version="1.0" encoding="UTF-8"?>
<project xmlns:xsi="http://www.w3.org/2001/XMLSchema-instance"
         xmlns="http://maven.apache.org/POM/4.0.0"
         xsi:schemaLocation="http://maven.apache.org/POM/4.0.0 http://
maven.apache.org/xsd/maven-4.0.0.xsd">
    <modelVersion>4.0.0</modelVersion>

    <artifactId>consoleApp</artifactId>
    <groupId>org.example</groupId>
    <version>1.0-SNAPSHOT</version>
    <packaging>jar</packaging>

    <name>consoleApp</name>

    <properties>
        <project.build.sourceEncoding>UTF-8</project.build.sourceEncoding>
        <kotlin.code.style>official</kotlin.code.style>
        <kotlin.compiler.jvmTarget>1.8</kotlin.compiler.jvmTarget>
    </properties>

    <repositories>
        <repository>
            <id>mavenCentral</id>
```

```
            <url>https://repo1.maven.org/maven2/</url>
        </repository>
    </repositories>

    <build>
        <sourceDirectory>src/main/kotlin</sourceDirectory>
...

</project>
```

Let's take a look at the main tags:

- `project`: Contains the basic information of the project, such as the package type, version, name, and model version (POM schema). It is the main tag where everything else is encapsulated to respect the XML format. For example, the version when you are going to release your project to production would be `1.0. 0`, indicating that it is the final version and you have completed the development. However, it's common for many projects to remain in a 0.x version during development, especially when still evolving or before reaching a stable release.
- `properties`: It contains the properties of the project. It can have, for example, the encoding and `jvmTarget`.
- `repositories`: Indicates which repositories we can use. In this case, it refers to `MavenCentral`. Maven Central is a repository that we are going to use a lot within the Kotlin and Java ecosystem.
- `build`: We can see that it refers to the directory that contains the Kotlin code, and also to the test directory. You will also notice that it has a section defined for the plugins.
- `dependencies`: We can say that, here, we place the libraries that we want to include in the project. For example, in this case, by default, it is `Junit5`.

As an example, we will modify the `pom.xml` file.

We will do something basic but very useful – adding the `log4j` dependency, which is a popular logging library for Java applications. We are not interested in testing code functionality, just in simply showing how we modified the file and the process.

In the `dependencies` section, we will add the Maven code. Normally, to find it, we simply go to the GitHub repository or the project's official website. In an internet search engine, we can type the name of the project plus the word "Maven" to locate it quickly.

For example, if we are looking for Log4j 2, we can go directly to its GitHub repository:

`https://github.com/apache/logging-log4j2`

Alternatively, we can go directly to the Maven repository to find the latest version and copy the dependency snippet, for example: `https://mvnrepository.com/artifact/org.apache.logging.log4j/log4j/2.23.1`

We are using **log4j Maven**.

The first result of the search or the first five will always refer to the project or a similar project. Here's the code to the reference of the **pom** file:

```
<dependency>
    <groupId>org.apache.logging.log4j</groupId>
    <artifactId>log4j-api</artifactId>
    <version>2.23.1</version>
</dependency>
<dependency>
    <groupId>org.apache.logging.log4j</groupId>
    <artifactId>log4j-core</artifactId>
    <version>2.23.1</version>
</dependency>
```

We added `Log4j` in our `dependencies` section, which we already had. Now the code looks like this:

```
<dependencies>
    <dependency>
        <groupId>org.jetbrains.kotlin</groupId>
        <artifactId>kotlin-test-junit5</artifactId>
        <version>1.7.21</version>
        <scope>test</scope>
    </dependency>
    <dependency>
        <groupId>org.junit.jupiter</groupId>
        <artifactId>junit-jupiter-engine</artifactId>
        <version>5.8.2</version>
        <scope>test</scope>
    </dependency>
    <dependency>
        <groupId>org.jetbrains.kotlin</groupId>
```

```
        <artifactId>kotlin-stdlib-jdk8</artifactId>
        <version>1.7.21</version>
    </dependency>
    <dependency>
        <groupId>org.apache.logging.log4j</groupId>
        <artifactId>log4j-api</artifactId>
        <version>2.23.1</version>
    </dependency>
    <dependency>
        <groupId>org.apache.logging.log4j</groupId>
        <artifactId>log4j-core</artifactId>
        <version>2.23.1</version>
    </dependency>
</dependencies>
```

In the last part of the code, you can see that the change has already been made. However, the dependency has been added to the document and not to the project. To properly integrate the new dependency, we need Maven to reload and apply the updated configuration. This process ensures that any new dependencies in the `pom.xml` file are downloaded and integrated into the project, and any removed dependencies are cleaned up.

To let Maven reload with the new configuration, follow these steps:

1. **Update dependencies**: Ensure that any new dependencies added to the `pom.xml` file are downloaded and available for the project. This may involve resolving and downloading new libraries.
2. **Remove unnecessary dependencies**: If any dependencies were removed from the `pom.xml` file, Maven needs to clean up and remove these from the project to prevent any leftover or unused elements. For this, we must let Maven do its job (see *Figure 2.1*):
    1. Right-click on the `pom.xml` file.
    2. Click on the **Maven** option.
    3. Click on **Reload project**.

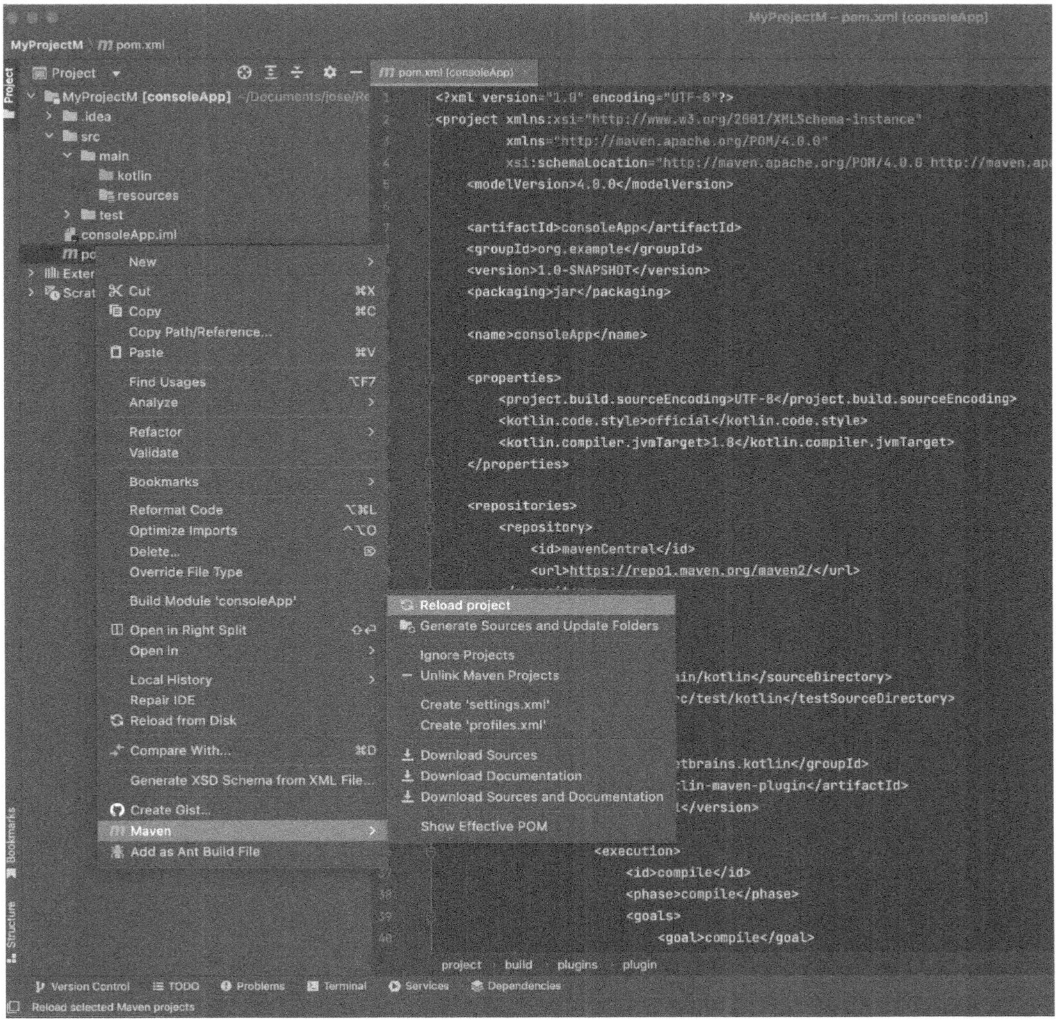

Figure 2.1 – Reload Maven project in IntelliJ IDEA

After reloading the project, we'll notice that if we add or remove the dependency, the changes will take effect. If we add a dependency to the file, it will become available for use in the project.

Congratulations on adding your first Kotlin dependency using Maven!

When using Maven with Kotlin, the setup process is quite similar to Java in terms of project structure, dependencies, and plugins. However, there are a few differences worth highlighting:

- **Kotlin plugins**: Kotlin requires specific plugins to handle the Kotlin compilation process.
- **Dependencies**: Kotlin projects may include additional libraries for Kotlin, such as the Kotlin Standard Library.
- **Interoperability**: Maven helps manage dependencies for both languages in a single build process, making it easier to migrate or integrate Kotlin.

Gradle

We can say that Gradle is a younger project within the Java ecosystem. There is a very big perception of Gradle being relatively new. This is because, at the beginning, it was not popular, until the moment when Android started to use it to manage projects that were Android applications, then Gradle began to be known.

Gradle can use scripting languages such as Groovy and Kotlin, and is very customizable. Gradle is based on DSL, so we can be much more specific if we compare it with XML.

Flexibility is one of its main differentiators. We can add condition logic, where complex projects can be more easily managed and configured.

Gradle handles incremental builds – probably its most important feature when compared to Maven. So, in performance, this makes Gradle superior. Incremental builds can significantly reduce build times, especially for large and complex projects, as they only recompile the modified components. Incremental builds consume less memory and processor resources.

Just like Maven, the recommendation is to decide which tool we are going to use for a project. To start, therefore, simply create a new project and select the name, language, and Gradle.

In the case of Gradle, we can normally choose between Groovy and Kotlin in the Gradle DSL option. In this case, we select Groovy.

Now we are going to check the main structure of the file where the Gradle file appears. In reality, the one that matters to us of all the options is the one called `build.gradle`.

Let's review the contents of the file:

```
plugins {
    id 'org.jetbrains.kotlin.jvm' version '1.7.21'
}

group = 'org.example'
version = '1.0-SNAPSHOT'

repositories {
    mavenCentral()
}

dependencies {
    testImplementation 'org.jetbrains.kotlin:kotlin-test'
}

test {
    useJUnitPlatform()
}

compileKotlin {
    kotlinOptions.jvmTarget = '1.8'
}
```

```
compileTestKotlin {
    kotlinOptions.jvmTarget = '1.8'
}
```

We can see that the script is divided into parts:

- **Plugins:** Indicate that we are going to support Kotlin in the JVM.
- **Group and version:** We define the group and version of the project.
- **Repositories**: We indicate that we are enabling `mavenCentral` to resolve dependencies.
- **Dependencies:** We include `kotlin-test` by default for testing.
- **Test configuration:** Includes `JUnit` for testing.
- **Compilation options**: We set at least or higher than, for example, JVM `1.17` for the main code and the test code in this example.

This is the default configuration. As we can see, it is much more practical, shorter, and easier to read if we compare it with Maven.

We are going to add the same `log4j` library (`https://logging.apache.org/log4j/2.3.x/maven-artifacts.html`), but now, using Gradle.

The recommendation is the same for adding a project. Most of the dependencies have their official website or repository that contains the instructions with the latest version available, just to copy and paste into our project, depending on whether it is Maven or Gradle. So, on the same website where we got the information, we looked for the Gradle section and copied and pasted it into our project, and the code now looks like this:

```
plugins {
    id 'org.jetbrains.kotlin.jvm' version '1.7.21'
}

group = 'org.example'
version = '1.0-SNAPSHOT'

repositories {
    mavenCentral()
}

dependencies {
    testImplementation 'org.jetbrains.kotlin:kotlin-test'
```

```
    implementation 'org.apache.logging.log4j:log4j-api:2.23.1'
    implementation 'org.apache.logging.log4j:log4j-core:2.23.1'
}

test {
    useJUnitPlatform()
}

kotlin {
    jvmToolchain(21)
}

compileTestKotlin {
    kotlinOptions.jvmTarget = '1.8'
}
```

When we modify the Gradle file, we will always notice that we are asked to sync, or a small pop-up window may appear where we are asked to synchronize or reload the project. Simply accept, and that's it. If we have new elements, then we may possibly see a time in which those new dependencies are downloaded, as is happening in our case, and when we remove a dependency from the dependencies file section, this dependency will no longer be available in the project, as it was removed. To conclude, we have already seen that we can use both Maven and Gradle in any project. Both are tools that continue to improve every day, so it's likely we will continue to receive news about them.

Summary

In this chapter, we delved into three fundamental pillars crucial for developers transitioning from Java to Kotlin: interoperability, Gradle, and Maven.

Kotlin's seamless integration with Java allows developers to utilize existing Java libraries, frameworks, and tools without any disruption. This interoperability enables a hybrid code base where Kotlin and Java coexist and interact efficiently, preserving established workflows and investments in Java infrastructure. Practical examples demonstrated how Kotlin and Java can work together within the same project, highlighting the simplicity and power of this integration.

Gradle, a flexible and powerful build automation tool, is fully compatible with Kotlin. It uses domain-specific languages such as Groovy and Kotlin to describe builds, offering a rich and expressive way to manage project configurations. Gradle's incremental build feature significantly enhances performance, especially for large projects, by only recompiling modified components. We discussed how to add and manage dependencies in a Gradle-based Kotlin project.

Maven, an XML-based build automation tool, has been a staple in the Java ecosystem since 2004. It uses the **Project Object Model (POM)** for project configuration and dependency management, following the convention over configuration principle. Maven's stability, extensive documentation, and robust central repository make it a reliable choice for Kotlin and Java developers. We covered how to integrate dependencies and manage project configurations using Maven.

Understanding these tools and their integration with Kotlin equips developers to manage Kotlin projects effectively, ensuring seamless dependency handling, build automation, and project configurations.

In the next chapter, we will explore the concepts of nullability and nulls in Kotlin. We will delve into how Kotlin handles null values, the syntax for dealing with nullable types, and the advantages of Kotlin's null safety features compared to Java. This will further enhance your ability to write robust and error-free code in Kotlin.

3

Null and Non-Nullable Types

In this chapter, we will dive into one of the most powerful features of Kotlin: handling nullability. For Java developers transitioning to Kotlin, understanding how Kotlin manages `null` and non-nullable types is crucial. This chapter is divided into three sections to give you a comprehensive understanding of Kotlin's approach to nullability and how it can help you write safer and more robust code. While Java allows nulls freely, Kotlin takes a different approach, emphasizing type safety and preventing null-related errors.

First, we'll explore how Kotlin approaches null values, and then we will provide you with the tools to write safer, more reliable code.

We will explore the concept of null in Kotlin. Unlike Java, Kotlin distinguishes between nullable and non-nullable types at the language level. You will learn how to declare nullable types and understand the implications of using them in your Kotlin code. This will set the foundation for understanding Kotlin's null-safety mechanisms.

After that, we will learn how Kotlin helps prevent the notorious **NullPointerException** (**NPE**) that often plagues Java programs. We will cover key features such as safe calls, the Elvis operator, and the not-null assertion operator. After covering this, you will know how to leverage Kotlin's null safety to write cleaner and more reliable code.

In the final section, we will focus on conditions and safe calls. You will learn how to use conditional statements to handle nullable types effectively. We will also explore the power of safe calls (?.) and the Elvis operator (?:), which allows you to navigate nullable types gracefully and avoid null-related errors. Practical examples will demonstrate how these features can simplify your code and enhance its readability.

By the end of this chapter, you will have a solid understanding of how Kotlin manages nullability and how you can use its null-safety features to write robust and error-free code. These lessons will not only make your code more reliable but also reduce the risk of runtime errors – leading to safer applications and fewer surprises once your code is running in production.

We're going to cover the following main topics:

- Decoding null in Kotlin
- Null safety
- Conditions and safe calls

Technical requirements

To begin, you can use any text editor or **Integrated Development Environment** (**IDE**) of your choice with the Java language. We recommend IntelliJ IDEA **Community Edition** (**CE**). This tool already comes with everything you need to work with both Java and Kotlin.

The software requirements for this chapter, which the versions, are as follows:

- Java JDK 17 or higher
- IntelliJ IDEA CE
- Kotlin 1.x or 2.x

The code used in the chapters can be found in the book's accompanying GitHub repository:

`https://github.com/PacktPublishing/Kotlin-for-Java-Developers.`

Decoding null in Kotlin

In the programming world, the concept of null values has been the cause of numerous errors and headaches. Null references have particularly been a critical source of bugs and crashes in Java, where the NPE is a common problem. Kotlin addresses this issue by incorporating null safety directly into the type system. In this section, we will explore how Kotlin handles nullability, ensuring that developers can write safer and more reliable code.

Before we discuss null from a Kotlin perspective, we will understand it from a Java perspective in order to later compare them. Let's look at the Java perspective of null.

What is null in Java?

In Java, `null` is a value that represents the absence of an object. We could also say that null is a literal value that can be assigned to any reference type variable. Any reference of the `type` object can be null, meaning that it does not point to any instance of a particular object. However, using `null` in Java can be error-prone. The exception that occurs is an NPE, which occurs when you try to access methods or properties of an object that is null.

So, we can say that *null is a value that can be assigned to any reference type variable.*

At a technical level, we could say that when we have a null, it means that we have an object reference that does not point to any object in memory.

Each object in Java is stored in a memory region called the **heap**. When an object is created, a unique memory address is allocated on the heap, and this address is used to access the object. Reference variables do not directly contain the object but instead store the memory address where the object is located.

A null value is represented as a special address, called a null address, which does not point to any valid object in memory.

The null address is a special memory address used to indicate the absence of an object. In most computer architectures, this address is defined as a predefined constant value. Typically, the value `0` is used, although in some architectures it may be `-1` or some other specific value.

For example, in architectures such as those based on `x86` processors, the memory address that represents null is implemented as the value `0`. This means that if a memory address containing `0` is accessed, it is interpreted as a null reference.

In other architectures, such as those based on PowerPC processors, the null address may be implemented as the value `-1`. In this case, accessing a memory address containing `-1` is interpreted as a null reference.

Understanding null in memory

In most architectures, null is represented as the memory address `0`. This value is predefined and reserved to indicate that the reference does not point to any valid object.

Let's create a string with Java:

```
String name = new String("Jose");
```

💡 **Quick tip:** Enhance your coding experience with the **AI Code Explainer** and **Quick Copy** features. Open this book in the next-gen Packt Reader. Click the **Copy** button **(1)** to quickly copy code into your coding environment, or click the **Explain** button **(2)** to get the AI assistant to explain a block of code to you.

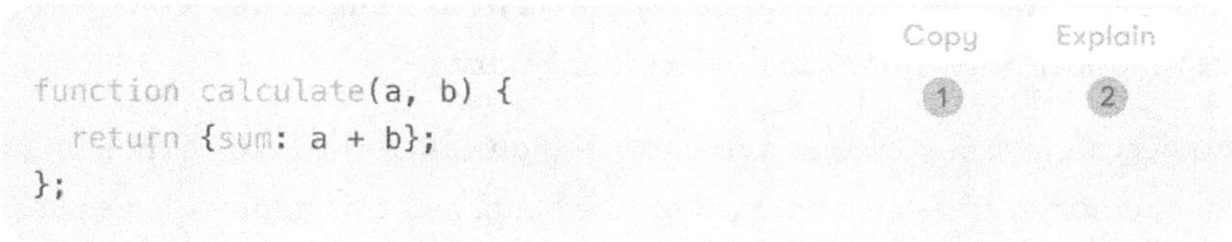

The next-gen Packt Reader is included for free with the purchase of this book. Scan the QR code OR go to `https://packtpub.com/unlock`, then use the search bar to find this book by name. Double-check the edition shown to make sure you get the right one.

This is the code we need if we want to create a text string in Java. We could put any text within the double quotes, and this would be considered the value of this object.

On a technical level, what happens is that a `String` object is created at some memory location, and this location is assigned to the `name` variable. So, `name` now points to the starting memory address where the string `"Jose"` is stored.

In Java, if we want the object to change the value to `null`, we simply have to add the next line of code. We assign the value in the following way:

```
name = null
```

First, we created a variable name and assigned it the address of the string `"Jose"`. That means the name was pointing to the memory location where the string data was stored.

After assigning `null`, the variable name no longer contains a valid memory address. Instead, it stores a special value known as the null address, which indicates that it doesn't point to any object. Normally, when we create an object, memory is allocated to store its data, and the variable holds the address of that memory location.

Let's print the value of `name`:

```
System.out.println(name);
```

This is the complete code:

```
public class Main {
    public static void main(String[] args){
        String name = new String("Jose");
        name = null;
        System.out.println(name);
    }
}
```

The result is as follows:

```
null
```

Let's now add a line of code twice to make the difference clear. Seeing `null` as a result can fool us if we don't look deeper. The line of code is as follows:

```
System.out.println(name.length());
```

We are going to add it two times, once after creating the string and then again when we change it to `null`. The complete code is as follows:

```
public class Main {
    public static void main(String[] args){
        String name = new String("Jose");
        System.out.println(name.length());
        name = null;
        System.out.println(name.length());
        System.out.println(name);
    }
}
```

The result is as follows:

```
4
Exception in thread "main" java.lang.NullPointerException: Cannot invoke
"String.length()" because "name" is null
at Main.main(Main.java:6)
```

First, it prints the number 4. This is because the string contains `Jose` and has four characters. So, this is correct; notice how the logic matches what we expect.

But after we assign *null* to the variable, the next call to `name.length()` throws an exception. This happens because we're trying to access a method on a variable that now holds null. Previously, it worked, but once the reference no longer points to a valid object, calling its methods results in an NPE. *This is a common error in Java, and it cannot be caught at compile time* – it only fails when the program is running.

When a string is `null`, it does not have a length because it does not represent a real object.

Calling `length()` on a null reference results in an NPE – a situation Java developers will be all too familiar with. This example serves as a reminder of why Kotlin introduces null safety as a core language feature.

What does null really mean?

`null` is not stored as a specific value in memory. Rather, it is a concept that indicates the absence of a reference to an object. When a variable is `null`, it means that it does not point to any object in memory.

We can also understand why it will generate an error when we execute the code through this logic: methods, such as `length()`, are actions that can be performed on objects. An object is an instance of a class that contains data and methods. For a method to be called on an object, the variable that refers to the object must not be `null`.

Our specific code can be fixed in two ways.

The first is simple, although it is not practical for code used in large projects: we remove the `null` assignment that we made ourselves. With this, the code will work without a problem. But this solution just works around the problem; we have just shared it in case you want to quickly execute the code.

The solution that is often used in general in Java is to be prepared for the possibility of null, and this is very easy; this would be the code:

```
public class Main {
    public static void main(String[] args){
        String name = new String("Jose");
        System.out.println(name.length());
        name = null;
        if (name != null) {
            System.out.println(name.length());
        } else {
            System.out.println("The name variable is null!");
        }
        System.out.println(name);
    }
}
```

We need to focus on the `if` condition. This condition will avoid the exception, since we can see that the condition is responsible for finding out whether `name` is `null` at this moment:

```
if (name != null) {
```

This helps us take the next step depending on whether it is `null` or not. If it is not `null`, then we can use the `length` instruction to find out the size of the string:

```
System.out.println(name.length());
```

If it is `null`, instead of using `length`, which we already know would cause an exception, we will then print only that it is `null`, and that is how we will know that this is the reason for not showing the size:

```
} else {
        System.out.println("The name variable is null!");
}
```

With this, we have made it clear that although we see the word `null` when accessing the object, this has no relation to it being a text string; a string is different from `null`. We shouldn't be fooled by the fact that the values displayed are both text strings.

Key takeaways

From the above operations, we can gather that following are the key takeaways of `null`:

- `null` is a keyword in Java that represents a special value.
- There is no distinction in the type system between references that can be null and those that cannot be `null`.
- There is no compile-time checking to prevent null errors.
- It will cause an NPE at runtime if you try to access a method or property of a null object.
- `null` can be assigned to any variable that is a reference type (objects, arrays, and interfaces).
- `null` is the only value that can be assigned to a variable of any reference type without causing a type error.
- Technically, null is of type null, which is a subtype of all other reference types.
- At the hardware level, `null` is represented as a special memory address.
- This address, called the **null address**, is a predefined value that the system recognizes as an indicator that there is no valid object at that location.
- An NPE helps prevent the program from continuing with potentially unexpected behavior.
- Using null is memory efficient as it does not require storing additional data.
- All null references share the same memory representation, regardless of the type of object they might refer to.

What is null in Kotlin?

In Kotlin, null is used to represent the absence of a value, just like in Java. However, Kotlin clearly differentiates between types that can contain null (nullable) and types that cannot contain null (non-nullable).

The main difference is that Kotlin forces developers to explicitly handle null cases, significantly reducing null-related errors at runtime. In Kotlin, the type system is designed to explicitly distinguish between references that can contain null and those that cannot. This distinction is made at the type level, meaning it is built into the language's type system.

We are going to use the same example of the name string but now in the Kotlin programming language, to be able to see what we mentioned:

```
fun main(args: Array<String> ){
    var name: String = "Jose"
    println(name)
    println(name.length)
}
```

We can see that we have two lines, one to print the name and another the size of the string. The result is this:

```
Jose
4
```

But then we will make name null as we did earlier in Java. We need to add this line at the end of the previous code:

```
name= null
```

This will be flagged as an error, and what we will notice is that depending on the editor or the development environment, the message will be the same: **Null can not be a value of a non-null type String.**

This is an error message that the Kotlin compiler displays when you try to assign a null value to a variable or parameter of a non-nullable type. As we have discussed, there is a clear distinction between nullable and non-nullable types. A regular String is a non-nullable type, meaning it cannot contain null.

So, now we understand that String is a non-null type, but if we really need this string to allow null, we will have to make a change in the definition.

In order to be able to use null, we will do this in the code:

```
    var name: String? = "Jose"
```

We have added the question mark so that we can then set the null value to the name text string. In fact, we can see that the line that was showing an error no longer shows an error:

```
name= null
```

Now we have the option to change the value of the string to null as many times as we want in our code.

But if you are observant, you will have noticed that we now have an error on another line within the same code. This is the line that marks an error:

```
println(name.length)
```

For now, this does not affect us, since we will solve it in the next section. But before finishing this section, we are going to share some key points that can be added to what was shared previously about what we should know about null in Kotlin.

> **Nullability in Kotlin**
>
> In Kotlin, `null` also represents the absence of a value.
>
> Kotlin introduces a nullable and non-nullable type system.
>
> By default, types are non-nullable.
>
> The ? operator is used to declare nullable types (for example, `String?`).
>
> The Kotlin compiler performs nullity checks and does not allow assigning null to non-nullable types.

We now understand how Kotlin handles nullability. Throughout this section, we've compared several aspects of Kotlin and Java. We've highlighted specific cases where their behavior differs, and shown how Kotlin simplifies many of these situations. This gives us a clear idea of what to expect when working with nulls in Kotlin. In the following section, we'll explore null safety in depth. We'll see how it brings significant benefits to our code, and also examine the concept thoroughly to understand everything involved in applying it effectively in real projects.

Null safety

Many times, when we talk about a feature of a programming language, we expect it to refer to just a character or a line of code. That is why when programmers are introduced to the concept of **null safety**, they are initially a little confused since it is not just one thing. Null safety is a concept encapsulating a set of characteristics of the programming language that are designed to prevent errors that can cause null references. These errors, as we are aware, are known as NPEs, and they occur at runtime.

Something we have already seen that we can include as part of null safety is the ability to have null and non-null types. It is very easy to distinguish whether we can have null by simply knowing the type, since if it is not of the nullable type, then we know that it cannot be null.

The following is example code with non-nullable types:

```
fun main(args: Array<String> ){
    var name: String = "Jose"
    var age: Int = 10
    var height: Double = 172.5
    var student: Boolean = true
}
```

We can see that they are only common definitions of what we have already done previously. If we want to use these same elements but as nullables, the code would be this:

```
fun main(args: Array<String> ){
    var name: String? = null
    var age: Int? = null
    var height: Double? = null
    var student: Boolean? = null
}
```

We have added, as previously mentioned, the question mark, ?, to the definition of the elements we are creating. With this, we are simply giving them the ability to be null. As we mentioned, this is just one of the concepts that make up null safety.

Another detail to notice is that the Kotlin compiler forces developers to explicitly handle the possibility of null when working with nullable types. This manifests itself in several ways.

The compiler does not allow direct access to properties or methods of a nullable type.

The other available features that make up null safety are the following:

- Conditions
- Safe calls
- Elvis operator
- `!!` operator
- Safe cast

Null safety in Kotlin is a set of tools that prevent NPE errors. The key is to distinguish between null (`String?`) and non-null (`String`) types, allowing the compiler to force explicit null handling. These tools, which we just introduced, allow Kotlin to handle null values in a safe and expressive way, reducing the risk of runtime exceptions and making our code more predictable.

In the next section, we will work with conditions and calls to be better prepared in handling and working with null. We will see everything in great detail as it will also allow us to understand and master all the concepts later on.

Conditions and safe calls

Let's remember that we left some code with an error when we were starting to understand how Kotlin uses nulls. The code is as follows:

```
fun main(args: Array<String> ){
    var name: String? = "Jose"
    println(name)
    println(name.length)
    name= null
}
```

Safe call

The error occurs on the line where we try to get the length of the string. The message is: **Only safe (?.) or non-null asserted (!!.) calls are allowed on a nullable receiver of type String?.**

This means we're trying to access a property or method on a variable that could be null, without using the proper safety operators. This line has an error:

```
    println(name.length)
```

This means that we have to be prepared in case this is null, because if it is, just like in Java, we will not have a size that we can display and we would end up with an error.

So, we have two possible situations:

- If the `name` string has a value, then everything will work fine.
- If the string contains a null, then this will throw an error.

This is where we can say that it is not safe to run the code because there is a possibility that it will stop abruptly.

So, we need to make what is called a **safe call**. We do this using the question mark operator (`?.`). It's the same operator we previously used to allow nulls in variable declarations. Now, we place it before the method call on an object that could potentially be `null`. Here's what the change looks like:

```
    println(name?.length)
```

Now, let's look at the two possibilities. The first one is if `name` has a `String`:

```
var name: String? = "Jose"
println(name?.length)
```

The result is as follows:

```
4
```

The second possibility is if `name` has `null`:

```
var name: String? = null
println(name?.length)
```

The result is as follows:

```
null
```

As we can see, both options are valid at the moment; neither of them ends the execution of the code abruptly. This is because we used a safe call.

So, let's recap what is happening:

```
println(name?.length)
```

The preceding code attempts to print the length of the `String` value stored in the `name` variable. However, it does this in a safe manner using the null-safe call operator. If `name` is not null, the operator proceeds to access the `length` property and print the value. If `name` is `null`, the operator simply returns null, preventing an NPE error and avoiding unwanted output.

Basically, the null check that we did in Java explicitly is done here for us by the compiler.

Conditions

We looked at two possible scenarios in the previous example, but surely some programmers have thought of the possibility of using `if`? We can use `if`, and although many times it is not the most elegant and clear option, sometimes we may have the need to do so. An example is to execute a few more instructions if we detect the possibility of it being null.

So, let's see an example of what the situation would be if we needed or wanted to work with null and conditions:

```
fun main(args: Array<String> ){
    var name: String? = "Jose"
    if (name != null)
```

```
        println(name.length)
}
```

As we see, we have the `name` string, which has the value `Jose`, and we are placing `if` which will prevent us from printing the size of the string if `name` is `null`. This is the condition:

```
    if (name != null)
```

The result is as follows:

```
4
```

Let's change the value `Jose` to null:

```
fun main(args: Array<String> ){
    var name: String? =  null
    if (name != null)
        println(name.length)
}
```

There will be no visible result of running this since we have no instructions in case it is null; we can add it with `else`:

```
fun main(args: Array<String> ){
    var name: String? = null
    if (name != null) {
        println(name.length)
    }else{
        println("Name is null")
    }
}
```

The result is as follows:

```
Name is null
```

Something important that we can mention is that we can do this more easily in a single line, as in the following example:

```
if (name != null) println(name.length) else println("Name is null")
```

Although it may seem a bit complex to read at first, we encourage you to start taking advantage of these Kotlin features to write more concise and robust code. It's one of the language's most powerful capabilities.

Elvis operator

In Kotlin, the Elvis operator is a concise and convenient way to handle nullable variables and provide default values if they turn out to be null. It's represented by the question mark followed by a colon (`?:`).

The Elvis operator (`?:`) provides a default value when an expression to its left is null.

We can say in simple words that it is a ready conditional prepared to work with nulls, so it makes dealing with them shorter in code, but also much easier and clearer to read.

Let's change the previous code using the Elvis operator:

```
fun main(args: Array<String> ){
    var name: String? = null
    val size = name?.length ?: "Name is null"
    print(size)
}
```

Observe that everything happens on this line:

```
    val size = name?.length ?: "Name is null"
```

The Elvis operator will return something; this something will be stored in the `size` variable, where we have two possibilities: if it is not null, then the first thing is executed, which is the instruction that is further to the left of where we ask for the size of `name`. But if the opposite is true, that is, if `name` is null, then we will execute the following instruction, which is then a text string that tells us that `name` is null.

As we can see, we can say simply that we already have a pre-made `if` ready to execute depending on the situation, whether it is null or not.

The Elvis operator is normally only used when we need to handle a value in a simple way. If we need to execute more than one instruction on a value or perform previous instructions a few more times, then the Elvis operator may be too short. In those cases, it would be recommended to use, as we saw previously, `if` that allows containing more complex operations in code and a large size. Another recommendation is to always think about whether there is the possibility of reducing the code by using this operator, since the simplicity achieved is very good and makes it easy to read.

Another situation where it is convenient to use the Elvis operator is if you want to provide a default value if the nullable variable is `null`.

We can compare the Elvis operator with the null-safe operator:

- **Null-safe operator (?.)**: Checks whether the variable is null before performing the operation. If null, it returns `null`.
- **Elvis operator (?:)**: Provides a default value if the variable is `null`. If not `null`, it returns the variable's value.

Just as a gentle reminder, this and the other mechanisms for working with nulls we're looking at are part of null safety.

Safe cast

To explain safe cast, we are going to use the code directly. This would be our example if we decided to use safe cast:

```
fun main(args: Array<String> ){
        var name: Any? = "Jose"
        val n = name as? String
        print(n)
}
```

This line declares a variable named `name` of type `Any?`:

```
var name: Any? = "Jose"
```

The question mark (?) after `Any` indicates that it's a nullable variable, meaning it can hold any type of value, including null. Here, it's initialized with the string value `Jose`.

This line is the key part:

```
val n = name as? String
```

It performs a **safe cast** using the `as?` operator. This operator attempts to convert the value stored in `name` to a `String` type, but it does so safely:

- If `name` actually contains a `String` value (`"Jose"`, in this case), the cast is successful, and the converted `String` value is assigned to the variable `n`.
- If `name` is null, or if it contains a value that cannot be converted to a string (e.g., an integer), the cast fails, and `n` will be assigned null. The `as?` operator prevents a `ClassCastException` error that would occur with an unsafe cast.

The `as?` operator allows for safe conversion of nullable variables, preventing crashes due to incompatible types or null values. Even though `name` is declared as `Any?`, the code attempts to convert it to a string using the safe cast. This is because the safe cast checks for compatibility before performing the conversion.

The safe cast operator (`as?`) in Kotlin is a valuable tool for working with types that may be null or unknown. It allows type conversions to be performed safely, returning null instead of throwing an exception if the conversion fails. This improves code robustness and clarity, making type handling safer and more predictable.

The !! operator

The `!!` operator in Kotlin, known as the non-null assertion operator, is a powerful but potentially dangerous tool. Unlike the other null-safety features we've seen so far, this one gives us more freedom – and with that, more risk.

The tools we explored earlier help us safely navigate around null values, adding useful constraints that prevent many common errors. However, `!!` bypasses those constraints. If we misuse it, we can still run into runtime exceptions such as an NPE, just as in Java.

In simple terms, we can say that the `!!` operator converts any value into a non-null type and throws an exception if the value is `null`.

We, as programmers, are telling the compiler to trust us and that we are sure that this is not a `null` value. From this, it is clear that we have explicitly told the compiler that we will take care of this now, and it is our responsibility.

It is important to be aware of the following:

- It can cause an NPE at runtime.
- It negates the advantages of Kotlin's nullable type system.
- It is often considered an "*easy way out*" and can hide design issues.

Of all the mechanisms we have mentioned, we can also say that it is the most insecure. We would first have to analyze the following:

- `.?`
- Conditionals
- Elvis operator, `?:`
- Safe cast

In fact, there are some companies or development teams that do not approve or allow the use of this operator. Or, if it is going to be allowed, the implementer requires a very good justification and to review whether it is the most viable option.

In our example, we will see an error if we apply it. We have better options, as we saw previously, but we need to see how we can use it:

```
fun main(args: Array<String> ){
    var name: String? = null
    print (name!!.length)
}
```

If we execute this code, the result is as follows:

```
Exception in thread "main" java.lang.NullPointerException
at MainKt.main(Main.kt:5)
```

As we mentioned, more often than not, this is a dangerous instead of a good option. It should be used in situations where there is absolute certainty that the value is not null or as a last resort when other, safer options are not viable.

Summary

In this chapter, we've explored the powerful nullability-handling features of Kotlin, which significantly enhance code safety and reliability compared to Java. As a Java developer transitioning to Kotlin, you have learned how Kotlin manages null and non-nullable types, providing a safer programming environment by reducing the risks of null-related errors such as NPE.

In Java, null values are permitted freely, which can result in NPE errors at runtime. Kotlin addresses this issue by distinguishing between nullable types, such as `String?`, and non-nullable types, such as `String`. This distinction is enforced at the type system level, ensuring greater safety by preventing null-related errors.

Kotlin offers several mechanisms to handle null safety effectively. Understanding how to declare and use non-nullable and nullable types is fundamental to avoiding unintended null values. Safe calls, denoted by `?.`, allow you to access properties or methods of a nullable type without the risk of encountering an NPE. The Elvis operator, `?:`, further enhances code clarity and conciseness by providing default values for null cases. Safe casts, represented by `as?`, enable safe type conversions, returning null if the conversion is not possible, thereby preventing exceptions. The non-null assertion operator, `!!`, forces a nullable type to be treated as non-nullable, though this comes with the risk of throwing an NPE if the value is indeed `null`.

Don't forget that when transitioning from Java-style null handling to Kotlin's safer approach, it's important to effectively use conditionals and safe calls to manage nullable types. The Elvis operator can be a powerful tool to simplify and clarify code logic. Finally, while the non-null assertion operator, `!!`, can be useful, it's crucial to understand its potential risks and apply it judiciously.

Understanding Kotlin's approach to nullability is crucial for writing robust and error-free code. By leveraging Kotlin's null-safety features, you can significantly reduce the risk of runtime errors, leading to more reliable and maintainable applications. These features promote better coding practices by making null handling explicit and integral to the code, rather than an afterthought.

In the next chapter, we will go into Kotlin's extension functions and learn how we can use them.

4

Extension Functions and the Apply Function

In the vast ecosystem of modern programming languages, **Kotlin** stands out as a beacon of innovation and pragmatism. Its carefully crafted design not only addresses the limitations of its predecessors but also introduces powerful features that transform the way developers approach everyday programming challenges. In this chapter, we'll dive into some of these features.

Extension functions represent one of the most significant advancements in object-oriented programming in recent years. These functions allow developers to extend the capabilities of existing classes without needing to inherit from them or modify their original source code. Imagine being able to add new methods to system classes or third-party libraries as if they were an intrinsic part of those classes. This capability not only improves code readability and maintainability but also opens new possibilities for designing fluent and expressive APIs.

On the other hand, the `apply` function belongs to a special set of utilities in Kotlin known as **scope functions**. These functions are designed to simplify and clarify code, especially when it comes to setting or modifying objects. The `apply` function provides an elegant way to work with objects, allowing multiple operations in a concise and readable context. Using it can transform verbose blocks of code into concise and self-explanatory expressions, significantly improving clarity and reducing the likelihood of errors.

Throughout this chapter, we'll explore in depth how these two features can be leveraged to elevate the quality of our Kotlin code. We'll begin by breaking down the syntax and inner workings of extension functions, examining how they integrate with the Kotlin type system and how they can coexist with regular methods. We'll analyze common usage patterns, discuss best practices, and warn about potential pitfalls to avoid.

In this chapter, we're going to cover the following main topics:

- What is an extension?
- Companion objects and properties
- The `apply` function

Technical requirements

To begin, you can use any text editor or **integrated development environment** (**IDE**) of your choice with the Java language. We recommend IntelliJ IDEA **Community Edition** (**CE**). This tool comes with everything you need to work with both Java and Kotlin. The list of requirements for this chapter is as follows:

- Java JDK 17 or higher
- IntelliJ IDEA CE
- Kotlin 1.x or 2.x

The code used in the chapter can be found in the book's accompanying GitHub repository: `https://github.com/PacktPublishing/Kotlin-for-Java-Developers`.

What is an extension function?

Function extensions in Kotlin are one of the most interesting features in the universe of possibilities that Kotlin provides. We can say that a function extension will allow us to extend the functionality of a class that already exists. This highlights that function extensions allow us to increase the capabilities of the classes that we already have in our code so that we don't have to modify them.

Imagine going to a restaurant where the chef has already prepared a set menu with fixed dishes – pasta, pizza, and salads. You love the pasta but wish it came with a special sauce that's not on the menu. You can't ask the restaurant to change the pasta for everyone, but you can bring your own special sauce and pour it on top of your dish without changing the restaurant's menu. The pasta remains the same for other customers, but for you, it has an extra flavor because of the sauce you've added.

This is similar to Kotlin's extension functions: you can extend the behavior of a class (like adding the sauce to the pasta) without modifying the class itself. The class stays unchanged for everyone else, but you get the extra functionality that you need.

To return to code, the classes that we have defined in Kotlin can be extended with additional features or capabilities by using extension functions or extension properties. **Extension functions** allow developers to add new methods to existing classes without modifying their source code or inheriting from them, while **extension properties** provide a similar mechanism for adding new properties.

In this section, we will focus on extension functions, but it's worth noting that Kotlin offers extension properties as well, which allow you to add new fields or computed values to a class without altering its original structure.

It seems like simply adding something, but remember that we often use third-party classes or libraries that are closed to prevent certain actions. With extensions, we will have the ability to interact with them in a different way and not simply use them, but improve them and adapt them to our needs without much complexity.

This adheres to the open/closed principle: classes are open for extension, but closed to change. This is an important software design principle.

How do function extensions work?

We need to make a few points clear, and we'll start with this one.

Extension functions in Kotlin don't actually modify the classes they are applied to. This means that they don't alter the original source code of the class. Instead, they provide new functionality to the class without altering its existing implementation.

Let's explain it in a more technical way so that we are 100% clear about what happens in Kotlin. The Kotlin compiler transforms extension functions into static methods, passing the receiving object as the first argument. This means that there is no runtime overhead and the extended class is not actually modified. Kotlin generates static functions that take the receiver object as their first argument.

We already know this. However, we could say that extension functions promote modular code by allowing us to extend the functionality of a class without modifying its original source code, improving organization and readability. While extension functions enhance modularity, it's important to note that when extending third-party classes, the logic is not entirely in one place, as the original class and its extensions are defined in different locations. Despite this, extension functions maintain backward compatibility by not altering the original class directly.

Something we should be aware of is that when we name an extension function, there is a chance that it could share the same name as an existing method in the class. However, it's not just the name that matters – it's also the signature, which includes the receiver type and parameters. If the extension function has the same name and a matching signature as an existing method, the class method will take priority. This ensures that the class's base behavior remains intact. To avoid conflicts, it's important to review the class methods and their signatures and check the documentation to ensure that your extension function doesn't unintentionally clash with an existing method.

One important limitation of extension functions in Kotlin is that they can only access the public API of the class they are extending. This means that extension functions cannot directly access or modify private or protected members of the class. As a user, it's crucial to be aware of this restriction, as it limits the scope of what extension functions can do. They provide a convenient way to add new functionality, but their access is confined to what is already exposed by the class, ensuring that the internal implementation remains encapsulated and secure.

On the subject of visibility and the scope of extension functions, they can be declared at the file level, meaning they are not wrapped in a surrounding class. These functions can be placed in separate files to keep the code modular and organized. Declaring extension functions at the file level allows us to extend classes without modifying their source code and keep related extension functions together. This approach is especially useful when adding functionality to third-party or existing classes while keeping the extension logic separate from the rest of the code, improving maintainability and clarity.

As we already know, extension functions are compiled into static methods. This means that when we use extension functions, there is no additional performance overhead compared to regular functions. In fact, since they are compiled as static methods, their performance is comparable to that of regular static methods in Java. The key point is that extension functions do not introduce any extra runtime cost or slow down the execution of the program.

Say we want to know whether a certain `String` value is a palindrome. This means that the value is the same front to back and back to front.

Consider this code:

```
fun String.isPalindrome() =  this.reversed().equals(this, true)

fun main() {
    println("Hello, world!!!".isPalindrome())
```

```
    println("Anna".isPalindrome())

}
```

We define an extension function, `isPalindrome`, on the `String` class. It will return a Boolean `true` value if the `String` value is a palindrome, or `false` otherwise.

We can access the `String` value using the `this` keyword. It holds the current value of the string on which this method is invoked. We take the following actions:

1. We reverse the order of the string, turning the value around.
2. Then, we compare this value to the original value, ignoring the case (as a palindrome is case-insensitive).

In the `main` function, we first call our new palindrome function on the `"Hello, World!!"` string.

In the same steps as previously, this is happening:

1. `"Hello, World!!!"` becomes `"!!!dlroW ,olleH"`.
2. As we compare ignoring the case, we compare `"hello, world!!!"` with `"!!!dlrow ,olleh"`.

The result is, of course, `false`; they are not the same.

Doing the same thing with the `"Anna"` string yields a `true` result.

Another way to organize extension functions is by creating a separate file specifically for them. While this can help keep the code organized, it's important to be cautious when doing so, especially if you're adding extensions for basic types such as `String`. Overusing top-level extension functions can pollute the namespace in the application, particularly if they're not offering generic or widely applicable functionality. Therefore, it's best to carefully evaluate whether an extension function truly adds value before placing it in a dedicated file such as `MyExtensions.kt`.

Inside the `MyExtensions.kt` file, we need to add the following line:

```
fun String.isPalindrome() =  this.reversed().equals(this, true)
```

We have just one line of code, and this line is our function extension called `isPalindrome`. We can call this second function in the `main` code without moving any previous lines of code. The code is as follows:

```
fun main(){
    val name:String = "Viena"
```

```
    val otherName: String = "Anna"
    println(name.isPalindrome())
    println(otherName.isPalindrome())
}
```

This runs without any problems. The result is the same as the previous example, where everything was in the same file. Now, let's explain how everything can be executed at the same time, even though the lines of code are separate:

- **Package-level visibility**: In Kotlin, by default, all declarations (functions, classes, etc.) are public and visible throughout the entire module, not just to other files in the same package. If you do not specify a package specifically in your files, all files in the same directory are considered part of the package by default.
- **Implicit imports**: Kotlin automatically imports all top-level declarations within the same package. This means that you do not need to specifically import functions or classes defined in other files in the same package.
- **Extension functions**: Extension functions, once defined, effectively become part of the type being extended (`String`). They are available anywhere the extended type is visible and the extension function is within reach.
- **Compilation**: During compilation, Kotlin processes all the `.kt` files in your module. This ensures that all public extension functions, regardless of where they are defined, are available across the module. However, keep in mind that their visibility follows the usual Kotlin rules (public, internal, etc.), and only functions with appropriate visibility modifiers will be accessible throughout the module.

In this example, we are using the `String` class to show how we can add a function extension without problems. Now, let's see a very similar example, but with a class created by us. We need to create a new file. This file is the new class; let's call it `MyClass`. This is the content:

```
class MyClass {

    fun printString(){
        println("Just a new String")
    }
}
```

Let's explain the code. On the first line, we are creating a class called `MyClass`, and inside this class, we have a definition to print a simple string. Note the instruction to print `"Just a new String"`. For now, we only need one method because the objective is to show how to use this class and how to add a function extension.

Let's return to the `Main` file because we have a `main` function that executes the Kotlin code. This is the new code:

```
fun main(){

    val newString = MyClass()
    newString.printString()
}
```

The first line is the `main` function definition. Inside the `main` function, we are creating a new instance of `MyClass` and then calling the `printString` method. The result of this execution is as follows:

```
Just a new String
```

We need to show how to do it. Let's add a function extension by adding this code:

```
fun main(){

    val newString = MyClass()
    newString.printString()

    fun MyClass.printInt() = println(10)
    newString.printInt()
}
```

The important part of the code lies in the last two lines. First, we define an extension function, `printInt()`, within `main()`, which prints the number `10`. Then, we call the `printInt()` method on the `newString` object, which is an instance of `MyClass`. Once executed, the code will print the value `10`, followed by the result of calling the previously defined `printString()` method:

```
Just a new String
10
```

The first line is the string definition, but the second line was added as a function extension, and as you can see, it's working.

As you can see, if we are adding an extension function to a class such as `String`, which already exists, or to a class defined by us in the program we are creating, there is no difference. Extension functions are simply code that we are adding, and they are extensions of the functionalities that we are giving to a specific class.

Even if we have full control over a class because we defined it ourselves, there are still valid reasons to use extension functions instead of regular member functions.

At first glance, it might seem unnecessary to define an extension when we could simply place the function inside the class as a method. However, Kotlin's extension functions offer several benefits that can make them a better choice in certain situations:

- **Separation of concerns**: Sometimes the behavior we want to implement does not belong to the core responsibilities of the class. By writing it as an extension, we keep the class clean and focused, while still providing additional functionality when needed.
- **Limited scope**: Extension functions can be declared only in the modules or files where they are needed. This allows us to avoid overloading the class definition with functions that might not be useful globally.
- **Fluent APIs and DSLs**: Extensions – especially when used with lambdas and receivers - can help us build more expressive APIs and domain-specific languages, which are harder to achieve with traditional methods inside a class.
- **Consistency with third-party or standard types**: Even for classes we own, it's sometimes useful to offer functionality in the same way we do for external or standard library types (such as `string`, `list`, or `date`), maintaining a consistent extension-based API across our code base.

In conclusion, using an extension function even on a class we wrote ourselves is not just syntactic sugar. It's a deliberate design choice that can improve modularity, readability, and code organization.

How to use Kotlin function extensions in Java

Now, we are going to show how an extension function can be used in a Java file. Remember that the declaration has to happen in a Kotlin file since we are talking about a Kotlin feature. So, first, we are going to create the Kotlin file that will contain the definition code. For this exercise, we are going to call it as we did before, or you can reuse the one from the previous example. The file is `MyExtension.kt`. This file will only contain the definition of a function.

This is the code:

```
fun String.isPalindrome() =  this.reversed().equals(this, true)
```

This is all the code in the file. In fact, it is the same functionality that we used before. Remember that what we are seeing is how to use this code in a Java file. Now, we are going to create the Java file that will have the `Main` class where we are going to create the executable code: the code that will be executed and will use this extension function. We are going to call the file `Main.java`, and this is the code:

```
public class Main {
    public static void main(String[] args){

        String name = "Anna";
        char secondChart = MyExtensionKt.isPalindrome(name);
        System.out.println(secondChart);

    }
}
```

The first line of code only has the definition of `Main`. In Java, we always need to place the code of the files inside a class; in this example, we have the `Main` class:

```
public class Main {
```

The second line is the declaration of the `main` method in a Java application. This method is the entry point of the application and is executed when the program starts:

```
    public static void main(String[] args){
```

The next line is just a definition. We create a string called `name` with a value of `Anna`:

```
        String name = "Anna";
```

The next line is where this Kotlin file is compiled. The extension function becomes a static method in a class with an automatically generated name – in this case, `MyExtensionKt`.

We place a variable where we want to place the result of executing this function, then we use the class to access the static method, which we already know is the extension function that we declared inside the Kotlin file. We pass it the `name` string so that it works on the right string:

```
        char secondChart = MyExtensionKt.isPalindrome(name);
```

On the last line, we are only sending the value to be printed if the result is correct:

```
System.out.println(secondChart);
```

The result we get is as follows:

```
true
```

So, while extension functions are a powerful feature in Kotlin, it's important to note that if you are working on projects that include Java, you can still use these functions, but the primary benefit is lost. In Java, extension functions are called regular static methods, which means you don't get the syntactic sugar that makes them so convenient in Kotlin. Essentially, the main advantage of Kotlin's extension functions is their concise syntax, but this is limited when interacting with Java code.

In this section, we explored the concept of extension functions in Kotlin, which allow developers to add new functionalities to existing classes without altering their source code. This is particularly useful when working with third-party libraries or classes where modification is not an option. We discussed how Kotlin handles these functions at the compiler level by turning them into static methods, ensuring no runtime performance penalty. Through various examples, we demonstrated how to extend built-in classes such as `String` and even custom classes.

The ability to extend existing classes without inheritance opens up new possibilities for modular, clean, and maintainable code. As we've seen, extensions add flexibility without compromising the original structure of your code base.

In the next section, we will dive into companion objects and properties. We'll see how companion objects allow you to define functions and properties that are tied to a class rather than instances of the class, similar to static members in Java. This will give you more control over the shared behavior in your classes.

Companion objects and properties

A companion object in Kotlin is a special object within a class that allows you to define functions and properties associated with the class, like static members in Java. However, unlike Java's static members, companion objects offer more flexibility. In Kotlin, you can implement interfaces, extend other classes, and maintain a clean object-oriented approach by encapsulating static-like behavior in an object. This makes companion objects more versatile, allowing you to retain all the benefits of Kotlin's object model, such as inheritance and interface implementation, while still providing static-like functionality.

In some ways, it is the equivalent of Java's static members, except that in Kotlin, the word *static* does not exist.

Let's use some simple code to explain the concept of companion objects. We need to create a simple class. We will use the name `MyClass`, and this is the code:

```
class MyClass {
    companion object {
        const val STATIC_VALUE = "this is a static value"

        fun printMsg(){
            println("Companion MSG")
        }
    }
}
```

We will explain this line by line. The first line is just the class name definition:

```
class MyClass {
```

The second line is the `companion object` definition. We need to use this instruction to indicate the beginning of the companion definition. We need to use curly braces to indicate the limit of the `companion object` block:

```
companion object {
```

Inside the companion object, we define a constant element called `STATIC_VALUE`, which is a string:

```
        const val STATIC_VALUE = "this is a static value"
```

The last element in our code is a function. This function prints a message, which is `Companion MSG`. In this example, we have two different kinds of elements. The first one is a property and the second is a function. We can have both types without any problems inside a `companion` object.

If we need to execute this code, let's do it separately, as we did before. We have the `main` function to execute the Kotlin code. This is the code:

```
fun main(){

    MyClass.printMsg()

}
```

The first line is the `main` function, and the second line shows us how we can execute the `printMSG` method without needing to create an object. We don't need an instance of `MyClass` to access this function; we can use the class name directly.

If we want to use the variable, we can add this line to the code:

```
println(MyClass.STATIC_VALUE)
```

Now, let's look at some details that we need to remember about properties when we use a companion object:

- **Static data storage**: This is used to store data that is common to all instances of a class and that does not change throughout the execution of the program, such as configuration constants and default values.
- **Direct access**: You can access these properties directly from the class name without needing to create an instance.
- **Avoid code duplication**: If a value is common to all instances, it is efficient and clean to store it in a companion object.

Here are some important details about companion objects:

- Companion objects are initialized when the class is loaded.
- A companion object is a single instance associated with the class, so the members are shared between all the instances of the class.
- Companion objects can extend interfaces.
- If we want access to companion object members outside the class, we need to use the class name.

It is a good idea to use a companion object in the following cases:

- Constants
- Utility functions
- Logger
- Extension functions
- Singleton pattern
- Factory method

The init block

We will go into more detail in *Chapter 5*, but since we can use `init` in companion objects, we will briefly explain how to use it. However, we will see the concept in more detail later.

The `init` block is a special block of code used to initialize objects. It runs immediately after the class's primary constructor is called and before any other code within that object is executed.

In the case of companion objects, this block is executed once, when the class is first loaded, and is used to perform any necessary initialization for the companion object's properties or variables.

We can initialize properties that require calculations or dependencies on other parts of the code. We can also use it for some configuration, for example, loading data from a file or establishing database connections.

This is an example `init` block with a companion object:

```
class MyClass {
    companion object {
        const val STATIC_VALUE = "this is a static value"

        fun printMsg(){
            println("Companion MSG")
        }

        init {
            println("init block")
        }
    }
}
```

We need to invoke the class or its companion object from a `main` function:

```
fun main() {
    MyClass.printMsg()
    println(MyClass.STATIC_VALUE)
}
```

We can see the definition of an `init` block. In our example, we simply add a `println` statement inside the `init` block to demonstrate its execution. This block executes immediately when an object of the class is created:

```
        init {
            println("init block")
        }
```

Running this code shows us these results:

```
init block
Companion MSG
This is a static value
```

We can see the order that we mentioned earlier: the first instruction in the list of results is the `init block` print instruction. We don't need to call the `init` block explicitly.

Now, let's look at a companion object that you can use to extend interfaces.

In the following code, we are defining an interface in Kotlin called `Printable`, which has a single method, `printInfo`. Interfaces in Kotlin are similar to those in other languages; they allow you to declare behaviors (methods) that must be implemented by the classes or objects that extend them:

```
interface Printable {
    fun printInfo()
}
```

In the following code, the companion object implements the `Printable` interface by providing a concrete definition for the `printInfo()` method. This is particularly useful when we want to expose certain behavior at the class level rather than through an instance:

```
class MyClass {
    companion object : Printable {
        const val STATIC_VALUE = "this is a static value"

        fun printMsg() {
            println("Companion MSG")
        }
        init{
            println("init block")
        }
```

```
        override fun printInfo() {
            println("Printing info from the companion object")
        }
    }
}
```

The companion object implements the `Printable` interface. This is interesting because, in Kotlin, a companion object can extend classes and interfaces, which is not possible in languages such as Java for static members.

The `printMsg` method overrides the `printInfo` method of the `Printable` interface. This method will be invoked when the companion object of the class is accessed and `printInfo` is called:

```
fun main() {
    MyClass.printMsg()
    MyClass.printInfo()
    println(MyClass.STATIC_VALUE)
}
```

In the `main` function, the `printMsg()` and `printInfo()` methods of `MyClass` are accessed directly without the need to create an instance of `MyClass`. This is possible because these methods are defined within the companion object. The `STATIC_VALUE` constant is directly accessible from the `MyClass` class. Companion objects allow you to have static properties and methods in Kotlin, with the advantage that they can extend interfaces, something that is not possible with Java static methods.

In this section, we explored the concept of companion objects in Kotlin, which allow us to define static-like properties and methods that can be accessed directly through the class without creating an instance. Companion objects are initialized when the class is loaded, and they are especially useful for constants, utility functions, and shared resources across all instances of the class. We also covered how companion objects can extend interfaces and briefly introduced the `init` block, which can be used to initialize properties or set up configurations when the class is first loaded.

Now that we understand how companion objects centralize shared functionality and static-like behavior within a class, it sets the stage for exploring how we can make our Kotlin code more concise and readable through the use of scope functions such as `apply`. Just as companion objects enhance the organization of common class-level properties and methods, scope functions allow for clean, readable code when initializing or modifying objects.

In the next section, we will dive into the `apply` function in Kotlin. We'll see how `apply` helps us streamline object initialization, improve code readability, and manage configurations more effectively by eliminating repetitive code patterns.

The apply function

The `apply` function is a scope function. Scope functions in the Kotlin standard library are designed to execute a block of code in the context of an object. When you call a scope function on an object using a lambda expression, it provides a temporary scope in which the object can be accessed without needing to refer to its name explicitly. There are five scope functions in Kotlin:

- `let`
- `run`
- `with`
- `apply`
- `also`

These functions are used for different purposes, but they all allow you to work more concisely and clearly with objects in Kotlin.

The `apply` function is an extension function that can be used with any object. It takes a block of code as an argument and returns the modified object after applying the block.

To explain `apply`, we are going to first create a new class, which we will call `Book`. As its name suggests, we are going to create a class that is the definition of a book. For now, we are not going to worry about the number of properties or actions that we are going to give the class. We are going to put a maximum of three properties since we only want to show how to use the `apply` function.

Normally, classes that only contain data should be modeled as data classes in Kotlin and use the primary constructor for initialization. The `apply` function is mainly used when the class comes from a third-party Java library. But in this case, we want a simple example that is consistent with the information we already know.

This is the `Book` class's code:

```
class Book {
    var title:String = "Everything about Kotlin"
    var author:String = "Jose Lujan"
    var isbn: String = "192838493"
}
```

We only have three properties: `title`, `author`, and `isbn`. These three properties are strings, to which we have assigned values.

In our `main` function, where we execute our code, we are going to create a `Book` object, and we are going to print the `author` property. This is the code:

```
fun main(){
    var myBook:Book = Book();
    println(myBook.author)
}
```

So, it is clear that we have two files: the `Book` file, which is a class that we define by referring to a `Book` object and that only has three properties, and the `main` function, which is responsible for executing our main code. In this function, we are creating the book and printing the `author` property of the book. If we execute the code, this is the result:

```
Jose Lujan
```

Now, we are going to focus on how to use `apply`. The `apply` function will allow us to have a block of code that will enable us to apply instructions to the object we are referencing. So, let's add this code block to our code:

```
myBook.apply{
    title = "The Best Java book"
    author = "Dimas Lujan"
    isbn = "10000000"
}
```

If we look at the syntax, we can confirm that it is a function extension. Inside, we are indicating that the `title` value will change to `The Best Java book`, the `author` value will change to `Dimas Lujan`, and `isbn` will change to `10000000`.

At first, it seems like it is just a simple assignment, but there are several small advantages:

- More concise and readable code
- Reduced repetition of the object name
- Useful for chain initialization

The `apply` function is an inline function, which means that the function's code is directly inserted at the call site during compilation, eliminating the need for a function call. This reduces the overhead at runtime and improves performance.

Not only do we have the ability to access the properties, but if we need to, we can also access the methods. If we need to change three properties of an object, we would have to write three separate instructions to access the three properties. We would have to use the name of the book followed by the name of the property (three times), so the code would become much smaller. Remember that we could find 10–20 objects in a normal code snippet, and each object could have 5–8 properties. This greatly increases the size of the code that we have, so we can achieve a lot of simplicity by simply knowing the capabilities that we have, thanks to Kotlin.

In a short and simple way, you can think of `apply` as an instruction that says "*apply the following to the object and return the object once we have applied it.*" This is a powerful tool in Kotlin that allows you to write cleaner and more concise code, especially when it comes to setting up objects. Its ability to directly access object properties and methods, along with its return from the original object, makes it ideal for chain initializations and configurations.

Summary

In this chapter, you have learned about two powerful features of Kotlin: extension functions and the `apply` function.

Extension functions allow you to add new methods to existing classes without modifying their source code. This improves the readability and maintainability of the code and opens up new possibilities for designing fluid and expressive APIs. You have learned how to create and use extension functions, looked at their internal workings, and seen how they can be used with Java code.

The `apply` function, one of Kotlin's scope functions, provides an elegant way of working with objects, allowing multiple operations in a concise and readable context. You have learned how to use `apply` to configure objects efficiently, reducing code verbosity and improving its clarity.

Additionally, this chapter covered the concept of companion objects, a Kotlin alternative to Java's static members, offering more flexibility and capabilities.

This information is useful because it allows you to write cleaner, more expressive, and more maintainable code in Kotlin. Extension functions and the `apply` function are powerful tools that can significantly improve code quality and readability, while knowledge about companion objects helps better organize code related to a class.

In the next chapter, we will delve into object-oriented programming concepts, the `Unit` type in Kotlin, primary and secondary constructors and their concise syntax, the default getters and setters generated by Kotlin for properties, various ways to initialize properties in Kotlin, and their impact on getters and setters.

Part 2

Object-Oriented Programming

In this part, you will explore Kotlin's **object-oriented programming** (**OOP**) paradigm, gaining a solid understanding of how Kotlin builds upon and enhances traditional OOP principles. You will start with the fundamentals, learning about classes, objects, inheritance, and encapsulation, and how Kotlin simplifies these concepts while maintaining flexibility. Next, you will dive into generics, which enable type-safe and reusable code by allowing parameterized types, ensuring robust and maintainable applications. Finally, you will explore data classes and sealed classes – two powerful Kotlin features designed for immutability, structured data representation, and controlled inheritance. By the end of this part, you will have a strong grasp of Kotlin's OOP model, equipping you with the skills to design clean, efficient, and scalable applications.

This part has the following chapters:

- *Chapter 5, Object-Oriented Programming Basics*
- *Chapter 6, Generics and Variance*
- *Chapter 7, Data and Sealed Classes*

5

Object-Oriented Programming Basics

When we start using Java, **object-oriented programming** (**OOP**) is one of the most important topics to understand, and lacking a solid foundation can lead to challenges. Even for something as basic as a `"Hello World"` program in Java, we need to understand the concept of **classes** and **methods**. Additionally, concepts such as **access modifiers** and **constructors** are just the beginning of the many topics that need to be understood as we dive deeper into Java.

That is why we want to explore some of these concepts in this chapter, taking into account their roles in Kotlin. However, we are also very interested in addressing topics that play a crucial role in getting the benefits of a programming language such as Kotlin, in which the goal is to not only eliminate the verbosity of the code but also to ensure clear and efficient programming.

Conversely, Kotlin introduces elements such as `Unit`, which differ from Java, and it's important to examine basic elements such as **data types**, **return types**, and **function structures** that play a crucial role in Kotlin's approach to programming. Additionally, we'll explore more detailed elements, such as constructors, which are key in OOP when we start creating, using, and manipulating objects.

Finally, we will discuss a topic that highlights how Kotlin excels at achieving more with less code. **Getters** and **setters** in Kotlin allow us to manage access to properties in a concise way. Instead of writing separate methods, Kotlin provides built-in support for property access, which can automatically apply logic when getting or setting values. This feature makes the code more flexible and concise, without compromising functionality or clarity.

In this chapter, we're going to cover the following main topics:

- OOP overview
- Unit and modifiers
- Constructors
- Getters and setters

Technical requirements

You can use any text editor or **integrated development environment** (**IDE**) of your choice with the Java language. We recommend the IntelliJ IDEA **Community Edition** (**CE**) IDE. This tool already comes with everything you need to work with both Java and Kotlin. The list of software requirements for this chapter is as follows:

- Java JDK 17 or higher
- IntelliJ IDEA CE
- Kotlin 2.x

The code used in this chapter can be found in the book's accompanying GitHub repository: `https://github.com/PacktPublishing/Kotlin-for-Java-Developers`.

OOP overview

OOP is one of the most widely used programming paradigms to create software. You could also argue that it is the most popular, but it is certainly one of the many paradigms that all programmers must learn at some point, which is why we have dedicated a chapter to it in the book.

Some programming languages only support one programming paradigm, and others support more than one. Kotlin is a multi-paradigm language, meaning that we can work with different programming paradigms such as OOP, functional programming, procedural programming, declarative programming, reactive programming, and data-oriented programming using the same language.

A **programming paradigm** can be defined as a type of solution that is already defined, with some established ways of doing things, so when we use a programming paradigm, we use existing rules and definitions to try to address a type of problem and solve it in a certain way, or with a certain technique. It is a distinct set of concepts or thought patterns.

So, using a programming paradigm provides us with a foundational way of thinking about problems and structuring solutions in code. Each paradigm, such as object-oriented, functional, or procedural, comes with its own principles and abstractions. Understanding these paradigms helps us approach problems more systematically and recognize how others have organized their code. While adapting a paradigm to a particular problem can be challenging, it guides us in identifying key components and designing solutions that align with well-established programming models.

Another issue is that, in the same software, we could use two or more paradigms for a solution. Of course, we would have to find a way to respect certain different rules, but it is possible. For example, a web page works with web technologies, but in the backend, the solution could use the object-oriented paradigm, so we would be using two paradigms, and more paradigms could be used if necessary.

Let's use a simple analogy. Two people can speak English, but one person speaks American English and the other British English. Both people speak the same language and can understand each other, but there are differences in accent, pronunciation and certain words. This is similar to paradigms; ultimately, the language is the same, but there are certain conventions that are different, depending on the paradigm. Additionally, certain technical aspects can increase the complexity of adapting our code to fit within the OOP paradigm. As a result, we can identify these challenges as inherent to the OOP approach.

Something we should remember in this chapter is that, in OOP, everything is an object.

Classes

Although there is a lot to discuss about OOP, the word *object* stands out generally. However, the most important concept within OOP is probably the concept of classes because, without a class, we cannot have an object. But what is a class?

A class is the definition of an object. To achieve this definition, we must go through the process of **abstraction**. Abstraction is another of the most important concepts within OOP, since it is the process that allows us to know and better understand what an object is, and after the abstraction, we will then be able to create it.

Think of abstraction as trying to explain what a tiger is to someone who has never seen one. You wouldn't go into every tiny detail, such as how many whiskers a tiger has or the exact number of stripes. Instead, you'd focus on the main characteristics that make a tiger a tiger – it's a large, wild cat with orange fur and black stripes, sharp teeth, and it hunts for food. This process of identifying only the most important details and ignoring unnecessary ones is called abstraction. In programming, abstraction works the same way – we focus on the key features of an object or concept and leave out the details we don't need to deal with right now.

This process may seem obvious, but as programmers, we know that it is not. We don't all understand things in the same way, and that is why OOP is complex. Abstraction helps by abstracting the characteristics and actions that allow us to create the definition of a class, which becomes a vital process in OOP.

A class is simply the definition of the characteristics and actions that we want an object to have. Simply put, we could say that it is a block of code where we define where we will place the properties and actions that an object can have and perform when it is created. So, there has to be a class in order to create an object. A class is a blueprint for an object.

To create a class in Kotlin, the most common method is to create a file that refers to the class. For example, let's say we are going to create a file called `Book`; the extension of the file is `.kt`. However, this is still technically not a class; it is just a Kotlin file with the name `Book`. Inside the file, we will have to define what we want to be considered a class for use later, so inside the file, we will write the following:

```
class Book {
}
```

It doesn't make much sense to just create a class without any more code, but for this example, we will stick to the minimum, and we will increase the code depending on the concepts to explain. For now, the code is very clear – we place the word `class` to indicate that we want to create a class, which is followed by the name of the class, which is `Book` in this case. By convention, the first letter of the class name is capitalized (which is a rule in many programming languages) and should be singular. Then, we place the curly braces to indicate the code block of this `Book` class. Congratulations, you have defined your first class.

Properties

So far, we have talked about objects and classes. To recap, we know that classes are the definition of an object, where we capture the properties and actions that this object will be able to do. In other words, it is the template with which we will create the object. Now, we are going to see how to define properties.

Properties within OOP are the characteristics of an object; in some programming languages, they are called **attributes**. In Kotlin, the standard term is *properties*, so that is what we will use throughout this book. These characteristics are what define an object; for example, a book may have a title and an author. Properties can be explicitly declared with their types, and that's the approach we'll start with to make everything clear.

Later in Kotlin, you'll see that specifying the type of a property is not always necessary. The compiler can automatically determine the type based on the assigned value. This is known as **type inference**, and it helps make the code more concise without losing type safety. For now, we'll focus on explicit declarations, and gradually introduce inference once the core concepts are in place.

Here is the code:

```
class Book {
    var title:String = "Everything about Kotlin"
    var author:String = "Jose Lujan"
    var isbn = "192838493"
    var pages = 250
}
```

As we can see, properties have the purpose of defining characteristics, but to define them, we have to do so with a programmer's mindset. This means we will use both types that already exist in Kotlin (such as `String` and `Int`) as well as custom types that we create ourselves, such as the `Book` class in this example. Kotlin allows us to combine built-in types and our own custom types to define objects and their properties. For example, a title or the name of an author could easily be defined as a string (that is, a text string), since it can be any type of character. Also, we can have different variable sizes; the ISBN could also be considered a string for ease, and the number of pages could be defined by an integer. We know that a page cannot be a number in fractions, so it would be impossible to find a book that has 250.5 pages, as page numbers are whole numbers, not fractions, which is why we can define pages as integers. These types of challenges, such as defining the type for `pages`, are what we face every day in programming. It is something that can be improved with practice, and we will not always agree with everyone, but it involves analyzing and thinking about what is best for the problems that we are solving.

Methods

When we refer to methods in OOP, what we mean is that they are the actions that an object can do. Just like properties, methods are defined within a class. By convention, properties are placed first and then the methods. Normally, actions are methods that are defined by name (such as `run`, `jump`, and `read`). These verbs help us get an idea of the action that is expected when the method is executed, such as *read data* or *select database*. You can provide parameters to methods if they require additional information in order to execute. On other occasions, those actions will return a value, so we will have to be prepared to use that data. For now, we will define a method that simply prints the title of the book:

```
class Book {
    var title:String = "Everything about Kotlin"
    var author:String = "Jose Lujan"
    var isbn = "192838493"
    var pages = 250

    fun printTitle(){
    println("Book title: $title")
    }
}
```

Methods and functions in programming share a close relationship. Both are blocks of code that can be invoked to perform a specific task or return a value. However, the main difference lies in their context. Functions are independent, meaning they don't necessarily belong to a class or object; they are more general and can exist on their own. On the other hand, methods are functions that are associated with a class or an object, and thus can only be called through an instance of that class (or directly through the class in the case of static methods). In short, every method is a function, but not every function is a method.

In Kotlin, functions are blocks of code that perform a specific task and can optionally return a value. To define a function, we use the `fun` keyword followed by the function name, parentheses for parameters, and braces for the body of the function.

When naming a function, if the name consists of two or more words, the words are written together, capitalizing the first letter of each word except the first one. This naming convention is called **camel case**. Examples are `calculateTotal()` and `printMessage()`.

In this example, the `printTitle` method contains a simple `print` statement that outputs the title of the book. This method accesses the `title` property of the `Book` class and prints it. While it may seem as if calling the method gives you access to the property, it's important to note that it is the method itself that has access to the `title` property. This is because the method is part of the class and can interact with the class's internal properties. The caller of the `printTitle` function does not have direct access to the properties; the method does, and it performs the action of printing the property value.

Methods with parameters

Now, we are going to see how we can have a method with parameters. It is actually very simple and follows the logic of the functions. We are going to add a property called `isRead` that lets us know whether a book has already been read. In addition, we will show another type of data. In this case, `isRead` is of the Boolean type; therefore, it can only have two values, `true` or `false`. First, we will create this method where we previously defined the properties:

```
var title:String = "Everything about Kotlin"
var author:String = "Jose Lujan"
var readDate:String? = null
var isbn = "192838493"
var pages = 250
var isRead = false
```

Now, we are going to add a method that changes the value of the `isRead` property. This is an indicator of whether the book has already been read or not, as shown in the following code:

```
fun markAsRead(readDate: String) {
    this.isRead = true
    this.readDate = readDate
}
```

In the `markAsRead` function, we update two properties of the book: `isRead` and `readDate`. The function receives one parameter, `readDate`, which represents the date when the book was read. Inside the function, we set the `isRead` property to `true` to indicate that the book has been read. Additionally, we assign the value of the `readDate` parameter to the `readDate` property of the book. This approach allows the method to perform multiple actions, marking the book as read and recording when it was read, making it more useful than a simple setter function.

This code is easy to read if we analyze the text line by line, and we have just seen how a method can use parameters and how they are used in code.

Methods that return values

Now, we will see how we can have methods that we need to return a value; in this case, we will use as an example a property that we already have to keep the code simple. The value that we want to return is the number of pages in a book, so we are going to create a method that allows us to return that value so that we can not only show it but also actually do something with it. The following code shows the methods that we've already seen, plus a new one:

```
fun printTitle(){
    println("Book title: $title")
}

fun markAsRead(readDate:String) {
    this.isRead = true
    this.readDate = readDate
}

fun getNumberOfPages(): Int {
    return pages
}
```

The new method is the last one, so we have continued using the base definition that we already know. The only thing that changes is that, after the parentheses, we have placed a colon, followed by the type of value that we are going to return; in this case, it is an integer. If we need to return a value, we need to add the reserved word `return`, followed by the element that we want to return, which is `pages`, although we could have more code before `return` without causing any problems. The important thing that we must understand is that we have to indicate that we are going to return a value by using the reserved word `return`. Here's a more concise version of the method using an expression body:

```
fun getNumberOfPages(): Int = pages
```

This is the preferred way in Kotlin when the function consists of a single expression.

We will discuss elements such as `get` and `set` later.

Unit and modifiers

Now, we will talk about two basic elements that help us understand Kotlin a little better when working with OOP: `Unit` and modifiers.

Unit

A quick way to explain `Unit` to a Java developer is to say that it is similar to what we refer to as `void` in Java – that is, it represents the absence of a value when a function or method is returned. On a technical level, there are differences, although the fundamentals are the same.

Let's look at a function that uses `Unit`; to do so, we will look at the previous code block for the functions we have defined:

```
fun printTitle(){
    println("Book title: $title")
}

fun markAsRead(readDate:String) {
    this.isRead = true
    this.readDate = readDate
}

fun getNumberOfPages(): Int {
    return pages
}
```

In this case, we can ask ourselves, which function returns a value? The answer is the last function, the one called `getNumberOfPages`. The first two functions, `printTitle` and `markAsRead`, are functions that actually use `Unit`, but we didn't know so until now.

In fact, if we do not indicate to a method or function that it has to return a value, we are already using `Unit`; hence, the use of `Unit` is implicit when we do not indicate a return. In fact, there is no need to declare it, which is why we do not see it in the previous definitions, but we are going to write it so that we can check it. We are going to modify the code as follows, placing the word `Unit` as if it were a value to be returned, as we did in the last function when we indicated that we wanted to return an integer. This is how the code looks:

```
fun printTitle():Unit{
    println("Book title: $title")
}

fun markAsRead(readDate:String):Unit {
    this.isRead = true
    this.readDate = readDate
}

fun getNumberOfPages(): Int {
    return pages
}
```

We can see that all three methods now have a return value of `Unit` – the first two as `Unit`, and the last one, `Int`. It is generally not a good practice to explicitly use `Unit` as a return type in Kotlin, as it is inferred by default in functions that don't return a value. However, for functions with an **expression body**, it is very important to explicitly set the return type. This helps prevent accidentally changing the return type if the function's body is modified, ensuring that the intended return type remains consistent. We can simply take it as a rule that we must learn very soon in Kotlin: in the case of not placing a return value, `Unit` is used by default, even if it is not written explicitly.

Another piece of information that we should know is that although `Unit` is similar to `void` in Java, in Kotlin, `Unit` is considered a real type. Another interesting detail that is worth knowing is that `void` is not considered an object in Java, while in Kotlin, `Unit` is a singleton object. At a more technical level, `Unit` is compiled to `Void` in Java bytecode, and `Unit` is translated by Kotlin when it is called from Java, and `void` in Java is seen as `Unit` when it is called from Kotlin.

Modifiers

We mentioned modifiers briefly previously in the book, and now, we will go into detail to explain them.

In Kotlin, we have four access modifiers that can be used in classes. They are as follows:

- `public`
- `private`
- `protected`
- `internal`

Currently, everything we have in our code is `public`, since, by default, none of the properties have a modifier.

We are going to set `pages` and `isRead` as `private`. By doing so, we are going to limit access; only the elements within the class will have access:

```
private var pages = 250
private var isRead = false
```

It's not only properties that can have modifiers; methods can too – for example, let's make the `markAsRead` method `private`:

```
private fun markAsRead(readDate:String){
    this.isRead = true
    this.readDate = readDate
}
```

With this change, `markAsRead` can only be accessed from within the `Book` class. This allows us to encapsulate data, ensuring that it cannot be manipulated from outside the class. This is called **encapsulation** or **information hiding**. Encapsulation is a key aspect of OOP that allows us to control access to certain properties or methods, thereby hiding the internal implementation details from code outside of the class.

Let's modify `isbn` to become protected:

```
protected var isbn = "192838493"
```

This allows access from the class where it is defined and from any subclass that inherits from it.

In simple words, `isbn` is accessible inside the `Book` class and in any class that inherits from `Book`. This is quite interesting and useful when, for example, we want some properties to be accessible according to their inheritance and not open to all elements in the code.

Now, we will modify `author` as `internal`:

```
internal var author:String = "Jose Lujan"
```

By marking `author` as `internal`, the property is accessible from anywhere within the same module but not from outside of it. This means that code within the same module (for example, a set of related classes or files) can access and modify this property. However, it won't be accessible to code from other modules or libraries. Internal visibility sits between `public` (accessible from everywhere) and `private` (accessible only within the class or file), allowing for a balance between exposing functionality and maintaining some level of encapsulation.

Side note

Modules are essentially a set of Kotlin files and other resources compiled together as a single unit. Modules help manage dependencies and organize your project into manageable pieces.

Let's summarize the modifiers so that everything is clear:

- `public`: When we do not specify a modifier, this is the default modifier. It is not necessary to place it, and all properties and methods that are declared as `public` allow access from any part of the code.
- `private`: When we use this, we limit visibility to the class where the element is declared, so the properties or methods that use `private` are not accessible from outside the class.

- `protected`: This is a bit similar to `private`, but it also allows visibility to inherited classes – that is, to subclasses.
- `internal`: If we use this modifier in a property or method, this causes us to be accessible only within the same module.

Constructors

Now, we will discuss constructors. A constructor is a special method within a class. This method is used when we want to create and initialize an object. In other words, the point at which we create an object is the exact moment we use a constructor, enabling us to execute the code to initialize the object.

In Java, the constructor has the same name as the class, so it is very easy to recognize. Here is an example:

```
public class Book {
    private String title;
    private String author;
    private String isbn;
    private int pages;

    public Book(String title, String author, String isbn,int pages) {
        this.title = title;
        this.author = author;
        this.isbn = isbn;
        this.pages= pages;
    }
}
```

We can see that in this Java code, we have a class called `Book`. This class has four properties: `title`, `author`, `isbn`, and `pages`. Immediately after these properties, we define something that, in this structure, looks like a method that has the same name as the class. This is a constructor. It is usual for a constructor to receive parameters and use their values to perform its work.

Remember that the main task of the constructor is to execute code or instructions to initialize an object.

Let's use an analogy. Imagine that we want to create 20 books in our program. We have only one class, `Book`, but the 20 books are different. Therefore, when we create an object, we need to supply different data, such as the title, author, ISBN, and number of pages.

In Kotlin, we define a constructor to receive those values as parameters. However, passing parameters alone isn't enough – we also need to assign them to the class properties. This can be done directly in the primary constructor or inside an `init` block. Once assigned, each object will hold its own specific values for those properties.

Normally, we have to be careful with the order and type of values – that is, if we have four properties of the `String` type, then we will have to pass four parameters of the `String` type when creating the object. If the types do not match, then it is simply an error.

By recognizing that a constructor shares the same structure as a function, we can deduce that it can either be a constructor without parameters or one with parameters. Unlike Java, Kotlin does not support traditional constructor overloading. Instead, Kotlin allows the use of default parameter values in constructors, which makes multiple overloaded constructors unnecessary in most cases. However, secondary constructors can still be defined if a different initialization path is required.

The following example has three constructors:

```
public Book(String title, String author, String isbn,int pages) {
    this.title = title;
    this.author = author;
    this.isbn = isbn;
    this.pages= pages;
}
public Book(String title, String author, String isbn) {
    this.title = title;
    this.author = author;
    this.isbn = isbn;
}
public Book(String title, String author) {
    this.title = title;
    this.author = author;
}
```

The obvious question that arises from this example is, how do we know which constructor to execute? The answer is very simple – Java analyzes the constructors and sees which one is the corresponding one. When calling the constructor, the parameters are analyzed so that we know which constructor we are going to use. The first option contains four properties (`title`, `author`, `isbn`, and `pages`), the second option contains three parameters (`title`, `author`, and `isbn`), and the third option contains only two properties, `title` and `author`. Note that the parameter types are part of the constructor signature. So `Book(String, Integer, String)` is considered different from `(String, String, Integer)`. But this only applies to parameter types. The actual names do not matter.

Kotlin constructors

The primary constructor is considered the main constructor when creating an object. It is called the primary constructor because it is the main or primary point where the object is initialized.

In Kotlin, the primary constructor is a constructor that is defined at the beginning of a class definition. Returning to our `Book` example, let's remember that the most basic way to define a class in the Kotlin programming language is as follows:

```
class Book {
}
```

If we want the properties we mentioned, we need to set them as follows:

```
class Book {
    var title:String = "Everything about Kotlin"
    var author:String = "Jose Lujan"
    var isbn = "192838493"
    var pages = 250
    var isRead = false

}
```

But first, we need to learn how to create our first object.

Creating an object

To easily create an object in Kotlin, we will use the two files from our example, and to make things practical, we have not only the `Book` class (which we have already seen the code for, so we will not repeat it), but also the class where the program starts. This is the code:

```
fun main(){
    val myBook:Book = Book()
    println(myBook.title)

}
```

We can see in the previous code that we have the `main` function that allows us to execute the code in Kotlin. We define the `myBook` object where we use the `Book` class to declare its type. We create the object as follows:

```
val myBook:Book = Book()
```

We continue with the `print` instruction, simply to have something visual. If we review the `Book` code, we can see that the title of the book is `Everything about Kotlin`.

Congratulations! You have created your first object. When printing the title, we access `myBook`, and therefore, it is the object we have created. We can be sure that this object is present when we look at the output, which is the title of the book that we have placed in the class definition.

As in many programming languages, creating an object is referred to more elegantly as creating an instance of a class, the instance itself being the object.

It's worth remembering that the default constructor always has the name of the class and no input parameters.

Primary constructor

Kotlin automatically generates a parameterless primary constructor (we can also call it a default constructor). We will use the same `Book` code as the starting point for the explanation of the primary constructor:

```
class Book {
    var title:String = "Everything about Kotlin"
    var author:String = "Jose Lujan"
    var isbn = "192838493"
    var pages = 250
    var isRead = false

}
```

This class has a default primary constructor. Although not explicitly written, Kotlin automatically generates a parameterless primary constructor.

The generated constructor would be equivalent to the following:

```
class Book constructor () {
    var title:String = "Everything about Kotlin"
    var author:String = "Jose Lujan"
```

```
    var isbn = "192838493"
    var pages = 250
    var isRead = false

}
```

We can see that, after the word Book, which is the class name, we have the reserved word constructor, indicating that we are defining a constructor. By using the word constructor, we are explicitly telling Kotlin that we are defining a constructor. In this case, constructor() is the explicit declaration of the primary constructor without parameters. However, the constructor keyword is optional in this case and could be omitted, leaving simply Book() to define the primary constructor.

So, by having a primary constructor without parameters and actually following Kotlin's logic, there is not much point in placing the word constructor. We could omit it and allow Kotlin to do this work for us.

If you do not explicitly define a constructor in your class, Kotlin automatically generates a public parameterless constructor. This is what occurs in the background when no constructor is defined in the class.

Now, let's create a primary constructor. This is the code:

```
class Book(var title: String, var author: String, var isbn : String, var
pages: Int, var isRead: Boolean){

}
```

We can see that we have removed several lines, including all of the property definitions. In Kotlin, if we want to define a primary constructor, we can place the parameters directly inside the parentheses after the class name. This automatically creates properties and assigns them based on the values passed. In this example, we are using this approach to simplify the code by combining property declarations and the constructor. We have the title, author, isbn, pages, and isRead properties listed inside the parentheses of the primary constructor. This indicates that when we create an object of the Book class, we will need to pass values for these properties in the constructor. We can also see in our code that, currently, the class has nothing. We simply open and close the brace, but we have no code inside it, so we have the class defined, and it only has one primary constructor.

Now, let's see how to create an object and use the constructor:

```
fun main() {
    val myBook: Book = Book(
        "The best Kotlin Book",
        "Jose Lujan",
        "192839ND39431",
        250,
        false
    )
    println(myBook.title)
}
```

In our `main` function, we are creating the `myBook` object using a primary constructor. When we create the object, we need to pass the five parameters that were specified in the constructor. This is because we have not defined another constructor, and we only have this constructor to work with, so we place the values that we are going to need.

This type of constructor can be a little confusing at first for developers who come from Java (specifically, it is the definition that is made in the code), but over time, they will be able to adapt and realize the benefit of reducing code and making it easier to define.

We are not finished with this primary constructor yet. If you come from the Java world, you'd know that it is common for a constructor to contain not only an assigned value that arrives through parameters. We also need, on some occasions, to perform extra operations to be able to assign values; they can be calculations, query operations, and so on. The type of operation is not important, but it is important to execute more complex instructions that are not only an assignment. In these cases, we must ask the question: how can we use code in a primary constructor?

The answer to this is very simple; let's look at the code:

```
class Book(var title: String, var author: String, var isbn : String, var
pages: Int, var isRead: Boolean){
    init {
        title = title.uppercase()
        author = author.uppercase()
        println("Created Book: $title by $author")
    }

}
```

In the preceding code, we see the definition of the primary constructor with the five parameters: `title`, `author`, `isbn`, `pages`, and `isRead`. To execute additional code during the initialization of the object, we use the `init` block. The `init` block is called every time an instance of the class is created, and it's useful for executing any setup or logic that needs to happen when the object is initialized.

For example, in our case, we are converting the `title` and `author` properties to uppercase using the `uppercase()` function. After performing this transformation, we print the modified values to verify the changes.

It's important to note that the `init` block is executed after the primary constructor, which means you can use or modify the properties initialized by the primary constructor. However, the `init` block is not suitable for defining new variables or properties. If you need to initialize additional variables, it should be done in the constructor or by defining them as properties of the class.

The `init` block in Kotlin is used to execute initialization code when an instance of a class is created. It is a special block that runs immediately after the primary constructor has been called, and it is useful for performing additional setup or initializations that cannot be handled directly in the constructor.

Examples of when to use the `init` block are as follows:

- Validating or transforming values passed to the constructor.
- Executing code that depends on all properties initialized by the constructor.
- Printing messages or performing tasks that need to happen every time an object of the class is created.

One important point is that you cannot declare new properties inside the `init` block; its purpose is to work with properties that have already been defined and initialized by the constructor.

Then, we will rely on `init` to place code, and thus, the primary constructor can have instructions that we need to execute when initializing an object.

Something that is important to mention here is that we can have multiple `init` blocks in code. It is possible to have multiple `init` blocks within the same class. All `init` blocks are executed in the order in which they appear in the code, immediately after the primary constructor has initialized the class properties.

Let's test this out with two `init` blocks:

```
class Book(var title: String, var author: String, var isbn : String, var
pages: Int, var isRead: Boolean){
    init {
        title = title.uppercase()
        author = author.uppercase()
        println("Created Book: $title by $author")
    }

    val publisher: String = "Packt"

    init {
        println("Second init Block")
    }

}
```

This code block seems to resemble the previous one; the main difference is that after the `init` block, we add a `publisher` property. In this, we place an element of the `String` type. We only do this to place an instruction before the next `init` block. Now, we see that an `init` block has been started. As previously mentioned, the `init` blocks will be executed after initializing the object. Also, they are executed in the order that they are defined in the class, so we could have even more than two, but in the file, they will be executed in the order of appearance. This was just a simple demonstration of how `init` blocks coexist.

Secondary constructors

We previously discussed the primary constructor, which is the first or main thing to consider when creating an object, but it is very normal in OOP to find ourselves in several scenarios when creating an object. For example, when creating our `Book` object, we will not always know all the information or values at the beginning when we want to create the object, and then if we have four elements and they are not all essential to create the book, we could create another constructor, where we could work with just two elements (e.g., `title` and `author`). This additional constructor would be called the secondary constructor.

Let's look at the code to visualize this concept:

```
class Book(var title: String, var author: String, var isbn : String, var
pages: Int, var isRead: Boolean){
    init {
        title = title.uppercase()
        author = author.uppercase()
        println("Created Book: $title por $author")
    }

    val publisher: String = "Packt"

    init {
        println("Second init Block")
    }

   constructor( title: String, author: String): this(
        title,
        author,
        "Unknown ISBN",
        0,
        false
    ){
       println("Secondary constructor")
   }


}
```

All the code is the same as in the previous example – we have a sequence of constructors in everything we see. The specific code that was added is this:

```
constructor( title: String, author: String): this(
    title,
    author,
    "Unknown ISBN",
    0,
    false
){
```

```
    println("Secondary constructor")
}
```

Here, we use the word `constructor`, which begins the instruction that we are going to use to define a secondary constructor. In this case, we're thinking about the possibility of creating an object but only receiving two pieces of data: the title and the author.

Here comes the interesting part. We can see that after the parentheses, we put a colon. This means that the secondary constructor delegates to the primary constructor of the class.

This is why, within the parentheses, we have to place five elements, which are needed by the primary constructor that was previously defined. If we need more complex code or instructions, we can place the necessary code within the braces. In our previous code, we only have the `println` instruction, but all the code we need could be there. Here is the order of code execution when using the secondary constructor:

- The secondary constructor is called.
- The secondary constructor delegates to the primary constructor.
- The `init` blocks will be executed in the order they appear in the class.
- The body of the secondary constructor is executed.

One thing we might ask ourselves is, why is it necessary to delegate?

In Kotlin, if a class has a primary constructor, every secondary constructor must delegate to it, either directly or indirectly. This ensures that initializations defined in the primary constructor are always executed.

This way of working allows us to have multiple ways to create an object while maintaining a consistent initialization.

It's worth mentioning that we could have more secondary constructors. Each secondary constructor provides a different way to initialize the `Book` class with different levels of detail, depending on the available data. You can define as many secondary constructors as you need in a Kotlin class.

Getters and setters

In the world of Java development, it is very common to hear about `get` and `set`, or getters and setters, which are methods that allow us to assign a value or obtain a value. The values refer to the properties of an object, so `Set` allows us to assign a value to the property of the object, and `Get` lets us know the value of the property of a certain object.

`Get` will always give us a value which means it will return a value, and we can already intuit that it will work like a return from a function. We will continue using the example of the `Book` class, and in Java, there is some simple and fast code to enter the `get` and `set` methods of a property:

```
public class Book {
    private String title;
    private String author;
    private String isbn;
    private int pages;

    public Book(String title, String author, String isbn, int pages) {
        this.title = title;
        this.author = author;
        this.isbn = isbn;
        this.pages = pages;
    }

    // Getter
    public String getTitle() {
        return this.title;
    }

    // Setter
    public void setTitle(String title) {
        this.title = title;
    }
}
```

The last two methods defined are the ones we are interested in. We can see that the first is `get` and the second is `set`. It is customary to use the same name of the property with the corresponding prefix if it is `get` or `set`. In the case of `get`, we know that we must return a value, and that is why we use `return`, and we refer to the object's property with `this` and the name of the property.

In the `set` case, we use `void` to indicate that we will not return something and define that we need a parameter to assign that value to the property. To assign the value, we access it again by referring to the same object with `this` and the name of the property, with the assignment operator referencing the parameter.

This is very simple, and the code is basic, but we have 50 properties. If we want to continue along this path, then we would have to make 100 methods, two for each property – get and set. Adding the lines of code to this would mean a lot of code for something that could be quite simple to solve.

Kotlin getters and setters

Getters and setters are a similar case to what happens with the primary constructor when it is used by default. This means that by default, we don't have to do anything extra. Kotlin creates the code for us; we just have to know that it exists in order to use it. `get` and `set` are generated, which reduces the use of code when creating the base of our project. We don't have to do anything and already have the corresponding `Get` and `Set` methods.

We have already seen the Java code of the `Book` class. Let's make the equivalent code with `get` and `set` and a constructor in Kotlin:

```
class Book(var title: String, var author: String, var isbn: String, var
pages: Int)
```

In this example, we can see the great advantage of Kotlin. In a single line, we are doing what we did before, but using fewer lines. Let's break this down to make it clearer:

- We are defining a `Book` class.
- We place a primary constructor when placing properties inside the parentheses.
- It is not necessary to use the word `constructor` for the definition, since we want one by default.
- By default, `Get` and `Set` are also defined for the properties.
- The getters and setters are automatically generated by the compiler due to `var`.
- You can access the getter `title` value directly using the book title.
- You can change the setter `title` value directly using `book.title = "My New Title"`.

Now, we will see how to use these getter and setter methods. We will go to the `main` function to create the `Book` object and use `get` and `set` as previously mentioned. This is the code:

```
class Book(var title: String, var author: String, var isbn: String, var
pages: Int)
fun main() {
    val book = Book("The Best Kotlin Book", "Jose Lujan", "1234567890",
250)
```

```
    //Getter
    println("Title: ${book.title}")

  //Setter
    book.title = "My New Kotlin Programming Book"
    println("Updated Title: ${book.title}")
}
```

As we can see under the specific comments where we placed the reference to `Get` and `Set`, we used both in two different cases. In the first `print` statement, we print the title, and to gain access to this property, we use the `get` method. We do not have to define this, since it is already defined by us; we simply use it, and that's it.

Conversely, in `Set`, we can see how we access the property just by placing the name of the object and the names of the properties. We have not had to define `set` for this to happen; it had already been generated by default, and for the same reason, we can see that in the following `print` statement, this title has been changed.

As previously mentioned, Kotlin can be an incredible way to reduce code if we learn how to use it. Although this may seem obvious, in reality, as we saw, we have saved ourselves from writing many lines of code, but it was not obvious that this could be achieved, which is why we have to spend time learning Kotlin. The Kotlin development team has worked hard to offer these types of possibilities, minimizing time and increasing the speed of development using this programming language.

Summary

In this chapter, we delved into the foundational concepts of OOP as they relate to both Java and Kotlin. You learned about the importance of classes and objects, the cornerstones of OOP, and how to define them in Kotlin. We explored how properties represent the characteristics of an object, and how methods define the actions that an object can perform. We also covered key concepts such as constructors – both primary and secondary – and how they initialize objects with specific states. Furthermore, we examined Kotlin's ability to streamline code by automatically generating getters and setters, reducing verbosity while maintaining clarity and efficiency.

The information in this chapter is crucial because a solid understanding of OOP is essential for any Java or Kotlin developer. Mastering these concepts allows you to write more structured and maintainable code. Moreover, understanding how Kotlin optimizes these OOP principles, particularly through features such as concise primary constructors and automated getters/setters, enables you to write code that is both efficient and easy to read.

In the next chapter, we will explore generics in Kotlin, a powerful feature that allows you to write more flexible and reusable code. You will learn what generics are, how to use them with functions, and the concept of variance, all of which will further enhance your Kotlin programming skills.

6

Generics and Variance

In this chapter, we will delve into the powerful world of **generics** in Kotlin. For those who are familiar with Java, it is important to note that generics in Kotlin offer a more robust and type-safe approach. Kotlin's type system handles variance more explicitly and eliminates issues such as raw types and wildcard complexity. In this chapter, we will explore the fundamentals of generics and cover essential concepts related to them. After that, we will delve into some important details and nuances that can help you better understand and effectively use generics in Kotlin.

Generics allow you to define classes, interfaces, and functions without explicitly specifying the type of data they will work with until they are instantiated or used. This offers greater flexibility and code reuse.

We will start with a summary of generics in Java. After that, we will explain the concept of Kotlin generics, starting with a couple of examples. This concept enables the creation of flexible, reusable, and type-safe code components. We will then explore how generics can be used with functions, with detailed examples and specific use cases. Once we have a clear understanding of generics and their use with functions, we will move on to how generics interact with properties. It is important to connect various Kotlin concepts to fully appreciate its benefits and apply them effectively in our projects.

Finally, we will cover a key point relating to generics in Kotlin, the concept of **variance**. This concept, in turn, compels us to explain other details and concepts that are usually difficult for developers when they get to know Kotlin. We will take special care by relying on code examples that are as short and concrete as possible.

While generics in Kotlin and Java share many similarities, Kotlin's approach is more robust and type-safe, offering clearer handling of variance and features such as reified types that eliminate issues such as raw types and wildcard complexity. These improvements result in a cleaner and more powerful way to work with generics compared to Java.

In this chapter, we're going to cover the following main topics:

- What are generics?
- Using generics with functions
- Variance

Technical requirements

To begin, you can use any text editor or **integrated development environment** (**IDE**) of your choice that uses the Java language. We recommend the IntelliJ IDEA **Community Edition** (**CE**) IDE. This tool already comes with everything you need to work with both Java and Kotlin. The list of software requirements for this chapter is as follows:

- Java JDK 17 or higher
- IntelliJ IDEA CE
- Kotlin 1.x or 2.x

The code used in this chapter can be found in the book's accompanying GitHub repository: `https://github.com/PacktPublishing/Kotlin-for-Java-Developers`.

What are generics?

Let's start by discussing what generics are. As the name suggests, something that is generic implies that we will have "something" that is defined in a general way, and we can use it depending on certain situations or characteristics.

The idea of defining something as generic has the advantage of making it more flexible and reusable. The principle behind this is straightforward: when we design our code to handle only specific types, we limit its applicability. However, by allowing more general type parameters, we expand the range of possibilities and make our code adaptable to different types and scenarios.

At first glance, we could say that *generics* is a concept that we normally find in programming when playing with the parameterization of types. But let's apply a more technical definition to understand the concept better – generics is a feature that can be applied to programming languages, in general, to define and use types/methods with non-specific types so that, later, during their compilation or execution, they are used in a specific way.

This may seem simple, but it is not. Many factors need to be considered, such as the interoperability of certain types and performance concerns related to the execution time of specific tasks. For instance, using generics with complex data structures can sometimes lead to overhead during type checking or when dealing with type erasure at runtime. Additionally, operations involving generic collections or type casting might introduce subtle performance costs that can impact the efficiency of critical sections of code.

A key question to ask when working with generics is: what do we want to achieve with them? Generics in Kotlin enable you to define classes, interfaces, and functions that can operate with a variety of data types while maintaining type safety. This flexibility allows for more reusable and adaptable code, which can be tailored to specific types during compilation or execution.

When we use generics with functions, we can see their main benefit: the code we write becomes more adaptable and can work with different types. For properties, generics allow us to handle values of various types, making our code more flexible and capable of supporting different use cases.

We can see that, in general, what we are looking for is flexibility, reusability, adaptation, expanding options, and adjusting to different situations.

Generics in Java

Now, we will briefly review generics in Java. While mastering Java generics is not our goal, understanding them helps highlight the differences and similarities with Kotlin. This book is focused on Kotlin, but as we have done in previous sections, reviewing certain Java concepts can provide better context for understanding specific details, advantages, and disadvantages of using generics in Kotlin.

Generics did not exist since Java's inception; they were added in version 5 and were a very promising feature. One of the main reasons for adding them was to try to eliminate the need to work too much with explicit casting.

Let's go to the code; this way, we will surely get a better understanding of generics in Java. This is the code of the `Container` class:

```
public class Container {
    private String content;

    public Container(String content) {
        this.content = content;
    }
```

```
    public String getContent(){
        return  content;
    }

    public void setContent(String content){
        this.content = content;
    }
}
```

💡 **Quick tip**: Enhance your coding experience with the **AI Code Explainer** and **Quick Copy** features. Open this book in the next-gen Packt Reader. Click the **Copy** button

(1) to quickly copy code into your coding environment, or click the **Explain** button

(2) to get the AI assistant to explain a block of code to you.

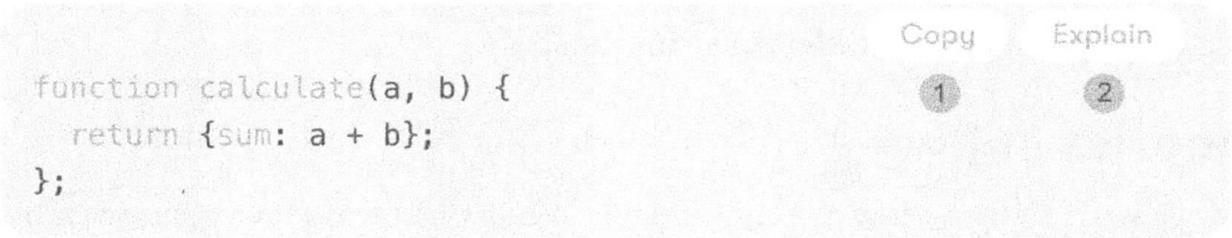

The next-gen Packt Reader is included for free with the purchase of this book. Scan the QR code OR go to `https://packtpub.com/unlock`, then use the search bar to find this book by name. Double-check the edition shown to make sure you get the right one.

Let's break down this code. First, we are going to define a class that we will call `Container`. For the time being, we want this example not to be a specific type, so we will give it a general name that does not refer to something specific.

We will only have a text string; we have content with a `String` type, and this limits the type of data we can use, which is the opposite of what we want to achieve in this chapter. While it might seem that using `Object` (or `Any` in Kotlin) could be a solution to allow more flexibility, it has its limitations. Using `Object` allows us to store any type of data, but we lose type safety. This means that every time we want to use the stored value, we would need to cast it to the appropriate type, which can lead to runtime errors if the cast fails or is forgotten.

On the other hand, generics provide a way to create classes or functions that are type-safe and flexible, allowing you to define the type of data they will work with when they are instantiated. This eliminates the need for type casting and makes the code more reliable and easier to maintain.

Generics allow you to work with any specific type, maintaining type safety and avoiding casting errors. In addition, the data type is specified at compile time, ensuring that the operations performed are safe and appropriate for the type.

We can see two methods and the constructor right after the property – the `Container` constructor, and the `getContent` and `setContent` methods.

`Container` is only the constructor; to this, we pass the string that we want to be the content of this container, and it sets the property value to the parameter received.

The `getContent` method simply returns the value of the `content` property.

The `setContent` method assigns a value to the `content` property, which is why it receives the content as a parameter and assigns it to the property, which currently is a string. As we can see, this example is very simple.

If we want to use this file, we will use a `Main` class with this code:

```
public class Main {
    public static void main(String[] args){
        Container myContainer = new Container("Jose");
        System.out.println(myContainer.getContent());
    }
}
```

Now, let's break down this code, which is very simple. We simply have the `Main` class, and inside that, we have the `main` function to be able to execute the code. Inside that, we create the container, which we call `myContainer`, and we pass a string in its constructor so that it assigns it to the `content` property. In the following line, we only send to print what we have in the content, since we use the `getContent` method, which returns the value. However, the `println` instruction is the one that shows it.

If we want to have the same functionality, but now for a different type, so perhaps an integer instead of a string, we need to write a class that is almost identical. This leads to much duplication of code, especially if more types are involved.

This problem can be solved by using generics.

If we want this example to involve generics, we can change the code to start the container like this:

```
public class Container<T> {
    private T content;

    public Container(T content) {
        this.content = content;
    }

    public T getContent(){
        return  content;
    }

    public void setContent(T content){
        this.content = content;
    }
}
```

Let's break this code down. At the beginning, it is clear that we have introduced `<T>`, indicating that this class is generic. The letter `T` is a type parameter, which can be replaced by any type when an instance of `Container` is created. Although `T` is commonly used, any valid identifier (such as `E`, `K`, `V`, etc.) can be used as a type parameter.

This type parameter allows the `Container` class to handle any type of data, making it more flexible and reusable. For example, when creating an instance of `Container`, a specific type (such as `Container<String>` or `Container<Integer>`) is specified, enabling the class to hold and manage data of that type safely.

This allows the container to be able to hold any type of data:

```
public class Container<T> {
```

In other words, `T` is a parameter of `Type`; in fact, it is a convention, it is a generic. To continue respecting the conventions, we will use the following well-known ones:

- `T` for type
- `E` for element
- `K` for key
- `V` for value
- `N` for number

Now, we have the following line, which is the definition of the `content` property. This property is private and is a generic type parameter, so you can have any object:

```
private T content;
```

The constructor is public and takes `T` as a parameter:

```
public Container(T content) {
    this.content = content;
}
```

Now, the `getContent` method is a public method that returns the content of the property:

```
public T getContent(){
    return  content;
}
```

Finally, we can see the `setContent` method. It is defined as `public`, which allows us to use it to modify the value of the `content` property:

```
public void setContent(T content){
    this.content = content;
}
```

There are two more points worth mentioning:

- The `Container` class is a generic class, which means that it can hold and work with objects of any type specified at the time of instantiation.
- The `T` type parameter makes the `content` variable, as well as the `getContent` and `setContent` methods, flexible so they can work with any specified data type, including in the constructor.

However, it's important to note that this flexibility has restrictions: once the `Container` object is created with a specific type (e.g., `Container<Boolean>`), you cannot retrieve the content as a different type, such as `String`. The type must remain consistent with the type parameter used when the object was instantiated.

Let's test whether this class is really generic because of what we did. Let's change the code that sends the object to be created:

```
public class Main {
    public static void main(String[] args) {
        Container<String> myAContainer = new Container<>("jose");
        Container<Integer> myBContainer = new Container<>(999);
        System.out.println(myBContainer.getContent());
    }
}
```

First, let's create two containers; the first will be called `myAContainer` and the second `myBContainer`. We can already see the difference here:

- In the first line, we create the object with a `String` type as a parameter for the constructor (`myAContainer`).
- In the second line (`myBContainer`), we use an `Integer` type.

Although both share the same class to create the object, we can create the object with different types, thanks to what we did previously.

Then, note that both objects will work depending on the type (`Integer` or `String`), but they are defined as generic:

```
Container <String>myAContainer = new Container<>("jose");
Container<Integer>myBContainer = new Container<>(999);
```

Now, we will see how to ask the property to print and see whether we have the expected result. Everything seems fine; in both cases, we have generics working, thanks to the definition of the element:

```
System.out.println(myAContainer.getContent());
System.out.println(myBContainer.getContent());
```

It works without any problems with a text string or an integer. As previously mentioned, `T` in this case is essential if we want to have `Container` as a generic element, thus allowing flexibility in the code.

Under the hood, the Java compiler generates code that uses `Object` as the parameter type and inserts casts wherever needed. While this works perfectly, we lose the ability to retrieve the type at runtime. This is called **type erasure**.

We are going to leave the Java part here, as we want to learn and understand how to do it in Kotlin, but what we have explained is necessary.

With this previous example, we only demonstrated one of the various uses of generics. The objective of this chapter, as in many others, is for Java developers to understand and notice the difference between implementing generics in Kotlin and Java. For this reason, we selected a very simple implementation of generics in Java – a class with only one property, a constructor, and the classic `get` and `set` methods – as our starting point for the Kotlin part. Now that we have that clear, let's start with Kotlin.

Generics in Kotlin

One of the main advantages of using generics in Kotlin is that the syntax can often be more concise and easier to read compared to Java. Kotlin eliminates boilerplate code and offers features such as type inference and a more straightforward declaration of generic types. To illustrate these benefits, we will revisit the same example we used previously with Java but rewritten in Kotlin. We will start by repeating the same example that we did previously with Java, but using Kotlin. This is the code:

```
class Container(var content: String)
```

Recall that our first definition of the `Container` class contained a `String` property, which was our starting point. Let's refresh on several details about the constructors and the `Container` class:

- When we define a class in Kotlin, a primary constructor is automatically provided by default. This constructor is what we use to create instances of the class. In this case, we define the class to have a property called `content`, which is of the `String` type.
- We already have the `get` method by default.
- We already have the `set` method by default as well, so we don't have to worry about defining it; both `get` and `set` were already explained in the previous chapter.

The code we need to execute that allows us to create the object and see that everything works correctly is this:

```
fun main(){
    val myAContainer = Container("jose")
    println(myAContainer.content)
}
```

We create our container, called `myAContainer`, and pass it the parameter it needs for the `String` type. In the following line, we send the content to be printed to see the value that we have in the console, which will be the string that we placed when creating the container.

Now, we are going to change the `Container` class using generics.

This is the code of the class that uses generics:

```
class Container<T>(var content: T)
```

It's just one line of code; as previously mentioned, it's very easy to write, but we must explain several things regarding Kotlin, some of which we have seen in previous chapters of the book:

- We start with the definition of the class. As previously explained, when we use the definition as we have it in the code, we already take advantage of Kotlin to have a primary and ready-to-use constructor.
- We have redefined the `Container` class as a generic class, meaning we have modified it so that it can store data of any type, represented by `T`.
- The letter `T` is a wildcard; it can be represented by any type of data.
- By declaring `<T>`, we create a type parameter that can be replaced by any concrete type when the class is instantiated.
- `T` is replaced by `Int`, `String`, and `List<String>`, respectively, when instantiating.
- For the definition, we can use `var` or `val` for properties. However, we must remember that if we use `val`, the contents cannot be modified after the object is created, which helps maintain data integrity.

This is the code we have to execute:

```
fun main(){
    val myAContainer = Container("jose")
    val myBContainer = Container(9999)

    println(myAContainer.content)
    println(myBContainer.content)

}
```

Here, we do the same thing we did in Java when running and checking that we can have two objects of the same `Container` class.

Note that we create two objects; the first receives a string as a parameter for the constructor, and the second receives an integer as a parameter. The constructor does not have any problem, since it is prepared by the definition we made for the class to work with generics, so everything will be fine.

In the last part of the code (last two lines), we just send the content to print, and then we can see that what we did in both cases is correct; both types are different (`String` and `Integer`), and they can be used without problems.

As we can see, it is very simple and useful – by simply using `T`, we can prepare ourselves and our code so that it is ready to work with generics and, thus, function without further complications.

When to use generics

Let's explain it with code, for example, for flexible data structures:

```
// Instead of creating multiple classes:
class StringBox(val value: String)
class IntBox(val value: Int)
class PersonBox(val value: Person)

// Create a single generic class:
class Box<T>(val value: T) {
    fun getValue(): T = value
}

// Use generic classes:
val stringBox = Box("Hello")
val numberBox = Box(100)
val personBox = Box(Person("Jose Lujan"))
```

Instead of creating a separate class for each data type you need to handle, such as `StringBox`, `IntBox`, or `PersonBox`, you can use a generic class that accepts a generic data type, `T`. This is accomplished by using the `<T>` syntax in the class definition, which tells the compiler that `T` is a type parameter to be specified when instantiating the class. In this approach, each class is specific to one data type, resulting in code duplication and less flexibility.

If we think about the approach of using a generic class, it is much simpler.

Here, `Box<T>` is a generic class that accepts any type, `T`, allowing a single layout to handle different types of data. The `getValue()` method returns the stored value of the `T` type, which makes the class flexible and reusable.

Each `Box` object stores a specific type of data, but the code for the `Box` class remains the same. This improves reusability and simplifies maintenance, as you can work with any type of data without duplicating class logic.

Generics can also be used for utilities. Let's see an example:

```
// Generic function to process lists
fun <T> List<T>.processEach(action: (T) -> Unit) {
    forEach { item -> action(item) }
}
// Use with different types:
val numbers = listOf(33, 3, 38)
numbers.processEach { println("Number: $it") }
val names = listOf("Noemi", "Viena", "Jose")
names.processEach { println("Name: $it") }
```

Let's go through the different elements of the code:

- `<T>`: This is a generic type parameter that represents any type of data. By using it, you tell the compiler that the function can work with a list of any type (`List<T>`), whether it is a list of integers, strings, objects, or so on.
- `List<T>.processEach`: This is an extension function that applies to the `List<T>` class, which means that you can use this function on any object of the `List` type.
- `action: (T) -> Unit`: This is a parameter of the function that represents a lambda function that receives an element of the `T` type and does not return any value (`Unit`). This allows the behavior of `processEach` to be customizable.
- `forEach { item -> action(item) }`: The function iterates through each element of the list using `forEach` and executes the action passed as an argument on each item.

This example shows how generics and extension functions in Kotlin can make code more flexible and reusable, allowing you to apply operations to lists of any type easily and efficiently.

When not to use generics

Generics are used when you need your class, function, or data structure to be flexible and able to handle different types of data. However, if you know in advance that your class or function will only work with a specific type, using generics can make your code more complex and less readable:

```
// BAD (overcomplicated):
class UserRepository<T : User> {
```

```
    fun save(item: T)
    fun find(id: Int): T
}
// BETTER (simpler and clearer):
class UserRepository {
    fun save(user: User)
    fun find(id: Int): User
}
```

In this example, `UserRepository` is defined as a generic class that will only accept types that inherit from `User`. However, if the `UserRepository` class is only going to work with the `User` class (and not with specific subclasses of `User`), the use of generics is unnecessary and complicates the declaration.

In the second definition of `UserRepository`, it is defined without generics and works directly with the `User` class, which makes the code clearer and easier to understand. The class fulfills its purpose without adding an unnecessary layer of complexity.

Another example of when not to use generics is when we have a simple action, such as just printing, and `Any` is sufficient. Let's see another example:

```
// If you only need to print items:
// BAD (unnecessarily generic):
fun <T> printItem(item: T) {
    println(item.toString())
}

// BETTER (simpler):
fun printItem(item: Any) {
    println(item.toString())
}
```

Generics are useful when you want your function or class to be flexible and able to work with different data types in a safe and specific way. However, if your function doesn't benefit from that extra flexibility and only needs to handle things in a general way, using `Any` is a better choice.

In this example (first block of the code), the `printItem` function is defined with a generic parameter, `T`, which implies that it can accept any data type. However, if the function is just going to print the item by calling `toString()`, there is no need to use a generic type parameter, since all types in Kotlin inherit from `Any`, which already has the `toString()` method.

In the second part of the code, the `printItem` function receives a parameter of the `Any` type, which is the superclass of all types in Kotlin. This is sufficient because `Any` guarantees that the item has a `toString()` method, and there is no need to use generics if no specific operation is to be done based on the type.

When to use Any instead of generics

You can use `Any` instead of generics in the following cases:

- **When you don't need to do type-specific operations**: If your function only requires using methods common to all types (such as `toString()`), `Any` is sufficient.
- **When you don't need type flexibility**: If you're not going to perform operations that depend on the specific type of the element, there's no need to use generics.
- **To simplify code:** Using `Any` makes code clearer and easier to understand in these cases.

If your function only needs to work with elements in a generic way and does not need to do specific operations based on the type, it is better to use `Any` instead of generics. This simplifies the code and makes it more readable, avoiding unnecessary complexities.

Let's explain this with code. This example shows a use case where using `Any` in a Kotlin class can lead to type issues and runtime errors. Let's break down why this approach is problematic and how it could be improved by using generics:

```
class ShoppingCart {
    private val items = mutableListOf<Any>()
    fun addItem(item: Any) {
        items.add(item)
    }
    fun calculateTotal(): Double {
        var total = 0.0
        items.forEach { item ->
            // We need to check the type of each item
            when (item) {
                is Product -> total += item.price
                is DiscountedProduct -> total += item.discountedPrice
                else -> println("Unrecognized product type")
            }
        }
        return total
```

```
    }
}
```

The `items` list is of the `MutableList<Any>` type, which means that items of any type can be added to the cart, even those that shouldn't be in the cart (such as a text string or a number). This causes the `calculateTotal` function to manually check the type of each item to avoid errors, and then we can see the lack of type safety.

Since the list allows any type, it is possible for invalid elements to be added, which would force those cases to be handled with additional checks and could result in runtime errors.

Type checking in `calculateTotal` makes the code less clean and more error-prone, since each element type has to be handled individually, so we can say that we have unclear code.

Here is an example of how to use the preceding code:

```
fun main() {
    val cart = ShoppingCart()
    cart.addItem(Product("Laptop", 999.99))
    cart.addItem(DiscountedProduct("Phone", 599.99, 0.1))
    cart.addItem("This shouldn't be here")// we can add any type
    println(cart.calculateTotal()) // Possible error
}
```

We already know that the `ShoppingCart` class allows adding items of any type because the items list is defined as `MutableList<Any>`. This means that we can add any object. When `calculateTotal()` runs, it iterates over each item in the `items` list and uses a `when` block to determine how to handle each type. If a type other than `Product` or `DiscountedProduct` is encountered, the function prints a message such as `"Unrecognized product type"`. In the worst case, if we try to access properties or methods that don't exist on an unexpected type, it could throw an exception. Or, if the code tries to access non-existent properties of an unexpected type, it might result in a runtime error.

To avoid such problems, it is better to use generics with restrictions. Redesigning the `ShoppingCart` class to only accept specific types (`Product` and its subtypes) would ensure that only valid items can be added to the cart.

This is the code:

```
// We define an interface for the products interface
interface PricedItem {
    fun getPrice(): Double
}
```

`PricedItem` is an interface that defines a contract for items that have a price. Any class that implements this interface must provide an implementation of the `getPrice()` method. The `getPrice()` function returns a `Double` type and is used to return the price of a product:

```
class Product(
val name: String,
val price: Double
) : PricedItem {
    override fun getPrice() = price
}
```

Here's how this code works:

- `Product`: This class represents a simple product with a name and price.
- `PricedItem`: The `Product` class implements the `PricedItem` interface, so it provides an implementation of the `getPrice()` method, which simply returns the value of the `price` property:

  ```
  class DiscountedProduct(
  val name: String,
  val price: Double,
  val discount: Double
  ) : PricedItem {
          override fun getPrice() = price * (1 - discount)
  }
  ```

- `DiscountedProduct`: This class represents a product with a discount applied.
- `PricedItem`: Like `Product`, this class also implements the `PricedItem` interface, so it provides its own implementation of `getPrice()`.

We also have the following properties and method:

- `name`: This is a `String` property that stores the name of the product.
- `price`: This is a `Double` property that stores the original price of the product.
- `discount`: This is a `Double` property that represents the discount as a fraction.
- `getPrice()`: This method calculates and returns the price after the discount has been applied by multiplying `price` by `(1 - discount)`. For example, if the price is `100.0` and the discount is `0.1` (10%), the method would return `100.0 * 0.9`, which is `90.0`.

This design allows both classes (`Product` and `DiscountedProduct`) to be handled uniformly when working with a collection of `PricedItem` (for example, in a shopping cart), making it easier to calculate prices and manipulate items that share the same basic data structure and behavior.

Now, we will see the `ShoppingCart` code:

```
// Generic cart that only accepts types that implement PricedItem
class ShoppingCart<T : PricedItem> {
    private val items = mutableListOf<T>()

    fun addItem(item: T) {
        items.add(item)
    }

    fun calculateTotal(): Double {
        return items.sumOf { it.getPrice() }
    }
}
```

Here, `items` is a mutable list that stores items of the `T` type. Since `T` is restricted to `PricedItem`, the list can only contain items that implement that interface. The `addItem` method accepts an argument of the `T` type, which must be a type that implements `PricedItem`. It adds the item to the `items` list, allowing new items to be added to the shopping cart.

`calculateTotal` calculates the total of all items in the cart by adding the values returned by `getPrice()` for each item.

Finally, the code to use the previous code is as follows:

```
fun main() {
    val cart = ShoppingCart<PricedItem>()

    cart.addItem(Product("Laptop", 999.99))
    cart.addItem(DiscountedProduct("Phone", 599.99, 0.1))
    // cart.addItem("This won't compile") // error: not a `PricedItem`

    println(cart.calculateTotal()) // Print the total of the prices
}
```

The cart is created to hold items of the `PricedItem` type. Both `Product` and `DiscountedProduct` objects can be added because they both implement `PricedItem`.

Attempting to add a type that does not implement `PricedItem` (for example, a text string) will result in a compilation error. This design ensures that the shopping cart only accepts valid items and allows the total to be calculated easily and securely.

Advantages of this implementation are as follows:

- **Type safety**: Using a generic type with constraints (`<T : PricedItem>`) ensures that only items that conform to the `PricedItem` interface can be added to the cart. This ensures that every item has a `getPrice()` method and eliminates the need for runtime type checks.
- **Reusability and flexibility**: The `ShoppingCart` class can be reused for different product types that implement `PricedItem`, such as `Product`, `DiscountedProduct`, or any other type that is implemented in the future.
- **Clean and safe code**: By restricting `T` to `PricedItem`, `getPrice()` can be safely accessed without the need for additional casts or checks.

In this scenario, where we distinguish between `Any` and generics, we can see how errors are prevented at compile time. In addition, the code is made cleaner and more maintainable, allowing for safe reuse of code, and this flexibility is provided without sacrificing type safety.

Using generics with functions

We have worked with classes, and something else that is also used often that can reinforce the importance and ease of working with generics are the functions that use them. Let's look at some example Kotlin code:

```
fun <T> printItem(item: T) {
    println(item)
}

    fun main(){
        printItem("Viena")
        printItem(50)
        printItem(true)
    }
```

One of the key features is the simplicity of the examples. The purpose is to make the content as practical as possible, allowing us to focus on understanding the concepts without getting bogged down in complex code.

We will work on the function that we are going to create and the `main` function in the same file, so let's go through the first part of the code, the `printItem` function.

We can see that the `printItem` function in its definition is already referencing `T`; this is for the same reason as when it did so in the `class` section. With this, we indicate that we want to work with generics, and we must be prepared so that they can be of different types.

In this example, we use the name `printItem`, but the name is irrelevant. We already know that between the parentheses, we have an element that we call `item`. This name can be whatever we want; it doesn't matter. The important thing is that we are referencing `T`, and we already know very well what that means at this point. `T` can be an integer, a string, or any of the other types that we already know we have available in Kotlin. The definition of the function shows how we can rely on generics to do what we want.

Finally, in this case, inside the function, we only send the element to print. This should work, regardless of the data type:

```
fun <T> printItem(item: T) {
    println(item)
}
```

In addition to classes, functions can also have type parameter declarations, which must be placed before the function name.

Now, we will see the part of the code where we call the function. With just three calls to the function, we can test whether it can really work with different types. In the first call, we place any string to test; in the second call, we place an integer; and in the third call, we place a Boolean. This is how to verify that the function works correctly, regardless of the type, by simply executing the specified instructions:

```
fun main(){
    printItem("Viena")
    printItem(50)
    printItem(true)

}
```

In Kotlin, we can then declare type parameters as several elements, as follows:

- Classes
- Interfaces

- Functions
- Methods
- Extension properties
- Extension functions
- Companions
- Type aliases
- Secondary constructors
- Higher-order functions
- Property delegates

Restrictions on type parameters

Everything has a price. This is something that we must accept in programming. If there were a best way to always do things, it would be very easy to have a definitive guide for everything, but the reality is that this is not the case. We always have a price to pay with each feature that we implement, or stop implementing it, but we must know whether the price is worth it, or we simply cannot afford it.

In our case, if we use type parameters, we could then place any type inside a function. However, there are three questions we need to ask that could be key in three different scenarios:

- If our function performs operations that involve adding data, would it make sense to add both numbers and text strings?
- If our function can receive more than one value, how can we prepare for operations if they are of different types?
- How do we design a function that can decide whether to perform certain actions based on the type of input it receives?

The reality is that the answers to the questions we posed earlier about type parameters are simpler than they might seem at first. There is the possibility of creating restrictions for the type parameters. We will start with our previous code, as follows:

```
fun <T> printItem(item: T) {
    println(item)
}

fun main(){
    printItem("Viena")
```

```
    printItem(50)
    printItem(true)

}
```

This code needs no explanation, as we have already explained it.

Let's make a change, as follows:

```
fun <T:Number> printItem(item: T) {
    println(item)
}
```

We can see that in the function definition, where we place the first letter, `T`, we place a colon and then a type. The type is a number; this is because we are indicating that we want to receive types, but we want them to be for the subtypes of the number, not for any class.

If we rely on the Kotlin documentation, we can see that the `Number` class is a superclass for all platform classes representing numeric values.

So, although as well as indicating to the function that we can use generics, we are also indicating that the generics used are only those that belong to numbers or are simply classes that inherit from the number. These are called restrictions, since we are delimiting or placing certain restrictions when it comes to options and types.

With this change in the code, if we then analyze the second part of the code, where we call the function, we will find two errors:

```
fun main(){
    printItem("Viena")
    printItem(50)
    printItem(true)
}
```

The errors that we find in the code are simple, since the function is now restricted by the `Number` type, so the first call, which is with a `String` type, and the call that uses a Boolean are the calls that will mark an error. Therefore, it makes sense and confirms that what we did is a restriction of the elements that are not of the type we indicated.

Now, let's look at one more detail, but first, let's go back to the code that has no restrictions:

```
fun <T> printItem(item: T) {
```

In the previous code, Kotlin avoids verbosity, which is the equivalent of having this:

```
fun <T:Any?> printItem(item: T) {
```

This is something important to note, since, as we can see, we could receive anything by default. In addition, we could also receive a `null` value; in fact, the following code would be valid:

```
fun <T> printItem(item: T) {
    println(item)
}
fun main(){
    printItem("Viena")
    printItem(50)
    printItem(null)
}
```

The last line does not generate any errors and works without problems. The following code would have the same result:

```
fun <T:Any?> printItem(item: T) {
    println(item)
}
fun main(){
    printItem("Viena")
    printItem(50)
    printItem(null)
}
```

As previously mentioned, they are equivalent. But if we wanted to allow any type except `null`, we would just need to change the code by removing the question mark, like this:

```
fun <T:Any> printItem(item: T) {
    println(item)
}
```

Now that we understand this detail of `Any` (that is, by default, not putting a restriction is equivalent to allowing everything with `Any?`), let's see how we could apply more than one restriction. If we want several restrictions, we would have to use the `where` instruction. Let's write the complete code and then break it down:

```
fun <T> printItem(item: T) where T: Number, T:Comparable<T>{
    println(item)
}
```

There are two restrictions:

- **Restriction one**: The restriction is `T: Number`, which means that the `T` type must be a subtype of `Number`.
- **Restriction two**: This restriction says that the `T` type must implement the `Comparable<T>` interface. This means that objects of the `T` type can be compared with each other, using the `compareTo` method.

The first restriction is about specificity, where we indicate the types we want it to work with, but the second constraint is about functionality, where we indicate the type of operations that can be used. This helps us make sure that we have a behavior that is appropriate to what we need in our programs.

Reified types

Now, let's discuss one of the features that can be confusing the first time we encounter them – reified types. When we work with generics, one of the limitations that frustrates developers the most is not being able to use a type directly.

Normally, solving this problem leads to very complicated solutions or excessively long code. If we use these approaches in Kotlin, we might not fully take advantage of Kotlin's features for writing cleaner and more efficient code.

In Kotlin, thanks to inline functions, which we have already discussed, we can use reified types within functions. Reified types allow you to preserve generic type information at runtime, overcoming the limitation of type erasure that occurs during compilation. By marking a type as reified, you can use that type inside the function without issues.

However, it is important that the function we want to enable is an inline function, as we need to indicate in the code that it should be replaced at the call site to work properly. In reality, this approach addresses a limitation of the **Java Virtual Machine (JVM)**; type information is erased at runtime, preventing its use in generic methods. This limitation is not exclusive to functions, as Java's generics face the same constraint across various contexts, including methods.

Let's look at the initial code for our example:

```
fun <T> printItem(item: T) where T: Number?, T:Comparable<T>{
}

fun main(){
}
```

We can see that the code is very simple; we have two functions to start our example.

In the first block of code, we define a generic function called `printItem`, which expects an element to be passed to it so that we can decide what to do with it.

We have two restrictions: one requires that the type must be a subclass of `Number`, and the other ensures that the type implements `Comparable`.

The `main` function does nothing; we simply have it there for when we want to execute something.

Now that we have explained the two blocks of code that we have, let's consider a situation. Let's imagine that, in the `print` function, we need to know the type to make decisions about what we want to do. That's where the role of a reified type comes in.

Now, we will learn something new. When you use generics, the type information is removed at compile time. This process is known as type erasure in Java and Kotlin. Generic type information is erased at runtime for backward compatibility reasons. This means that you cannot do certain operations that depend on knowing the exact type at runtime.

Now, let's add the `when` statement that allows us to work depending on the class we need. This is the code:

```
fun <T> printItem(item: T) where T: Number, T:Comparable<T>{

    when(T::class){

    }

}
```

Currently, we can see that we have only one new block of code; the block is `when`. What `when` does is compare a value against multiple conditions. You can compare a value against a series of conditions and execute the corresponding block of code if any of them are met. It's like having several `if` statements that take different paths, depending on what you want:

```
when(T::class){

}
```

This means that we make a switch on the type of `T`.

Why are we using `T::class`? It is for when we need to perform different actions that depend on the exact `T` type, regardless of the specific value of the item.

`T::class` is how Kotlin accesses the class reference of the generic type, `T`. This syntax is used when you need to obtain the class corresponding to the `T` type at runtime. It is particularly useful in scenarios involving reflection or when the behavior of your code depends on the exact type of `T`, rather than just its value.

The `::` operator is known as a member reference operator, and in this case, we use it to get a reference to the class of `T`. This allows us to work with the class in contexts such as when expressions or in functions that require metadata about the type.

We'll need to modify the code to read like this:

```
inline fun <reified T> printItem(item: T) where T: Number,
T:Comparable<T>{
    when(T::class){
    }
}
```

We have used `inline` and `reified`. Let's break down the changes:

- We add the `inline` keyword before `fun` to make the function inline.
- We use `reified` before `T` to make the generic type reified.

Key concept – inline and reified types in Kotlin

When we mark a function as `inline` in Kotlin, the compiler copies the body of the function to each place where it is called, rather than creating an actual function call. This mechanism allows the use of `reified` types. By using `reified` with a generic type in an `inline` function, you instruct the compiler to retain type information during compilation. This enables type-specific operations that would not be possible with regular generics due to type erasure.

Now, we are ready to place the options inside `when`; we have already explained the modifications and what happens with `inline` and `reified`. This is the code:

```
inline fun <reified T> printItem(item: T) where T: Number,
T:Comparable<T>{
    when(T::class){
        Int::class -> println("Integer")
        Float::class -> println("Float")
        else -> println("Unknown")


    }
}
```

We have three paths that can be taken in our case; when we have an integer, we will print a string indicating it. All paths print something.

We also consider `Float`, and print the text `"Float"`. Finally, we have an `else` case if there is anything else we want to print as unknown.

The implementation of `inline` and `reified` is not a major problem; the important thing is simply to understand the reason why we are using them.

What we wanted to know was what `reified` is; now we know it.

`reified` is a powerful feature in Kotlin that allows you to work with generic types at runtime, overcoming the limitations of type erasure. It is especially useful when we need to perform operations that depend on the exact type of the generic parameter. However, this feature comes with its limitations: `reified` types can only be used within `inline` functions, and `inline` functions should be used thoughtfully, as inlining increases the size of the generated bytecode and may impact performance if overused.

In summary, using `reified` types with `inline` functions allows type checking at runtime, which is not possible with standard generics. This is particularly useful when we need to dynamically check whether an item is of a compatible type, as it enables operations involving reflection or type checking at runtime. However, it is important to note that `reified` types can only be used within `inline` functions, which have their own restrictions. `inline` functions should be used with care, as inlining increases the size of the compiled code and may affect performance. Therefore, `reified` types should not always be seen as a substitute for basic generics.

Variance

We are approaching the final part of this chapter We will now discuss **variance** and other concepts that are related to it.

Variance in Kotlin is an important concept when working with generics.

Variance helps us understand how generics relate to inheritance and how values can be assigned from one type to another. It refers to the way generics behave with respect to inheritance and type relationships.

Concretely, variance determines whether a generic type can be replaced by another generic type. This then helps us understand and manage the possible or incompatible types in generics and other elements, where there is an inheritance relationship between types.

If we want to give a slightly more formal definition, we could say that variance refers to the relationship of generic types and the relationship of subtypes between type parameters.

When approaching the topic of variance, there are three new concepts that we have to understand; these concepts describe the aforementioned relationships:

- Invariance
- Covariance (`out`)
- Contravariance (`in`)

The fundamental problem here is that if we allowed generics to be variants by default, the following could happen:

- We could end up with type violations at runtime.
- We would lose the type safety that is one of the main advantages of strongly typed languages.

To address the need to manage the relationship between generic types and inheritance, the concepts of covariance and contravariance were introduced. Covariance, denoted by `out`, allows mappings from more specific types to more general types and is useful when only reading data. On the other hand, contravariance, denoted by `in`, allows mappings from more general types to more specific types and is useful when only writing data. These concepts help to manage type relationships safely in different scenarios.

Invariance

By default, generic types are invariant in Kotlin.

Invariance refers to a property of generic types in Kotlin (and other programming languages) where a type parameter does not allow for subtype substitution. This means that when a type is invariant, one cannot use a type with a different generic type, even if there is a parent-child relationship between them.

In simpler terms, if a certain type is defined as invariant, it is treated strictly as that specific type and cannot be automatically replaced with a more specific or more general type. This ensures type safety by preventing potentially unsafe assignments, but it also limits flexibility when working with related types.

In Kotlin, generics are invariant by default, so an invariant type can only be used with the exact type it was defined with.

Let's suppose we have four different types. `Figure` will be the main class, or the parent class of everything. We will then have three more classes that are child classes of `Figure`. The classes are `Triangle`, `Circle`, and `Square`.

This is the code:

```
open class Figure
class Triangle: Figure()
class Circle: Figure()
class Square: Figure()
```

The code is very simple; we define the `Figure` class and then, in the following lines, we define the `Triangle`, `Circle`, and `Square` classes, all inheriting, as we already mentioned, from `Figure`.

In traditional inheritance, we can use polymorphism to substitute instances of subclasses such as `Triangle`, `Circle`, or `Square` wherever `Figure` is expected. However, with generics, this is not possible by default. This is because generics in Kotlin (and most other languages) are invariant, meaning that even if two types have a subtype relationship, their corresponding generic types do not; as a result, you cannot pass `List<Circle>` where `List<Figure>` is expected, for example.

We can't see this currently; we just explain it now, as we will encounter this situation later in the code.

Now, we are going to define `Container`, which is the class that will allow us to use generics. This is the code:

```
class Container<T>(var content: T)
```

This code should be very easy to read by now; it is what we have used throughout this chapter. We define a `Container` class, and inside that, we just place `content`. As we can see, we use `T` to be able to work with generics.

This is the code for the `main` function, which is what allows us to execute the code:

```
fun main(){
    val triangleContainer = Container(Triangle())
    val circleContainer = Container(Circle())
    val squareContainer = Container(Square())
    val figureContainer: Container<Figure> = Container(Figure())
    val figureContainer1: Container<Figure> = triangleContainer
}
```

We can see that we have the `main` function, where we will place everything we want to be executed. Inside that, we have the first three lines, where the elements corresponding to the figures that we have are created (`Triangle`, `Circle`, and `Square`), and we are using the `Container` class with generics.

The following code declares a variable called `triangleContainer` and initializes it with an instance of the `Container` class that holds an object of the `Triangle` type:

```
val triangleContainer = Container(Triangle())
```

Now, what is this line of code doing? Let's see:

- `Container` is a generic class that can store any type of object.
- `Triangle()` is an instance of the `Triangle` class, which is passed as an argument to the `Container` constructor.
- `triangleContainer` is therefore a `Container` object that specifically holds `Triangle`.

This line shows how to create a generic container that stores a specific type (`Triangle`, in this case). This is useful for working with specific types within a generic structure, while maintaining flexibility and type safety in the code:

```
val figureContainer: Container<Figure> = Container(Figure())
```

This line creates a container specifically for the `Figure` class, which is valid because both the variable declaration and the created instance share the same generic type, `Container<Figure>`. This means that `figureContainer` can hold objects of the `Figure` type and operate according to the rules defined in the `Container` class for that type.

The last instruction is where we see the invariance; this is because we can see that the container we are creating, where we rely on the `Container` class with `Figure`, will not be marked as an error, since we are using the previous `Triangle` container. In terms of inheritance, an error should not be thrown. However, as previously mentioned, invariance is the default behavior for generic types in Kotlin:

```
val figureContainer1: Container<Figure> = triangleContainer
```

So, by using generics, if we have a generic `T` type, you cannot assign an object of a `T` subtype to a variable of the `T` type, and vice versa. Therefore, this last line is an error, but it allows us to check and understand invariance.

Covariance (out)

Covariance is a little easier to see; this is because we will use the word out in the code. By using covariance, we can indicate that we want to maintain the relationship between the child class and the parent class, or between the subtype and the supertype.

We can do this because we also have to ensure that the T value will only be read and that we will not modify its value. We can do this, as you may have guessed, by using out. So, let's now look at the code; we will use the previous code as a starting point:

```
open class Figure
class Triangle: Figure()
class Circle: Figure()
class Square: Figure()
```

The Figure class remains the same; it is not necessary, we don't need to modify the inheritance. Triangle and Circle are subtypes of Figure.

Now, let's see the Container class. This is the code:

```
class Container<out T>(val content: T)
```

In the previous code, we can see some changes. Remember that we are creating a container that will allow us to use generics.

We can see that the first change from what we saw previously is the use of the keyword out, which allows type parameters to be substituted by their subtypes without breaking type safety. This is typically useful when we need to create instances that will be read-only. There's a restriction: we cannot modify the content of the generic type when using out. This makes sense because modifying it could break the consistency of the types.

The second change is that we change var to val. This is always necessary, since covariant types, as mentioned, can only appear in output positions. In fact, this plays a bit with the meaning of the word out that we have used.

This is the code of the function that allows us to execute this example:

```
fun main(){
    val containerTriangle:Container<Triangle> = Container(Triangle())
    val containerFigure: Container<Figure> = containerTriangle
}
```

We only have two instructions. The first line is the one that allows us to create a `Triangle` container. It is quite straightforward, as we have already seen.

The second line is the one that shows us the covariance. We can see that we are creating a `Figure` container, which would be the superclass or supertype, but we use `Triangle` itself to do this when we assign the element. This does not generate an error, thanks to what we did previously with the word `out` and using the definition of the `content` property in the `Container` class with `val`. We did all this in the `Container` class.

Let's not forget the following regarding covariance:

- Covariant types can only appear in output positions, meaning they are used where data is returned or accessed, but not modified.
- Covariance is useful for types that produce data (e.g., collections or functions that return items), but not for types that act as consumers, which modify or accept data as input.
- When we use covariance, it implies that we cannot modify the content, which guarantees type safety, as it prevents accidental changes that could break the consistency of type hierarchies.

Contravariance (in)

Contravariance is easier to define at this point, especially since we have something direct to compare it to. Contravariance is the opposite of covariance and is used when we want a generic type to act as a receiver or accept input (i.e., to consume data). Another way to explain it is that contravariance allows us to work with a more general type when a more specific type would normally be expected. This is why contravariance is considered the opposite of covariance.

Remember that we are using the same code example in this final section. The initial code remains the same:

```
open class Figure
class Triangle : Figure()
class Circle: Figure()
class Square: Figure()
```

Now comes the code for the `Container` class:

```
class Container<in T> {
    fun setContent(content:T){
        println(content)
    }
}
```

We can quickly see the change: where before we had `out`, we now have `in`. This is the instruction that allows us to immediately know what we are implementing. The `in` keyword before `T` declares that `Container` is contravariant in `T`.

This is the code that we run next:

```
fun main(){
    val figureContainer: Container<Figure> = Container()
    val triangleContainer: Container<Triangle> = figureContainer

    triangleContainer.setContent(Triangle())
    figureContainer.setContent(Square())
}
```

In the first part, we can see that we defined two containers of figures; one is a `Figure` container, and the other is a `Triangle` container. Remember that we rely on the `Container` class to use generics:

```
val figureContainer: Container<Figure> = Container()
val triangleContainer: Container<Triangle> = figureContainer
```

In the second part of this code block, we can see how we assign an element to `content`. In the first line, we use `Triangle`, and in the second line, `Square`:

```
triangleContainer.setContent(Triangle())
figureContainer.setContent(Square())
```

We can see that we reverse the subtyping relationship, even though `Triangle` is a subtype of `Figure`, because of how we define inheritance. We can see that `Container<Figure>` is considered a subtype of `Container<Triangle>`.

Finally, we can see that it is safe to use `Container<Figure>` where `Container<Triangle>` can be expected, as anything that can consume `Figure` can also consume `Triangle`.

The flexibility we have achieved is something we have never seen before, and it allows certain parts of the code to be more reusable.

In this section, we explained variance, invariance, covariance, and contravariance. We must remember invariance when we need to read and write values of the generic type.

Covariance is used for reading only, value producers, or when we only need to return values of the generic type. Contravariance is used when we need value consumers or comparators, or when we only need to accept values of the generic type as input.

Summary

In this chapter, we explored the powerful concept of generics in Kotlin, a key feature that allows us to create flexible, reusable, and type-safe code components. We began with an overview of Java generics and discussed how generics in Kotlin offer a more concise and robust syntax. You learned how generics enable the definition of classes, interfaces, and functions that can handle different data types without compromising type safety, allowing for more efficient and reusable code.

We delved into the application of generics in functions, highlighting how generics improve code flexibility by enabling functions to work with multiple types. We also explored how generics work with properties, providing further flexibility when defining class attributes. A crucial part of this chapter was the introduction to variance (covariance and contravariance), which enables developers to manage type relationships effectively, ensuring compatibility between different generic types.

The information covered in this chapter is valuable because it allows developers to write more flexible and reusable code while maintaining type safety. Understanding how generics work in Kotlin helps to create robust, maintainable programs that can adapt to various use cases. Additionally, mastering variance concepts is essential for understanding how Kotlin handles type hierarchies in generic classes and functions.

In the next chapter, we will explore data and sealed classes, focusing on how Kotlin provides specialized constructs to handle immutable data and restrict class hierarchies, enhancing the management of data structures in our programs.

7

Data and Sealed Classes

In this chapter, we will dive into two essential features of Kotlin that greatly simplify and enhance the way developers model data and manage class hierarchies: data classes and sealed classes. These constructs play a critical role in making your code more concise, readable, and easier to maintain, while also providing robust solutions for type safety and immutability. Additionally, we will explore **enums**, another powerful feature for handling predefined sets of constants, which can simplify decision-making processes in your applications. We will also learn other important concepts within Kotlin that will be explained in detail.

Kotlin's data classes offer a streamlined way to create classes whose primary purpose is to hold data. Instead of manually implementing boilerplate code such as `equals()`, `hashCode()`, `toString()`, getters and setters, and `copy()`, Kotlin generates these functions automatically. This chapter will teach you how to use data classes effectively, showing you how to reduce redundancy and increase the maintainability of your data models with minimal effort.

We will then shift focus to sealed classes, which are an advanced type of class hierarchy that restricts inheritance, allowing you to model a closed set of possible types. Sealed classes are particularly useful when you need exhaustive handling of different cases, especially in combination with Kotlin's powerful **when expression**. They provide you with full control over subclassing, ensuring that only a predefined set of subclasses can be instantiated, which improves type safety and readability in complex scenarios.

Finally, we will explore enums, which allow you to define a collection of constant values, providing a clear and efficient way of representing a fixed set of related options. Enums are commonly used for managing state, settings, or commands in applications, and understanding their proper use can help you design cleaner and more organized code.

We're going to cover the following main topics:

- Data classes
- Sealed classes
- Enums

Technical requirements

You can use any text editor or **Integrated Development Environment** (**IDE**) of your choice with the Java language. We would recommend IntelliJ IDEA **Community Edition** (**CE**). This tool already comes with everything you need to work with both Java and Kotlin. The software requirements for this chapter, with the versions, are as follows:

- Java JDK 17 or higher
- IntelliJ IDEA CE
- Kotlin 1.x or 2.x

The code used in the chapters can be found in the book's accompanying GitHub repository: `https://github.com/PacktPublishing/Kotlin-for-Java-Developers`.

Data classes

We will start by briefly talking about what a data class is, then take a break to go to Java to do some code, and then continue with the explanation of a data class. Let's begin the explanation.

One of the key features of Kotlin data classes is their support for immutability through the use of `val` properties. By defining properties as `val` (read-only), you ensure that their values cannot be modified after the object is created, which aligns with the principles of functional programming and leads to safer, more predictable code. While Kotlin allows the use of `var` for mutable properties, this is generally discouraged in data classes, as it undermines immutability and can lead to unintended side effects. To maintain immutability while making changes, Kotlin provides the copy function, which allows you to create a new instance of the data class with modified properties while keeping the original object unchanged. This balance of immutability and flexibility is one of the reasons data classes are so powerful in Kotlin.

There are times when we need objects to perform the function of an entity. Let's imagine that we have software that allows us to manage a library. Then, we could think about what entities we can find. Thinking quickly, we could define what we will need as follows:

- Book
- User
- Loan
- Author
- Category
- Reservation

We don't need to be precise with all the elements; we just want to have a general idea. So, we can say that we have those six elements. Each of those entities can be used for different purposes, as follows:

- A book loan
- Repayment of loans
- Penalty for non-repayment or late return

Again, we will not going into all of this in detail as we just need a general idea. So, let's think that in these actions, for example, two or more entities may be involved. Let's analyze the action of a book loan.

In the book loan action, we have at least three elements involved:

- Book
- User
- Loan

A book can be made up of data such as the following:

- Author
- Title
- Pages
- Publisher
- ISBN
- Publication date

A user can be made up of something such as these:

- ID
- Name
- Email
- Address
- User type

The two entities – book and user, can be said to be easy to define in a certain way. Let's not forget that we don't need to get into the details, since we already understand the concept. Loans are a combination of these two entities, so we might think that they are more complex, and they are.

We say that it is a combination because a loan needs to have information from both entities:

- Knowing who the person is who makes the loan.
- Knowing which book the person requested.
- More details of the loan, such as the loan date, the delivery date, and whether there is more than one book (loan).

As we can see, these entities need a definition that allows us to maintain information about them in the properties of the objects.

If we define a book in code, we will then have to add all the properties that we will need. The same goes for all the other entities. These would be accompanied by actions or methods that we would apply to change the state of the object, that is, the values of the properties.

In summary, we can say that data classes are designed to represent data in a concise and efficient way. The main purpose is to simplify the work of creating objects, which we want to have data and have access to it, such as writing and deleting it. These objects are used to define entities.

We haven't seen this in code yet; the reason is that we are first going to see how it is done in Java.

Plain Old Java Object (POJO)

In Java, there are no data classes; in fact, this is a concept introduced by Kotlin and appears only in this programming language.

In Java, the concept of a **Plain Old Java Object** (**POJO**) originated to describe simple objects that do not depend on third-party frameworks or libraries.

A POJO is simply a Java class that has no dependencies on any frameworks. The term was coined to contrast with classes that required inheriting from specific framework classes or implementing special interfaces.

The following are characteristics of a POJO:

- It is framework-independent.
- It has no special restrictions on its structure.
- It is not required to follow specific conventions.
- It can have any constructor.
- Fields can be public or private.
- It is not required to implement any specific method.

JavaBeans

A JavaBean is a class that follows specific design conventions.

JavaBeans can commonly be confused with POJOs. POJO is simply a framework-agnostic class that does not rely on predefined structures or annotations. To clarify the distinction from POJOs, the following conventions are typical for JavaBeans:

- A JavaBean does not extend from predefined classes, only from an object.
- It has no framework annotations.
- It does not implement predefined interfaces.
- Properties should be private to encapsulate the data.
- Getters and setters are public since they are the way to access and modify properties.
- JavaBeans should have the implementation of the equals, `hashCode` and `toString` methods.

POJOs are more flexible and lightweight, suitable for modeling data without any imposed rules, while JavaBeans are designed to integrate with tools and frameworks that rely on these conventions, such as Java EE, serialization libraries, or data mapping. In short, JavaBeans are a more structured and standardized form of POJOs, geared toward scenarios where interoperability and tooling are essential.

Records

Records in Java are a feature introduced in Java 16 (previewed in Java 14) that provides a concise way to declare classes that act primarily as holders of immutable data.

This simple code automatically generated has the following conventions:

- Canonical constructor
- Getter methods (without the get prefix)
- `equals()` and `hashCode()`
- `toString()`
- Final (immutable) fields

Records in Java have a specific purpose: they are designed solely for modeling data in a concise and efficient manner. They are not suitable for implementing complex logic or for use in extensible models, as their primary focus is on the straightforward representation of immutable data. Java records are the most similar to what we want to use a data class in Kotlin for. In fact, many programmers see data classes as an evolution of POJOs and records.

We could say that POJOs were Java's initial approach to handling data. However, the JavaBeans specification went further than simply acting as containers for data. JavaBeans introduced a structured way to define classes with private fields, along with public getters and setters, enabling frameworks to access and manipulate data through reflection. For example, libraries such as Jackson use these methods to map JSON data to Java objects. In this section, we will show how classes are structured in Java to understand the changes and improvements when transitioning to Kotlin and using features such as data classes. Let's look at the parts that a simple Java object would have.

This is the definition of the `Book` class, with five properties:

```
public class Book {
    private String title;
    private String author;
    private String isbn;
    private int pageCount;
    private double price;
```

This is the constructor; the constructor needs five values to set for the five properties:

```
public Book(String title, String author, String isbn, int pageCount,
double price) {
    this.title = title;
    this.author = author;
    this.isbn = isbn;
    this.pageCount = pageCount;
```

```
        this.price = price;
    }
```

We need to define `getter` method, since they are what allow us to access the properties. There is one for each property we have. The `get` methods always return a value of the same type as the property they refer to and are public:

```
    public String getTitle() {
        return title;
    }

    public String getAuthor() {
        return author;
    }

    public String getIsbn() {
        return isbn;
    }

    public int getPageCount() {
        return pageCount;
    }

    public double getPrice() {
        return price;
    }
```

We also have `setter` method. These methods allow us to assign a value to the property. They are also always public and always receive a parameter at the same time as the property:

```
    public void setTitle(String title) {
        this.title = title;
    }

    public void setAuthor(String author) {
        this.author = author;
    }

    public void setIsbn(String isbn) {
```

```
        this.isbn = isbn;
    }

    public void setPageCount(int pageCount) {
        this.pageCount = pageCount;
    }

    public void setPrice(double price) {
        this.price = price;
    }
```

Within a POJO, we will always find an equals method, which is used to compare whether two instances of an object are logically equivalent. Instead of comparing only the references of the objects (that is, whether they point to the same object in memory, which is what the == operator does by default), the equals method compares the contents of the objects:

```
    @Override
    public boolean equals(Object o) {
        if (this == o) return true;
        if (o == null || getClass() != o.getClass()) return false;
        Book book = (Book) o;
        return pageCount == book.pageCount &&
           Double.compare(book.price, price) == 0 &&
           Objects.equals(title, book.title) &&
           Objects.equals(author, book.author) &&
           Objects.equals(isbn, book.isbn);
    }
```

We also have a `hasCode` method, which generates an integer value (`hash`) that uniquely represents that object based on its attributes. This value is mainly used in data structures such as HashMap, HashSet, and other hash-based collections to determine the location of objects and facilitate quick lookups:

```
    @Override
    public int hashCode() {
        return Objects.hash(title, author, isbn, pageCount, price);
    }
```

We also always have a `toString` method. Its purpose is to return a string representation of the object. This method is useful to obtain a readable description of the object and its state (the values of its attributes):

```
@Override
public String toString() {
    return "Book{" +
            "title='" + title + '\'' +
            ", author='" + author + '\'' +
            ", isbn='" + isbn + '\'' +
            ", pageCount=" + pageCount +
            ", price=" + price +
            '}';
    }
}
```

In general terms, we can say that there are five properties that are defined as private: `title`, `author`, `isbn`, `pageCount`, and `price`.

We have a public constructor. This constructor initializes all the properties. We have a getter and setter for each of the properties, so we can access them. We have the implementation of the equals method to be able to compare `Book` objects. We have the implementation of the `toString` method to be able to make a representation of the object in a text string.

We can also see that the conventions of POJOs that we previously mentioned are followed.

The code is somewhat long, especially considering it's only for a single object – the `Book` object. If we refer back to the library example, we'd need to create something similar for each of the other entities we've identified. This gives us a sense of the code's overall size, considering that this portion only defines the object and its characteristics. We have not yet added any of the business logic and other elements that would increase the code of our project even more.

Here, we have the equivalent of the `Book` class using a Java record:

```
public record Book(String title, String author, String isbn, int
pageCount, double price) { }
```

Fields declared in parentheses are automatically private and final.

The following are automatically generated:

- A public constructor that accepts all fields.
- Equals, `hashCode`, and `toString` methods.
- Getters for each field, called "accessors," with the same name as the field (e.g., `title()` for `title`).

This record is much more concise and eliminates the need to manually write getters, constructors, and other repetitive methods.

Records in Java are designed to model data in a concise and efficient manner, and feature key characteristics: they automatically generate the `equals()`, `hashCode()`, and `toString()` methods; all of their properties are immutable (final); they cannot inherit from other classes or be inherited, as they are implicitly final; and they do not allow adding additional fields outside of those defined in their declaration, thus maintaining their focus on simplicity and consistency.

Defining a data class

The code of what the `Book` object would look like using Java and the POJO concept has already been shown.

Next, we will show what the equivalent of this code would be using the Kotlin programming language:

```
data class Book(
    val title: String,
    val author: String,
    val isbn: String,
    val pageCount: Int,
    val price: Double
)
```

It may seem like very little code and that there is no possibility that it could have the same function as the previous one, but we are going to explain how it does. In fact, some of the concepts that we are going to explain we have already seen and explained in the book previously. So, we are going to go through it step by step to make it as clear as possible that this code, even if it is very short, is doing the same thing.

To create a data class in Kotlin, we have to place the word `data` before the word `class`. This is the instruction for Kotlin to understand that we are generating a data class and not just a regular class:

```
data class Book(
```

The difference is that with the data class, we are indicating that we will need, for example, the equals, `hashCode`, and `toString` methods. By default, these methods are already implemented with this instruction; Kotlin generates them automatically.

Everything inside the parentheses represents the properties we need. At this point in the book, we also know that Kotlin is creating a constructor for us by default, which means it is generating additional code automatically.

To this default code, we can add the getter and setter, which, as we saw previously, are generated when we make the declaration in this way.

If we analyze what is happening, we see that we already have all the elements that we would need. So, with this code, note the following:

- We can create a book object.
- We have a constructor with all the properties.
- We have `getter` and `setter` to access the properties.
- We respect the encapsulation of the properties.

We have, by default, the equals, `hashCode`, and `toString` methods, so we will be able to compare objects and generate the hash code and the string representation of the object.

We also have a method that we did not have in Java, the copy method. This method allows us to modify some of the properties of the object if necessary.

The `copy()` method in Kotlin data classes creates a new instance with some properties modified while keeping others identical to the original object. Unlike using `var`, it preserves immutability by generating a new object instead of modifying the existing one, ensuring consistency, especially in collections and concurrent environments.

With this, we confirm that this small amount of code is equivalent to what we had to do in Java in many more lines of code. This is something many developers who come from the world of Java find very surprising the first time they see it.

This is the code to use the `Book` class:

```
val book =
Book("The Best Kotlin Book", "Jose Lujan", "0395415152", 510, 99.99)
```

If we look at how to create this object, it does not change at all from how we have created objects previously in Kotlin. We simply indicate the name of the object, which in this case is `book`, and we use the constructor that we have by default. That constructor will need us to pass it the values of all the properties that we have placed, and that's it. With this, we have created the object using the `Book` data class that we have defined. Comparing the concepts of Java POJOs and Kotlin data classes, we can say a few things:

- Both can be used for the same purpose, creating entities and storing their data.
- Data classes in Kotlin are primarily used to store immutable data with properties that are accessed through getters. When modifications are needed, rather than using setters, the recommended approach is to create new instances using the automatically generated `copy()` method, which preserves immutability while allowing targeted property updates.
- POJOs and data classes use the same three methods: equals, `hashCode`, and `toString`. These are inherited from the `Object` or `Any` class.
- In Java, the previous methods have to be implemented by the programmer; in Kotlin, they are implemented by default.
- Only data classes contain the copy method.
- In data classes, we have the possibility through `var` to allow mutability in properties and, with the use of `val`, to implement immutability.
- When the Kotlin code is compiled to bytecode, the data class is a regular Java class with the methods and properties that we have added.

Although both classes have a similar purpose, they are slightly different, so we cannot say that they are equivalent.

The advantage of data classes is quite evident when seeing the great reduction in code compared to Java. It is by far one of the most significant reductions you can achieve when migrating to Kotlin. The cleaner syntax is another highlight, as many components, such as `equals`, `hashCode`, `toString`, and the primary constructor, are generated automatically.

When comparing data classes to Java records, several benefits stand out:

- **Flexibility**: While Java records are strictly immutable, Kotlin data classes allow properties to be mutable (`var`) or immutable (`val`), offering more versatility depending on the use case.
- **Default property values**: Data classes support default values for properties, eliminating the need for multiple constructors.
- **Copy function:** Kotlin data classes include a copy function, which makes it easy to create a modified version of an object without altering the original.
- **Compatibility with functional programming**: Just like Java records, Kotlin data classes integrate smoothly with functional operations such as `map`, `filter`, and `reduce`, making them ideal for transforming and processing data in a concise and expressive way.

In summary, while Java records and Kotlin data classes share some similarities in their goal of reducing boilerplate code for modeling data, data classes offer greater flexibility and functionality, making them a more powerful tool in many scenarios.

We have explored data classes in Kotlin and compared them with the concept of POJOs in Java. We have learned that data classes are designed to simplify the work of creating objects whose primary role is to hold data. By using data classes, Kotlin automatically generates common methods such as `equals()`, `hashCode()`, and `toString()`, which in Java would need to be manually implemented for POJOs. We also introduced Kotlin's unique `copy()` method, which provides additional functionality that POJOs do not have.

The comparison showed how Kotlin reduces the amount of boilerplate code significantly while maintaining functionality equivalent to Java POJOs. The automatic generation of methods and constructors makes Kotlin's data classes not only concise but also highly efficient for handling data entities.

Just like Java records, Kotlin data classes integrate smoothly with functional operations such as `map`, `filter`, and `reduce`, making them ideal for transforming and processing data in a concise and expressive way.

Let's look at the similarities:

- Concise syntax
- Automatic generation of useful methods
- Focused on data management

- Automatic generation of constructors
- Automatic getters

There are also differences:

- Mutability:
  - **Data class:** Supports mutable and immutable properties
  - **Record:** Only supports immutable properties
- Inheritance:
  - **Data class:** Allows inheritance
  - **Record:** Does not allow inheritance
- Additional methods:
  - **Data class:** Includes `copy()`
  - **Record:** Does not include `copy()`

Therefore, Java records are the closest implementation to Kotlin data classes, albeit with some additional limitations.

Sealed classes

Unlike many, this concept is very easy to explain since we can summarize it in very few words, and it is easy to understand. Sealed classes are used to represent restricted class hierarchies.

If we want to give a more detailed explanation, we can say that sealed classes allow us to represent limited data types through a restricted hierarchy of classes. We can also use them to represent states.

We can explain sealed classes in two ways for Java developers. For developers using Java versions prior to Java 15, the concept might seem somewhat similar to enums, as both can represent a restricted set of types. However, they are fundamentally different: enums are singleton objects that represent a single state, while sealed classes can define hierarchies of objects or classes. In Kotlin, we also have enums, and we will cover them later. In this chapter, we will not compare the concepts. For developers who have worked with Java version 15 or higher, it is possible that you will know the concept of sealed classes already, as Java introduced this feature as a preview in version 15 and made it a standard part of the language in Java 17. While the idea is similar between Java and Kotlin, the implementation details differ slightly.

Moving forward, let's try to understand the concept of a closed hierarchy to deepen the explanation.

A closed hierarchy can be defined by the characteristic that all its subclasses must be known at compile time. This allows the compiler to perform exhaustive checks, which is especially useful in `when` expressions.

To declare a sealed class, we will have to declare a class using the `sealed` and `class` keywords. Take the following example:

```
sealed class Book
```

Another element to consider is that all direct subclasses must be declared in the same file as the sealed class. But in addition, the subclasses can be simple classes like any other that we define, without anything special, just using the word `class`. They can also be data classes or object classes.

Something important to remember is that sealed classes are implicitly abstract, so we don't need to use the word `abstract` in their definition; they are abstract by default. Additionally, like any other class in Kotlin, sealed classes are public by default unless a different visibility modifier is specified. You can change their visibility as needed, using the same syntax as for other elements in Kotlin.

Now we are going to see an example of what a sealed class looks like. We will continue using the library example as a reference. Let's assume that we need several types of books. This is the beginning of the definition of the sealed `Book` class; it has three properties. Inside the sealed class, we define our first data class, and it is `Fiction`. It has four properties:

```
sealed class Book {
    abstract val title: String
    abstract val author: String
    abstract val year: Int

    data class Fiction(
        override val title: String,
        override val author: String,
        override val year: Int,
        val genre: String
    ) : Book()
```

We will add two data classes: `NonFiction` and `TextBook`. They have different properties, as we can see. The idea of this exercise is to demonstrate that we can customize classes as we need. In some cases, we can write that we want to override the property:

```
    data class NonFiction(
        override val title: String,
        override val author: String,
        override val year: Int,
        val subject: String
    ) : Book()

    data class TextBook(
        override val title: String,
        override val author: String,
        override val year: Int,
        val subject: String,
        val grade: Int
    ) : Book()
```

We add one more data class to refer to a `ComicBook` type. This will be our last data class:

```
    data class ComicBook(
        override val title: String,
        override val author: String,
        override val year: Int,
        val illustrator: String
    ) : Book()
}
```

We define a sealed class, `Book`, with four subclasses:

- `Fiction`
- `NonFiction`
- `TextBook`
- `ComicBook`

The subclasses have common properties to what we have previously used in the `Book` example, `title` and `author`, and a different one that we added, which is `year`. Then, we have specific properties for each type; for example, we have `illustrator` for `ComicBook` and `genre` for `Fiction`.

In this case, to demonstrate that the subtypes can be different, we use a data class for the subclasses. We won't go into this in detail as we have already discussed data classes.

Now, let's move on to the next part of the code:

```
fun getBookDetails(book: Book): String {
    return when (book) {
        is Book.Fiction -> "${book.title} by ${book.author} (${book.year})
- Genre: ${book.genre}"
        is Book.NonFiction -> "${book.title} by ${book.author} (${book.
year}) - Subject: ${book.subject}"
        is Book.TextBook -> "${book.title} by ${book.author} (${book.
year}) - Subject: ${book.subject} for Grade ${book.grade}"
        is Book.ComicBook -> "${book.title} by ${book.author} (${book.
year}) - Illustrated by ${book.illustrator}"
    }
}

fun recommendBook(book: Book): String {
    return when (book) {
        is Book.Fiction -> "If you like ${book.genre}, you'll love this
book!"
        is Book.NonFiction -> "Great for learning about ${book.subject}."
        is Book.TextBook -> "Essential for students in grade ${book.grade}
studying ${book.subject}."
        is Book.ComicBook -> "A visual treat illustrated by ${book.
illustrator}."
    }
}
```

We have two functions in the code, `getBookDetails` and `recommendBook`. In `getBookDetails`, we return a string with the details of the book regardless of the type of book. The `recommendBook` function will provide a recommendation based on the type of book.

Now, we go to the `main` function. Let's explain it:

```
fun main() {
    val books = listOf(
        Book.Fiction("I, robot", "Isaac Asimov", 1950, "Fantasy
literature"),
```

```
        Book.NonFiction("The Theory of Everything: The Origin and Fate of
the Universe", "Stephen Hawking", 2002, "Physics"),
        Book.TextBook("Basic Mathematics", "Jose Lujan", 2010, "Science",
10),
        Book.ComicBook("Spiderman", "Stan Lee", 1986, "Steve Ditko")
    )
    books.forEach { book ->
        println(getBookDetails(book))
        println(recommendBook(book))
        println()
    }
}
```

In the main function, we are going to create a list with different types of books. As we can see, the way to create them is very simple. We put them in a list, which makes it easier to pass them around to other functions. We create four books, one for each case to have a complete example.

After creating them, we use the list of books with the functions that we already mentioned for each of the books that are part of the list.

This was a simple but clear implementation of a sealed class.

Here, we see several benefits of using sealed classes:

- **Flexibility**: Each book, for example, can have its own unique properties and behaviors.
- **Expressiveness**: The code is clearly structured, showing the relationships between different types of books. However, it's important to consider that if the hierarchy becomes too deep or the classes grow large, the code might become harder to read and maintain. Additionally, for developers coming from Java, the Kotlin approach of having multiple classes in a single file may feel unfamiliar, as Java typically enforces one class per file for better organization.
- **Security**: The compiler can give us the security that we are handling all the possible types of `Book` through our `when` expression in the code.
- **Extensibility**: In a basic class hierarchy, we can add new types of books by extending the `Book` class. However, sealed classes go a step further by enforcing that all subclasses are explicitly handled in `when` expressions. This ensures that no type is accidentally missed, providing stronger guarantees and better safety compared to a basic hierarchy.

This way of working allows us to have the code ready to work with some design patterns; for example, a design pattern that could be easily implemented with this way of working is the State pattern.

Sealed interfaces

In Kotlin, sealed interfaces give us the ability to define a limited set of implementations, as with sealed classes, but with the advantage of focusing on behavior rather than shared state or properties. This is ideal for organizing type hierarchies that rely more on actions than common data.

For example, let's say we're still on the topic of books and we're working on a book management system where user roles with the following profiles have different access levels: administrator, guest, and registered user. This is where sealed interfaces come into their own, as they allow us to model these differences in a clear, controlled, and secure way.

Here's how they work and what they benefit from:

- **Controlled hierarchies**: All classes or objects that implement a sealed interface must be declared in the same file or, depending on the version of Kotlin you're using, within the same package. This restriction ensures that the compiler has complete knowledge of all possible implementations, allowing for greater code security and clarity.
- **Exhaustive checking in when**: A major benefit of sealed interfaces is their integration with `when` expressions. When you use a `when` expression with a sealed interface, the compiler makes sure that all implementations are accounted for. If you forget to handle one, the compiler will show you an error, helping you prevent runtime crashes.
- **Flexibility with multiple inheritance**: Unlike sealed classes, sealed interfaces allow a class to implement multiple interfaces. This makes them an ideal tool for modeling shared behavior in complex systems, where a class may need to inherit functionality from multiple sources.

In short, sealed interfaces combine the advantages of controlled hierarchies with the flexibility of multiple inheritance, making them a perfect choice for structuring behavior-focused systems while ensuring that the code is robust and maintainable. Let's look at some code for more details:

```
sealed interface UserRole
object Admin : UserRole {
    fun addBook(title: String, author: String) {
        println("Book '$title' by $author added.")
    }
```

```
    fun deleteBook(title: String) {
        println("Book '$title' deleted.")
    }
}
object Editor : UserRole {
    fun editBook(title: String, newDetails: String) {
        println("Book '$title' updated with new details: $newDetails")
    }
}

objectReader : UserRole {
    fun readBook(title: String) {
        println("Reading book: $title")
    }
}
```

`Admin` has permissions to add and delete books. `Editor` can modify the details of existing books. `Reader` can only read books.

Now we can handle the different behaviors of each role using an exhaustive `when` expression:

```
fun handleUserAction(user: UserRole, action: String, bookTitle: String,
details: String? = null) {
    when (user) {
        is Admin -> {
            if (action == "add") user.addBook(bookTitle, details ?:
"Unknown Author")
            if (action == "delete") user.deleteBook(bookTitle)
        }
        is Editor -> {
            if (action == "edit") user.editBook(bookTitle, details ?: "No
details provided")
        }
        is Reader -> {
            if (action == "read") user.readBook(bookTitle)
        }
    }
}
```

We can see that this code defines a `handleUserAction` function that handles actions of a user (`user`) based on their role (`UserRole`) and the type of action (`action`). It uses an exhaustive `when` expression to check the role:

- `Admin`: Can add or delete books
- `Editor`: Can edit book details
- `Reader`: Can read books

If we decide to add a new role, the compiler will force us to update this `when` expression, ensuring that everything is covered.

Sealed interfaces and sealed classes have key differences that make them suitable for different scenarios. Sealed interfaces allow multiple inheritance, making them an ideal choice for modeling shared behaviors across types. In contrast, sealed classes do not support multiple inheritance but are better suited for handling complex hierarchies that combine both state and behavior. While sealed interfaces focus on representing behavior-focused hierarchies, sealed classes are more useful when you need to work with defined data and state.

In summary, sealed interfaces are a powerful tool in Kotlin that, although similar to sealed classes, stand out when we want to model behavior-based hierarchies in a flexible and controlled way.

In this section, we have explored sealed classes and how they allow us to represent restricted class hierarchies. We have seen how sealed classes provide flexibility by letting us create subclasses with their own unique properties, and how they ensure safety by allowing the compiler to exhaustively check types when used in expressions such as `when`. Additionally, we've demonstrated the use of sealed classes in a practical example involving different types of books, showing how they can simplify code while enhancing clarity and maintainability.

Sealed classes give us the ability to handle various related types in a secure and expressive way, making them ideal for scenarios where the types of objects are known and controlled at compile time. We've also discussed their inherent extensibility, which allows us to add new types as needed, making sealed classes a valuable tool for managing complex data hierarchies.

In addition to sealed classes, we have also explored sealed interfaces, which bring the same level of safety and controlled hierarchies but with the flexibility of allowing multiple inheritance. Sealed interfaces are particularly useful when modeling behavior-focused hierarchies, enabling us to define polymorphic behavior for a set of related types. This makes them an excellent choice for scenarios where shared behavior is the primary focus, without needing to handle shared state or properties.

We will build on the concept of controlling a fixed set of types by exploring enums. Enums are a great tool when we need to define a finite set of constant values, offering a simpler alternative to sealed classes in certain cases. We'll dive into how enums can be used to represent fixed options and how they compare to sealed classes. This will help us further understand the different ways Kotlin supports controlled type hierarchies.

Enums

Enums are one of the most popular concepts within programming. They are not very difficult to explain or understand, and they are widely used when programming systems that have a complexity above what we can consider as something basic.

In general, the definition of an enum is that it is a special type of data that represents a fixed set of values. That is, we have a list of possible and unique values for a type of variable. A classic example of this is the days of the week (Monday, Tuesday...) but why use an enum instead of constants? Enums provide several advantages over constants: they are type-safe, ensuring that only valid values are used; they group related constants into a single type, making the code more organized and readable; and they can include additional properties or methods, adding more functionality compared to plain constants.

We know that the days, for example, do not change, and if we use them within a program, we could manage them in a fixed way; this would be a great example of the use of an enum. Other classic examples are the months of the year and the cardinal points.

In Kotlin, we can say that an enum is a special class since it represents a set of constant elements. In fact, as we mentioned, enum is a general programming concept, but an enum in Kotlin is different from what we normally know. In fact, if we compare it with enums in Java, we will confirm that it is different. One of the important features of enums in Kotlin, similar to Java, is that they are instances of the `Enum` class itself, so they can also have properties and methods.

This is important because we can associate specific data or behavior with each enum value. For example, we can define methods in the `Enum` class that all enum constants will share, but it also allows for methods to provide customized functionality for specific constants. However, it's essential to note that this customization applies to the enum as a whole, not to individual values with their own methods. Enums are not typically used for abstraction; their primary purpose is to represent a restricted set of constant values in a clear and type-safe manner. By leveraging their features, we can write more expressive and structured code.

To explain more details, we will use this code:

```
enum class Weekday(val isWorkday: Boolean) {
    MONDAY(true),
    TUESDAY(true),
    WEDNESDAY(true),
    THURSDAY(true),
    FRIDAY(true),
    SATURDAY(false),
    SUNDAY(false);

    fun isWeekend() = !isWorkday

    companion object {
        fun getWorkdays() = values ().filter { it.isWorkday }
    }
}
```

To define an enum, we use the word `enum` before the word `class` as we have in the first line of this code. Then, we define a value that will tell us if that day is a workday. This is just to add a little detail to the example:

```
enum class Weekday(val isWorkday: Boolean) {
    MONDAY(true),
    TUESDAY(true),
    WEDNESDAY(true),
    THURSDAY(true),
    FRIDAY(true),
    SATURDAY(false),
    SUNDAY(false);
```

In the following part of the code, we define a method that we call `isWeekend`. This method would return the opposite of the `isWorkday` property, which makes perfect sense since we know that by definition, we are defining certain days as workdays (true) and others as non-workdays (false):

```
    fun isWeekend() = !isWorkday
```

This method provides a simple way to check whether a day is a weekend by negating the `isWorkday` property.

In the next part of the example, we add a companion object. The getWorkdays method allows us to filter and return the working days. In Kotlin, methods inside a companion object can be called directly on the class, similar to static methods in Java, even though Kotlin's approach is more flexible:

```
companion object {
    fun getWorkdays() = values().filter { it.isWorkday }
```

To use our enum class, we are going to use this code, which is also quite descriptive and simple:

```
fun main() {
    println("Days of the week: ${Weekday.values().joinToString()}")

    val day = Weekday.SATURDAY
    println("Is $day a workday? ${day.isWorkday}")

    println("Is $day a weekend? ${day.isWeekend()}")

    println("Workdays: ${Weekday.getWorkdays().joinToString()}")

    when (day) {
        Weekday.MONDAY -> println("Start of the week")
        Weekday.FRIDAY -> println("TGIF!")
        Weekday.SATURDAY, Weekday.SUNDAY -> println("Weekend!")
        else -> println("Midweek day")
    }
}
```

We are going to explain what the lines that we have inside the main function do, so that it is clear what each one does and how we implement it.

In the first line, we are sending all the values of the enum to be printed:

```
println("Days of the week: ${Weekday.values().joinToString()}")
```

The joinToString function is an extension function in Kotlin that converts a collection or array into a single text string. By default, it separates the elements with a comma and a space (,). However, you can customize the output by providing optional arguments, such as the following:

- separator: Defines the string used to separate the elements (default: ", ").
- prefix and postfix: Add text at the beginning and end of the resulting string.

- `transform`: Allows you to specify how each element should be represented in the string.

In the next part of the code, we show how to access a specific property. First, we assign the element to a variable called `day`. Then, we retrieve the value of the property name, which in this case is `Workday`. We would do it directly like this:

```
val day = Weekday.SATURDAY
    println("Is $day a workday? ${day.isWorkday}")
```

In the following line, we show how to access a method that we define ourselves, a custom method, only again with the name of the variable and the name of the method, as we would do with any regular object:

```
println("Is $day a weekend? ${day.isWeekend()}")
```

We can access what we defined inside the companion object since we are working with `getWorkdays`, and as we see, we take advantage of `joinToString`. In this example, we are using the default separator (a comma followed by a space), which is why no separator argument is specified in the method call:

```
println("Workdays: ${Weekday.getWorkdays().joinToString()}")
```

This results in the workdays being displayed as a single string, separated by the default format.

We also see the use of `when`, where the program's flow is determined by the day. If needed, an `else` block can be added to handle any remaining cases. There's nothing special about using `when` with enums; it's simply a convenient way to handle different enum values:

```
when (day) {
    Weekday.MONDAY -> println("Start of the week")
    Weekday.FRIDAY -> println("TGIF!")
    Weekday.SATURDAY, Weekday.SUNDAY -> println("Weekend!")
    else -> println("Midweek day")
}
```

To finish this chapter, we are going to share some differences between an enum in Java and Kotlin.

The enum in Java is more limited; it cannot implement interfaces directly. It looks more like a set of constants due to the same limitations. In Kotlin, it is much more complete since we can have methods, properties, and interfaces, and we can say that it seeks to be object-oriented.

In Kotlin, enum values can have anonymous classes, and we can also use extension functions for enums.

Another important detail about enums in Kotlin is that by default, some methods and properties are defined:

- `name`: This property returns the name of the enum constant as a string.
- `ordinal`: This property returns the position of the constant in the declaration and works with logic 0.
- `entries`: This is a static property (introduced in Kotlin 1.9) that returns an `EnumEntries<E>` object containing all constants of the enum. It's more efficient because it doesn't create a new array on each access and provides a more idiomatic way to work with enumerations in modern Kotlin.
- `values()`: This is a static method that returns a new array containing all constants of the enum each time it's invoked. It's the traditional way, available since the earliest versions of Kotlin.
- `valueof()`: This is a static method that returns the enum constant that matches the name provided between parentheses. If it does not find a match, it throws `IllegalArgumentException`.
- `compareTo`: This is a method that compares two enum constants based on their ordinal.
- `toString`: This is an automatic implementation that returns the name of the constant.

Sealed classes and enums

In Kotlin, we have two options for representing controlled sets of values: sealed classes and enums. Sealed classes are more flexible because they allow us to define subclasses, each with unique properties and methods. This makes them ideal for modeling complex states or hierarchies, where each state can have its own behavior or additional data. On the other hand, enums are better suited for simpler scenarios where we need a predefined and limited set of constant values, all of the same type. Enums are typically used to represent different states of an entity, such as the days of the week or traffic light colors, or the status of an order. They provide type safety and clarity without the complexity of sealed classes.

Another feature is that enums are serializable by default and we can use an implementation of equals and `hashCode`. We must not forget that although all these elements are available by default, we could overwrite them if we need different behavior in some situations, although it is not common to do so.

Summary

In this chapter, we explored two foundational features of Kotlin: data classes and sealed classes, which simplify data modeling and managing class hierarchies. Data classes are designed to reduce boilerplate code, automatically providing methods such as `equals()`, `hashCode()`, and `toString()`. This makes them ideal for representing simple entities such as `Book` or `User`, allowing developers to focus on the logic without manually implementing repetitive code.

We also covered sealed classes, which enable a restricted class hierarchy, ensuring that all subclasses are known at compile time. This feature is particularly useful in combination with `when` expressions, providing exhaustive handling of different types or states, improving code safety and readability. Enums were another topic, where we learned how they represent fixed sets of constants, which are useful for managing states or options in applications.

This information is valuable because it helps developers write more concise, readable, and maintainable code by leveraging Kotlin's built-in support for immutability and type safety. It also ensures that your applications are less error-prone and easier to extend.

In the next chapter, we will delve into inline functions, which are another powerful feature of Kotlin that allows for efficient function calls, particularly in the context of lambda expressions. These functions optimize performance by reducing overhead and improving how Kotlin handles higher-order functions.

Part 3

Functional Programming

In this part, you will delve into Kotlin's functional programming capabilities, learning how it enhances code expressiveness and efficiency. You will start with inline functions, which optimize higher-order functions by reducing runtime overhead and improving performance. Next, you will explore lambdas, a core feature that enables concise and flexible functional constructs, making operations on collections and functional pipelines more intuitive. Finally, you will dive into collections and sequences, understanding how Kotlin differentiates between eager and lazy evaluation to optimize performance and memory usage. By the end of this part, you will have a strong foundation in functional programming in Kotlin, allowing you to write cleaner, more efficient, and more maintainable code.

This part has the following chapters:

- *Chapter 8, Basics of Functional Programming*
- *Chapter 9, Lambda*
- *Chapter 10, Collections and Sequences*

8

Basics of Functional Programming

This chapter covers the basic principles of functional programming, focusing on how Kotlin supports this paradigm. This includes concepts such as higher-order functions, lambdas, immutability, and the use of functions as first-class citizens. It will also explore how Kotlin eases the transition from an object-oriented approach to a functional one, emphasizing the advantages that functional programming brings in terms of flexibility and code maintainability.

We will explain what inline functions are in Kotlin and how they allow for improved performance. The key point is that functions marked as inline avoid the overhead of function calls by "inserting" the body of the function directly into the code where it is called. This becomes especially useful when working with lambdas or higher-order functions, since inlining reduces the additional object creation and call overhead normally associated with them. We will also provide examples that show in which situations using inline functions is beneficial.

We will then focus on functions that cannot or should not be marked as inline. The `noinline` keyword will be introduced, explaining how it is used to prevent the inlining of certain lambdas in a function marked as inline. Examples will be given here of situations where inlining is not desirable or necessary, such as when a higher-order function stores lambdas.

Finally, we will focus on how Kotlin translates inline functions into Java bytecode. We will discuss how the Kotlin compiler handles optimizations in terms of bytecode, comparing how inline and non-inline functions impact code efficiency at the JVM level. We will also cover a brief explanation of how to analyze the generated bytecode and what implications it has for performance and the final structure of the program.

This chapter will offer a combination of theory and practice, explaining the benefits of using inline functions within the context of functional programming and the impact at the bytecode level.

In this chapter, we're going to cover the following main topics:

- What is functional programming?
- The `inline` function
- The `noinline` function
- Translation to Java bytecode

Technical requirements

To begin, you can use any text editor or **Integrated Development Environment** (**IDE**) of your choice with the Java language. We recommend IDE IntelliJ IDEA **Community Edition** (**CE**). This tool comes with everything you need to work with both Java and Kotlin. The list of requirements for this chapter is as follows:

- Java JDK 8 or higher
- IntelliJ IDEA CE
- Kotlin 1.x

The code used in this chapter can be found in the book's accompanying GitHub repository: `https://github.com/PacktPublishing/Kotlin-for-Java-Developers`.

What is functional programming?

In *Chapter 5*, the focus was on object-oriented programming. In this chapter, it will be on functional programming. We will also investigate other concepts to understand and be able to use the related concepts.

Functional programming is a programming paradigm that treats computation as the evaluation of functions. It avoids changes in state and mutable data. The programming that we normally use is different. It is known as imperative programming, and it does just the opposite; its emphasis is on changes in the state of the program.

Something that we must always remember when we are trying to understand functional programming is that this programming paradigm focuses on "what" we are doing. If we use the opposite approach, which would be the imperative one, we would then be focused on "how" we are doing it.

Probably one of the key details of functional programming that stands out to programmers is that traditional cyclic instructions are discouraged. In other words, constructs such as `for`, `while`, and `do while` loops are generally not used. Depending on the language, there may be alternatives, but the common approach in functional programming is to replace cycles with recursion or higher-order functions. This is quite significant, as since the inception of programming, these cycles have been among the most used and taught topics.

If we wanted to relate Java and functional programming, we could say that the most important change came with Java 8, where three crucial elements were introduced that gave Java the capacity to support the functional paradigm. These three elements were as follows:

- Lambdas
- Streams
- Functional interfaces

Something important to mention is that Java is not a pure functional programming language, and this made the implementation of functional programming a bit verbose. Tail recursion optimization is not a possible implementation in Java due to its limited immutability. For this and other reasons, Java programmers had to do a bit more work if they wanted to apply this paradigm, unlike pure functional programming languages. But this did not stop the adoption of the functional paradigm in the Java community; it began to be used and is still being implemented. Of course, there have already been several improvements and changes that have gradually facilitated its implementation in Java for programmers.

There are four pillars of functional programming:

- Functions as first-class citizens
- Immutability
- Purity
- Higher-order functions

Under functions as first-class citizens, we will look at the following cases:

- Assigning functions to variables
- Passing functions as arguments
- Returning functions from functions
- Storing functions in data structures

Functions as first-class citizens

The concept of first-class citizens means the following:

- Assigned to variables
- Passed as arguments to functions
- Returned as the result of a function
- Stored in data structures

Talking specifically about Kotlin and functional programming, when we say that functions are first-class citizens, it means that functions can be treated like any other data type, that is, as integers, objects, and so on. We are going to rely on code to explain these four points.

Assigning functions to variables

The following is example code to illustrate the concept of assigning functions to variables:

```
val greet: (String) -> String = { name -> "Hello, $name!" }
println(greet("Noemi"))
```

We have broken down the components of this code here:

- `val greet`: This declares an immutable variable called `greet`, meaning that it cannot be reassigned after it is declared.
- `(String) -> String`: This is the type of the `greet` variable. It indicates that `greet` is a function that takes a parameter of type `String` and returns a value of type `String`. Basically, it defines the type of the lambda function.
- `{ name -> "Hello, $name!" }`: This is a lambda (or anonymous function). Inside the brackets, `name` is the parameter of the lambda (`String` type in this case). The part after `->` is the body of the lambda, which in this case returns a string that includes the value of the parameter name.

Passing functions as arguments

Now let's look at some code that passes functions as arguments:

```
fun applyOperation(x: Int, y: Int, operation: (Int, Int) -> Int): Int {
    return operation(x, y)
}
```

We have broken down the code and provided explanations of each part here:

```
fun applyOperation(x: Int, y: Int, operation: (Int, Int) -> Int): Int:
```

Here, you declare a function called `applyOperation` that takes three parameters:

- `x: Int`: The first number, of type `Int`.
- `y: Int`: The second number, of type `Int`.
- `operation: (Int, Int) -> Int`: This is a parameter that represents a lambda function that takes two integers, `(Int, Int)`, and returns an integer, `Int`.

The return type of `applyOperation` is also an integer, `(Int)`, which will be the result of applying the operation to the numbers x and y:

```
return operation(x, y):
```

This line executes the lambda function operation by passing it the x and y arguments. The value resulting from the operation will be returned by the `applyOperation` function. Here's what that would look like:

```
val addition: (a: Int, b: Int) -> Int = { a, b -> a + b }
val result = applyOperation(5, 7, addition)
```

Returning functions from functions

The following is example code to see how to return functions from other functions:

```
fun createMultiplier(factor: Int): (Int) -> Int {
    return { n -> n * factor }
}
val double = createMultiplier(2)
println(double(5))
```

Now, let's understand the code:

```
fun createMultiplier(factor: Int): (Int) -> Int:
```

Here, a function called `createMultiplier` is declared, which takes a parameter of type `Int` called `factor`. The return type of this function is another function that takes an integer as a parameter (`(Int)`) and returns an integer (`-> Int`):

```
return { n -> n * factor }:
```

The function returns a lambda (anonymous function). This lambda takes a parameter, `n`, of type `Int` and returns the product of `n` multiplied by the value of the factor that was passed to `createMultiplier`. In short, this lambda creates a multiplier. For example, if the factor is 2, the returned lambda will multiply any number, `n`, by 2.

`createMultiplier` is a function that returns a function (lambda). This lambda takes a number and multiplies it by the factor value that was passed to `createMultiplier`.

An example is if we call `createMultiplier(2)`, which generates a function that multiplies any number by 2. That function is stored in a double. Finally, when we call `double(5)`, the lambda multiplies 5 by 2, resulting in 10.

Storing functions in data structures

Now, let's look at the last point mentioned, which refers to first-class citizens, which are stored in data structures. The following is example code:

```
val operations = listOf<(Int, Int) -> Int>(
    { a, b -> a + b },
    { a, b -> a - b },
    { a, b -> a * b }
)

println(operations[0](10, 5))
println(operations[1](10, 5))
println(operations[2](10, 5))
```

Let's try to understand this code:

```
listOf<(Int, Int) -> Int>:
```

This indicates that the operations are a list containing lambda functions. Each lambda in the list takes two parameters of type `Int` and returns an `Int` type. Basically, each element of the list is a mathematical operation between two integers.

```
{ a, b -> a + b }:
```

This is the first lambda in the list, which takes two integers, `a` and `b`, and returns their sum (`a + b`).

```
{ a, b -> a - b }:
```

This is the second lambda in the list, which takes two integers, a and b, and returns their difference (a - b).

```
{ a, b -> a * b }:
```

This is the third lambda in the list, which takes two integers, a and b, and returns their product (a * b).

In the three print instructions, we are calling elements 0, 1, and 2 of the list.

In short, being able to treat functions as first-class citizens in Kotlin allows us to do the following:

- Write more flexible and reusable code.
- Implement functional design patterns more naturally.
- Create more expressive and powerful APIs.
- Facilitate function composition.

Immutability

Immutability is probably the easiest principle to explain. As the name suggests, the idea is that data should not change after it is created. We know that data can change during the execution of programs, but the idea here changes a bit since instead of modifying existing data, new data is then created. This seems very simple and even unnecessary, but if applied well, it can reduce many errors since the possibility of the state being modified in an unexpected or incorrect way in other parts of the software is reduced.

The use of immutable variables and data structures is promoted when working with functional programming languages.

As we already know, in Kotlin, we have two possibilities when declaring variables: one is to declare immutable variables and another is to declare mutable variables. So, we know that if we need to use immutable variables, we will rely on the definition using the val reserved word, which is what defines them as immutable variables. This code should be familiar to us since we have used a definition with val many times throughout the book:

```
val x = "Jose"
```

Another detail in Kotlin is that we also have data structures that are immutable by default. These are List, Set, and Map. As we know, this means that we cannot add or remove elements once they have been created. This is an example of the implementation of an immutable list:

```
val list = listOf(1,2,3,4,5)
```

```
//List.add(100) This uncommented Line of code would be an error since the
List is immutable
```

If we need to add or remove an element, but we must respect immutability, we need to create a new list.

It should be noted that in Kotlin, we also have the possibility of using this type of data collection in a mutable way. We do this with `MutableList`, `MutableSet`, and `MutableMap`. This is only when mutability is really necessary, but the recommendation, as we have already mentioned, is to use the immutable versions whenever possible. Remember, however, that if it is functional programming, we must use immutability. We only mentioned these data structures to help you learn more about the options that Kotlin offers us.

Now, thinking about immutable classes and data, we can create immutable objects in Kotlin by using data classes and defining their properties as `val`. This makes the properties read-only, meaning they cannot be reassigned after the object has been created. However, it is important to note that true immutability is guaranteed only if the property type itself is immutable (for example, primitive types, `String`, or other immutable classes). If the property refers to a mutable object, the reference cannot change, but the internal state of that object can still be modified.

Here is some example code:

```
data class  User(val name:String, val email: String)
val user = User ("Viena", "viena@example.com" )
//user.name = "Madison"  This Line would cause a compilation error because
properties defined with val are read-only.
```

To finish our explanation of immutability, we are going to provide an example of what we mean when we say that instead of modifying a variable, we must create a new one, that is, relying on operations that return new instances instead of modifying existing ones. We will use an example of a list with several numbers. Assuming that we want to add a new element, this is the code:

```
val list = listOf(1,2,3,4,5)
val myList = list + 10 // we have a new List[1,2,3,4,5,10]
```

Purity

Purity in programming – it sounds a bit strange, but to explain it better, we will use the concept of pure functions. When we talk about purity or pure functions, we are saying that these functions must have these important elements:

- It should be deterministic. This means a function must always return the same result for the same arguments, no matter how many times we execute it.
- No external state should be modified. In other words, we should not change global variables, databases, or any other external data source. It is also important to note that if a pure function calls a non-pure function, then the calling function itself is no longer pure.
- No external state should be modified. In other words, we should not change global variables, databases, or any other external data source. It is also important to note that if a pure function calls a non-pure function, then the calling function itself is no longer pure. In simple words, a pure function should only have one effect: returning a value.
- Here, it is useful to distinguish between external state modification and side effects. External state modification is one kind of side effect, referring specifically to changing something outside the function, such as a global variable or a database record. Side effects, however, cover a broader range of behaviors, such as printing to the console, throwing exceptions, or reading the current time. This distinction helps clarify why purity is stricter than just avoiding changes to the external state.

Now, we are going to see the concepts in code to understand them better. A pure function is as follows:

```
fun add(a:Int, b:Int): Int {
return a + b
}
```

In the preceding code, we can see that we have defined a pure function. It is easy to see this because the `add` function always returns the same result for the two elements that are received. If we set `a=10` and `b=1`, it always returns `11`, regardless of what is happening; it will always be `11`.

Another element that we already explained and that doesn't have side effects is easy to notice, as we see the function does not change the global state of anything.

Finally, we do not perform any external operation; we only take the two arguments that we have, which are `a` and `b`, and return the result of the operation without modifying anything else.

With this, we can then confirm that the `add` function that we have defined can be considered a completely pure function.

To make clear the subject of what a side effect is, we are going to demonstrate with code. A side effect occurs when a function interacts with what we can consider external context or the outside world. In simple terms, this can be the modification of the external state, such as updating a global variable, changing a database record, writing to a file, or mutating an object that exists outside the scope of the function. Remember that in a pure function, this should not happen. All we expect in a pure function is that everything happens within the function and depends only on its parameters. Of course, it can also return a value, which is considered the output of the function, but all within its scope and context. This is the code of a function with side effects; we can also say that it is a non-pure function:

```
var result = 0
fun add(a:Int){
result += 1
}
```

Now, we can see that the `add` function is modifying the `result` variable. If this `result` variable is outside the function, then the behavior of the `add` function is dependent on an external factor. This results in the function not being considered pure.

Understanding what makes a function pure and identifying pure functions in code, as we have discussed previously, is relatively straightforward. A pure function is one that, given the same input, will always produce the same output without causing or depending on any side effects (such as modifying a global state). This predictability is one of its greatest benefits. With pure functions, you can always be certain of their behavior, which eliminates the need to track changes in external states or worry about unexpected side effects.

Another advantage is the ease with which tests can be done since we do not need to prepare anything special. As you'll remember, we focus only on the function and do not depend on external states. Finally, another advantage is that models modularize the code in a simple way; we have isolated code that is completely functional just by passing parameters and waiting for some output, so we can modularize most of the code without problems.

Higher-order functions

In Kotlin, functions are treated as first-class citizens. This means they can be assigned to variables, passed as arguments, returned as values, or even stored in data structures. Building on this property, higher-order functions are simply functions that either take other functions as parameters or return them as results. This close relationship makes it easier to understand higher-order functions as a natural consequence of treating functions as first-class citizens.

In simpler terms, functions as first-class citizens is the general principle that allows functions to be stored in variables, returned as results, or passed around like any other value. Higher-order functions are a specific use of this principle: they are functions that either take other functions as parameters or return them as results. In other words, higher-order functions are possible because functions are first-class citizens.

While this may remind us of the idea that functions are first-class citizens, it's important to clarify that we're not just referring to passing functions around; we're also highlighting how they can be returned, stored, and manipulated like any other value in Kotlin.

The concepts of functions as first-class citizens and higher-order functions are very closely related. However, there are differences that we must be aware of.

In the case of functions as first-class citizens, remember that the following apply:

- They are assigned to variables.
- They are passed as arguments to other functions.
- They are returned from functions.
- They are stored in data structures.

In short, this implies that functions will be treated as values or first-class objects.

In the case of higher-order functions, they are a specific type of function that accepts one or more functions as parameters and can also return a function as a result.

A key feature of Kotlin is that it treats functions as first-class citizens. This means higher-order functions are functions that can accept one or more functions as parameters, return them as results, and even be stored in variables or passed around like any other value. However, this does not imply that every higher-order function is necessarily a pure function.

Higher-order functions build on the idea that functions in Kotlin are first-class citizens. In practice, this means we can pass functions as arguments, return them as results, or assign them to variables. The benefit for a Java developer is that, instead of relying on static methods or utility classes, higher-order functions allow us to express behavior more directly and concisely. For example, operations on collections such as `map`, `filter`, or `reduce` let us declare what we want to achieve without having to write repetitive boilerplate code. This leads to cleaner, more reusable, and expressive programs.

In simpler terms, we can summarize it as follows – not all first-class citizen functions are of a higher order, but all higher-order functions are treated as first-class functions, since they manipulate functions as values.

This is an example of a higher-order function:

```
fun operate(a: Int, b:Int, operation: (Int, Int) -> Int): Int{
    return operation(a,b)
}
val sum = operate(10,1) { x, y -> x + y }
val product = operate(10,1){ x, y -> x *y }
```

As we can see, the `operate` function is a higher-order function because it receives another function as a parameter, named `operation`. This means that `operate` can take any function that matches the required signature as an argument, making it a flexible and reusable tool for various operations.

In summary, higher-order functions are a powerful tool within functional programming that allow us to write very expressive code. In fact, Kotlin can very efficiently handle collections thanks to higher-order functions. Some of the most common operations are reduce, map, and filter.

Higher-order functions are commonly used in Kotlin to do the following:

- **Control data flow**: Pass different functions to a higher-order function to define specific behaviors at runtime.
- **Process collections**: `reduce`, `filter`, and `map` allow manipulating collections in a declarative way.
- **Dynamic functions**: By returning functions from other functions, we can generate custom behavior at runtime depending on the parameters.

Many of these operations are implemented as **extension functions** on collections. It is important to note that not all extension functions are higher-order functions; an extension function only qualifies as higher order if it accepts or returns another function. For example, `fun String.isEmail(): Boolean` is a simple extension function, while `fun <T> Iterable<T>.filter(predicate: (T) -> Boolean)` is both an extension function and a higher-order function.

Another useful clarification is that in Kotlin, we generally talk about **functions**, even when they are declared inside a class. However, when compiled to bytecode, they become **methods** from the perspective of Java.

All this is possible thanks to the ability to abstract behavior, compose functions, and build modular code capabilities that make higher-order functions such a central feature in Kotlin.

Inline functions

If we are talking about functional programming in Kotlin and higher-order functions, it is inevitable that we will talk about inline functions in Kotlin. The "inline" concept means that the body of the function is placed directly in the place where it is called; that is, a new function instance is not created at each invocation. Explaining it in another way, we could say that an inline function is one whose body is going to be copied right to the space where it is called at compile time. For that, we will have to use the word `inline` in the function declaration.

So, instead of calling the function, the compiler removes that call and inserts the code of the function itself at that point.

This is an example of code for an inline function:

```
inline fun operate(a: Int, b:Int, operation: (Int, Int) -> Int): Int{
    return operation(a,b)
}
val sum = operate(10,1) { x, y -> x + y }
val product = operate(10,1){ x, y -> x *y }
```

Let's walk through the code. In the first line, we can see how this function is now inline. This is because we have placed the `inline` reserved word at the beginning of the function, before the word `fun`.

This means that instead of making a call to the `operate` function during execution, the compiler will replace each call to operate with the body of the function and the provided lambda.

We have already seen the same function previously without `inline`, so now we will describe the difference between with and without `inline`:

- Without `inline`, the compiler will have to generate an object for the lambda – `{ x,y -> x + y }` – and pass it to the `operate` function.
- With `inline`, the compiler will insert the body of the function and the lambda directly into the part of the code where the function is called, thus eliminating the need to create the lambda object or make a call to the function.

When we use `inline`, we can find these improvements:

- We improve performance. Since inline functions indicate a copy and paste of the body, we are eliminating the creation of function objects and calls to the function. Therefore, there are blocks or functions to be executed.

- It reduces the overhead of lambdas. In Kotlin, when we use lambdas, an object is created that is passed directly to the function. So, if we use `inline`, this object is no longer created since we are using `inline` to place it in the place of the call.

There aren't just advantages to using `inline`; everything comes at a price. So, we need to know when it is convenient or not to use `inline`.

Using inline functions is sure to increase the size of the bytecode. Although the size will vary, remember that if the function is called many times, the body will then be copied and pasted in all those places where the function is called. If the code for that function is large, then the bytecode will also be large.

You should not always use `inline`. A misconception is that it is a great option and so it should always be used. The reality is that the performance benefit is what should dictate whether or not we use `inline`. We have to consider the number of calls and the size of the code that will be added. This is the only thing that will tell us if it is really an improvement for our code.

To help, we can pose the explanation as a question: when do we use inline functions?

- If we have small functions, it is a good option, since they do not have much code.
- If we frequently call functions, then the benefit can also be positive.
- If we have lambda functions, it could also be a good idea to use `inline`, since they are usually small, and performance is important in them.

The noinline function

Continuing with Kotlin and the context of functional programming, when we declare a function as inline, we already know that the function's body and its associated lambda parameters are inlined at the call site; in other words, their code is copied directly into the calling function. However, this behavior might not always be suitable for every parameter or every scenario we face. In some cases, we may not want certain parameters to be inlined. For such situations, Kotlin provides specific mechanisms to exclude parameters from being inlined.

We can say that `noinline` is a modifier used in inline function parameters to indicate that a specific function parameter should not be made inline.

Let's go back to the previous example where we created an inline function. Now we will use `noinline` as well. This is the code:

```
inline fun operate(a: Int, b:Int, noinline operation: (Int, Int) -> Int):
Int{
```

```
    return operation(a,b)
}
```

We can see in the code that the main function, which is `operate`, is still inline as before, but there is a change. This change is in `operation`. In `operation`, we place the `noinline` instruction before the parameter that we want to ensure is not inline. What this will mean for Kotlin is that the function itself will be inlined, but the lambda operation will not be inlined. In other words, it is treated as it is normally treated.

Among the important considerations when we want to use `inline` are the following:

- We can only use `noinline` in function parameters that are already clearly marked as inline.
- `noinline` will help us reduce the size of the bytecode if a lambda is used many times within a large inline function.

The use of `inline` and `noinline` is key to having precise control over what we are doing. Combining them allows us to optimize the code in terms of performance improvement in a great way. The important thing is to keep learning and using them to notice and analyze the differences in their use in different situations. This will never be easy, and even less so when we first begin to use them. Only with practice can we learn and understand in which cases it is better or not to apply them.

Translation to Java bytecode

In this last section of the chapter, we are going to see something that will always be useful to us; in fact, it is something that we can always take advantage of if we are curious and want to see what is the same or different between Java and Kotlin. This topic is bytecode.

Bytecode is a code format that is generated after compiling a program written in a high-level language. In this case, both Kotlin and Java are languages that are considered high-level.

Another characteristic of bytecode is that it is code that is designed to be executed by a virtual machine, and we know that both Java and Kotlin use virtual machines. This is what allows bytecode to be executed on any system that has a virtual machine that can read this code, that is, that can interpret it.

We could also describe bytecode as the midpoint between the code we are writing and machine language code, which is the code that computers execute.

Java, especially in its early days, owes its growth and popularity to the use of bytecode, since it was a way of allowing software created with Java to be portable. By this, we mean that software created with Java could be executed on different operating systems thanks to the use of bytecode and a virtual machine compatible with the operating system found on the computer or device.

In this last part, we are going to analyze several code examples in the Kotlin language and examine the generated bytecode. This analysis will help you understand not only the concepts discussed in this chapter but also those introduced in previous chapters. By examining the bytecode, we can confirm details that are not immediately visible in the source code, such as default methods generated by the compiler or how properties with specific modifiers are defined. This process allows us to use the bytecode as a tool to verify and deepen our understanding of Kotlin's behavior at a lower level. This section will be particularly interesting for those who enjoy delving into the inner workings of the code and reviewing its finer details.

Let's start with a classic `hello world` in Kotlin and analyze its bytecode. This is the code:

```
fun main(){
    println("Hello world")
}
```

We have created a `Main.kt` file in which we have placed the previous code. As we can see, it is the main function to be executed, and inside, we have the `print` instruction, which prints `Hello world`. This code should be quite easy to read and understand at this point in the book.

Now we are going to see the bytecode. To see the bytecode inside the IntelliJ IDEA editor, we are just going to press the following keys:

- **Windows**: *Ctrl + Shift + A*
- **Mac**: *Command + Shift + a*

This will open a window on the right side by default, where you will see the bytecode of the code you have in the foreground.

These are the first lines of code of the hello world bytecode:

```
// ================MainKt.class =================
// class version 52.0 (52)
// access flags 0x31
public final class MainKt {
```

We are just going to focus on the important lines from which we can learn, observe, and confirm some things.

We will start by explaining these two lines:

```
// access flags 0x31
public final class MainKt {
```

Access flags describe the class modifiers, such as public, final, or static. Here, `0x31` indicates that the class is public and final.

This indicates that the compiler has generated a class named `MainKt`. In Kotlin, when we don't define an explicit class (for example, if we define only file-level functions), the compiler generates a class named after the Kotlin file (in this case, `Main.kt` becomes `MainKt`).

In fact, remember that we talked about this at the beginning of the book when we ran through our first Hello world example. In the case of Java, we always needed a class that encapsulates the code within a file. However, this has changed in Java 25 with the unnamed classes and instance main method feature finalized there. In the case of Kotlin, this was never necessary; it is done by the Kotlin compiler. That is why we can find files in Kotlin that do not explicitly contain a class, but in reality, in the bytecode, it does exist, even if we are not aware of it.

As we can see, bytecode allows us to see much more easily what we have described. By looking at the bytecode, we will be able to confirm many of the things that Kotlin omits or decides to do for us by default to take away some work for the programmer. That is why we have decided to study some examples in detail using bytecode.

Now let's look at the code of the `main` function:

```
// access flags 0x19
public final static main()V
   L0
    LINENUMBER 4 L0
    LDC "Hello world"
    ASTORE 0
   L1
    GETSTATIC java/lang/System.out : Ljava/io/PrintStream;
    ALOAD 0
    INVOKEVIRTUAL java/io/PrintStream.println (Ljava/lang/Object;)V
   L2
   L3
    LINENUMBER 5 L3
    RETURN
   L4
    MAXSTACK = 2
    MAXLOCALS = 1
// access flags 0x1009
```

```
  public static synthetic main([Ljava/lang/String;)V
    INVOKESTATIC MainKt.main ()V
    RETURN
    MAXSTACK = 0
    MAXLOCALS = 1
```

This is the main method that the compiler generates from the Kotlin code. Let's see how it works.

```
public final static main()V
```

`main()V` means that it is a method called `main` that has no parameters (`()`), and does not return any value (`V`, which represents void):

```
  LDC "Hello world"
  ASTORE 0
```

The `"Hello world"` string is loaded onto the operand stack (with `LDC "Hello world"`) and stored in the first local variable (`ASTORE 0`):

```
GETSTATIC java/lang/System.out : Ljava/io/PrintStream;
```

The method then calls `System.out.println` to print the message `"Hello world"`.

`GETSTATIC` gets the static value of `System.out`, which is an output stream to the console.

`ALOAD 0` loads the value we stored earlier, the `"Hello world"` string, from the local variable `0`:

```
INVOKEVIRTUAL java/io/PrintStream.println (Ljava/lang/Object;)V
```

`INVOKEVIRTUAL` calls the `println` method on the `System.out` object to print the string:

```
RETURN
MAXSTACK = 2
MAXLOCALS = 1
```

`RETURN` ends the method, indicating that it does not return any value.

`MAXSTACK = 2` indicates that the operand stack can have a maximum of two elements at a time.

`MAXLOCALS = 1` indicates that the method uses a single local variable (where it stores the `"Hello world"` string).

```
public static synthetic main([Ljava/lang/String;)V
    INVOKESTATIC MainKt.main ()V
    RETURN
```

```
MAXSTACK = 0
MAXLOCALS = 1
```

This is the main method that takes a `String[]` array. Although in Kotlin you can define a main function without arguments, the JVM needs a main method that accepts `String[]` arguments. That's why the compiler generates this "synthetic" main method. Notice that this might differ if you use modern Java versions such as 25 and higher.

The `([Ljava/lang/String;)` parameter in `main([Ljava/lang/String;)V` represents a `String[]` array in Java. The method does not return any value (`V` means void).

Note

The JVM specification is where all these details are specified. If you want to take a look at some of the elements we are discussing here, you can find them in the specification – `https://docs.oracle.com/javase/specs/jvms/se24/html/index.html`.

`INVOKESTATIC MainKt.main ()V` calls the `main()` method without the arguments that we defined previously, which means that it simply delegates the execution to the other main method.

`MAXSTACK = 0` means it does not use the operand stack.

`MAXLOCALS = 1` means it has a local variable, which is the `String[] args` array.

In simpler terms, we can summarize it as follows:

- `MainKt.class` is the class generated from a Kotlin file called `Main.kt`. In Kotlin, if you don't define an explicit class, the compiler generates a class with the `Kt` suffix.
- It contains two versions of the main method: one with no arguments and one with a `String[]` array, which is required by the JVM.
- The code calls `System.out.println("Hello world")`, which corresponds to the classic `hello world` program.

The purpose of this hello world example was to help you become familiar with the process of reading and interpreting bytecode. This foundational understanding will prepare you for the more complex examples and specific details covered later in this chapter, where we will analyze bytecode to verify how Kotlin handles features such as inline functions, default parameter values, and property modifiers.

This is the Book class that we used earlier in the book as a data class:

```
data class Book(
    val title: String,
    val author: String,
    val isbn: String,
)
```

We can see in the bytecode that a Book class is generated:

```
// access flags 0x31
public final class Book {
```

The Book class is public and final, meaning that it cannot be extended. This is something we already learned when we looked at data classes, but we can confirm it here. As we mentioned, the bytecode will give us many answers to things that we don't see directly at first but know that they happen. Here, we are confirming something that we have already learned.

The access flags part in access flags 0x31 indicates that the class is public and final.

Regarding the properties of the Book class, we see the following:

```
// Title field
// access flags 0x2
private Ljava/lang/String;
title @Lorg/jetbrains/annotations/NotNull;() // invisible
// Author field
// access flags 0x2
 private Ljava/lang/String; author
@Lorg/jetbrains/annotations/NotNull;()
// invisible
// isbn field
// access flags 0x2 private Ljava/lang/String; isbn
@Lorg/jetbrains/annotations/NotNull;() // invisible
```

These are the private fields that correspond to the title, author, and isbn properties of the Book class. Each field is of the String type and is marked as private, meaning it can only be accessed within the class itself.

There is also the `NotNull` annotation added to each of these fields. This is because we defined them as such. If we had used "`val title: String?`", for instance, this annotation would not appear here.

Being a data class, we will find the following in the bytecode that resolves the getter issue:

```
// Getter for title
public final getTitle()Ljava/lang/String;
L0
ALOAD 0
GETFIELD Book.title : Ljava/lang/String;
ARETURN
// Getter for author
public final getAuthor()Ljava/lang/String;
L0
ALOAD 0 GETFIELD Book.author : Ljava/lang/String;
ARETURN
// Getter for isbn public final getIsbn()Ljava/lang/String;
L0
ALOAD 0 GETFIELD Book.isbn : Ljava/lang/String;
ARETURN
```

Let's remember that by default, in the data class, Kotlin adds `Get` and `Set` methods, but we don't see them. In this case, we can see how `Get` appears in the bytecode for each property, so this is again a confirmation of what we have learned.

Each property has a public getter automatically generated by Kotlin. These methods return the value of the corresponding field (`title`, `author`, or `isbn`).

The `GETFIELD Book.title: Ljava/lang/String;` instruction accesses the private `title` field and returns it.

The `ARETURN` instruction returns the value loaded onto the JVM stack, which in this case is a string.

In this case, since in Kotlin the `title`, `author`, and `isbn` properties are defined with `val`, they are immutable; there are no setters. However, if they were `var` properties, the compiler would also generate setters.

Another of the default methods that is added is copy, which is automatically generated by Kotlin when a class is defined as a data class. The `copy()` method allows you to create a copy of the `Book` object with the possibility of modifying some of its values. This is the bytecode of this method:

```
public final copy(Ljava/lang/String;Ljava/lang/String;Ljava/lang/String;)
LBook;
   L0
    NEW Book
    DUP
    ALOAD 1
    ALOAD 2
    ALOAD 3
    INVOKESPECIAL Book.<init> (Ljava/lang/String;Ljava/lang/String;Ljava/
lang/String;)V
    ARETURN
```

In short, this bytecode represents a Kotlin `Book` data class with three properties (`title`, `author`, and `isbn`). The class includes the following:

- Getters for the properties
- A constructor to initialize the properties
- The `componentN` methods that allow destructuring
- The `copy()` method, which allows creating a copy of the object
- The automatically generated `toString`, `hashCode`, and `equals` methods

All of this code is generated by the Kotlin compiler from a simple data class definition in the Kotlin source code. This shows how the Kotlin-generated bytecode optimizes the creation of common classes and functions.

We have already reviewed two examples. Now we will proceed with the last one, which is directly related to the content of this chapter. Let's use an inline function. This is the code that we are going to analyze:

```
inline fun execute(action: () -> Unit) {
    try {
        action()
    } catch (e: Exception) {
        println("An exception occurred: ${e.message}")
    }
```

```
}

fun main() {
    execute {
        println("This code runs without problems")
    }
    execute {
        val res = 1 / 0
        println("This message will never be printed")
    }
    println("The program continues to run after the exception")
}
```

Before seeing the bytecode, let's explain the code in parts:

- `inline`: The inline modifier indicates that the body of the `execute` function will be embedded in the call, rather than invoking a normal function. This optimizes performance by avoiding the overhead of the function call and the creation of lambda objects.
- `action: () -> Unit`: This is the lambda type parameter, which takes no parameters and returns no value (`Unit` is the equivalent of `void` in Kotlin). That is, `action` is a function that is passed as an argument and will be executed within the body of `execute`.
- `try-catch`: Within `execute`, an attempt is made to execute the `action()` lambda within a `try` block. If an exception occurs during the execution of the lambda, the `catch` block catches the exception, and the corresponding error message is printed.
- `e: Exception`: Catches any exception that is a subclass of `Exception`. The `catch` block then prints a message indicating that an exception occurred, displaying the exception message using `${e.message}`.

Now let's see how this code would be executed step by step:

1. First call to `execute`:
    - `"This code runs without problems"` is printed.
    - No exception occurs.
2. Second call to `execute`:
    - An exception occurs when trying to divide by 0 (1 / 0).
    - `"An exception occurred: / by zero"` is printed.
    - The line `println("This message will never be printed")` is not executed.

3. Final message outside of `execute`:

    - `"The program continues to run after the exception"` is printed.

Using `inline` in this context helps optimize performance. Instead of making a call to the `execute` function and creating a lambda object for `action`, the compiler embeds the `execute` code directly where it is called. This eliminates the overhead of the function call and lambda creation.

The bytecode for this example is long, almost 300 lines, so we are going to concentrate only on the details that we want to confirm by reading the bytecode.

The inline modifier in Kotlin does not appear explicitly in the bytecode; that is, you will not see the word "inline" anywhere in the bytecode. However, the effect of using `inline` can be observed indirectly by analyzing how the bytecode is generated. When an inline function is used, the Kotlin compiler "expands" the code for that function at the place where it is called, rather than generating a function call. In a normal (non-inlined) function, we would see an explicit call to the function, like this:

```
INVOKESTATIC MainKt.execute (Lkotlin/jvm/functions/Function0;)V
```

This line indicates a call to the `execute` function. If the function were not inlined, each time `execute` was called, the bytecode would generate an instruction to invoke that function, as in this example.

However, when the function is inlined, that explicit call disappears from the bytecode, because the compiler directly inserts the function code where it is called.

In short, when a function is marked as inline, its body is inserted directly at the call site, and we won't see a typical function call in the generated bytecode. We'll confirm this shortly when we look at the bytecode output; if the call is missing, it means the inlining worked as expected.

Although something important is happening behind the scenes, it is *not displayed* in our code. So, is `inline` not working as expected?

This is the method that was declared as inline in the original Kotlin code. However, in the bytecode, we still see a separate method definition. This is because the Kotlin compiler generates this method for cases where inlining is not possible (for example, if the function is passed as a reference).

Another way to explain it would be to say that seeing the definition in the bytecode indicates that the compiler has generated a callable version of the method in scenarios where inlining is not possible, for example, when the function is passed by reference, invoked from Java code, or involves non-inlineable lambdas.

That is why it is important to rely on bytecode in times like these, since it shows what is really generated, and that will help us better understand Kotlin.

The following bytecode is generated from the previous code:

```
L3
NOP
L25
LINENUMBER 26 L25
L26
ICONST_0
ISTORE 1
L27
LINENUMBER 14 L27
ICONST_1
ICONST_0
IDIV
ISTORE 2
```

These blocks appear to be the content of the lambdas passed to `execute`, but they are directly inside the main method instead of being called into the `execute` method. This is exactly what inlining does; it inserts the body of the inline function directly into the place where it is called.

With this, we can then check that we can see the body of the inline function directly in the place we expect.

In short, although we don't see the word `inline` directly in the bytecode, the structure of the generated code, especially how the contents of `execute` seem to be expanded directly into `main`, is strong evidence that `execute` was declared as an inline function in the original Kotlin code.

As we can see, having access to the bytecode allows us to clarify some issues that are not always visible in the direct code and some concepts of functional programming that we can use to see what is happening specifically.

With these three examples, we have started to delve deeper into how we can read and understand bytecode. The main objective, however, was to demonstrate how examining bytecode can help us understand what is happening in detail, especially when using specific features such as inline functions. This allows us to see how the compiler handles these functions and what changes occur at the bytecode level.

Summary

In this chapter, you learned about **inline functions** in Kotlin and their role in improving the performance of functional programming. The chapter began by explaining the basics of functional programming in Kotlin, including key concepts such as higher-order functions, immutability, and functions as first-class citizens. These ideas will help you understand how Kotlin's functional paradigm differs from object-oriented programming.

The focus then shifted to **inline functions**, highlighting how Kotlin's inline modifier helps reduce the overhead of function calls and lambda creation by embedding the function body directly where it is invoked. You saw when to use inline functions, such as when passing lambdas frequently, and understood how inline functions optimize performance. However, the chapter also explored **non-inline functions**, explaining when certain lambdas should not be inlined and why it's important to manage the trade-offs between performance and bytecode size.

Finally, the chapter covered how Kotlin translates inline functions into Java bytecode. You learned how to analyze bytecode to understand the implications of using inline and non-inline functions, gaining insight into the performance and structure of their programs at the JVM level.

The information in this chapter is useful because it provides you with practical ways to write more efficient Kotlin code by leveraging inline functions, especially in functional programming scenarios. By understanding the impact on bytecode, developers can make informed decisions on when to use inline functions for optimization.

In the next chapter, you will explore lambda expressions, delving deeper into how they work in Kotlin and their role in functional programming.

9

Lambda

In this chapter, we will dive into one of Kotlin's most powerful and expressive features: lambda expressions. Lambdas bring a functional programming approach to Kotlin, simplifying complex operations and enabling concise code. We will keep exploring **higher-order functions**, which are key to understanding how Kotlin allows functions to be passed around just like data. These functions set the foundation for more advanced techniques.

Next, we will introduce the concept of receivers, which allow us to make the code more readable and declarative by defining operations that seem native to the objects they operate on. This enables a cleaner and more intuitive way to extend functions, further enhancing the flexibility of Kotlin code.

Finally, we will focus on collections, where lambdas truly shine. You'll see how operations such as filtering, mapping, and reducing can be done effortlessly with lambdas, making Kotlin both powerful and elegant when working with data structures.

By the end of this chapter, you will understand how to wield lambdas effectively, transforming your code into a more efficient, flexible, and streamlined version of itself.

In this chapter, we're going to cover the following main topics:

- Higher-order functions
- Receivers
- Collections

Technical requirements

You can use any text editor or **Integrated Development Environment** (**IDE**) of your choice with the Java language. We recommend the IntelliJ IDEA **Community Edition** (**CE**) IDE. This tool already comes with everything you need to work with both Java and Kotlin.

The list of software requirements for this chapter is as follows:

- Java JDK 17 or higher
- IntelliJ IDEA CE
- Kotlin 1.x or 2.x

The code used in this chapter can be found in the book's accompanying GitHub repository: `https://github.com/PacktPublishing/Kotlin-for-Java-Developers`.

Lambdas and higher-order functions

Although we have already discussed higher-order functions earlier in this book, in this section, we aim to explore additional related concepts in more detail. Specifically, we will focus on understanding how lambdas, receivers, and collections play a role in enhancing the flexibility and efficiency of higher-order functions in Kotlin.

Let's start with what we already know. We know that these are functions that can accept other functions as parameters or return them as results, allowing us to write more reusable and modular code.

In the world of programming, functions are essential because they allow us to abstract common behaviors and make them reusable across different parts of our code. This approach provides greater flexibility, as we can pass functions as arguments to other functions, enabling us to dynamically adjust their behavior. By doing so, we effectively customize the functionality at runtime, adapting it to specific scenarios or requirements.

We are going to address this topic again because in this section, we want to clear up some very specific doubts. The first is: Are lambda functions higher-order functions?

Are lambda functions higher-order functions?

To answer this question, we are going to rely heavily on code. Our example will be a dynamic menu, something that is usually common in the industry – for example, in application development.

So, here is the code to fully understand higher-order functions:

```
class MenuBuilder {
    private val items = mutableListOf<MenuItem>()
    fun item(name: String, action: () -> Unit) {
        items.add(MenuItem(name, action))
    }
    fun build(): List<MenuItem> {
        return items.toList()
    }
}
```

💡 **Quick tip**: Enhance your coding experience with the **AI Code Explainer** and **Quick Copy** features. Open this book in the next-gen Packt Reader.

(1) Click the **Copy** button to quickly copy code into your coding environment.

(2) Click the **Explain** button to get the AI assistant to explain a block of code to you.

🔒 **The next-gen Packt Reader** is included for free with the purchase of this book. Scan the QR code OR go to `https://packtpub.com/unlock`, then use the search bar to find this book by name. Double-check the edition shown to make sure you get the right one.

In this code, the `MenuBuilder` class is designed to help dynamically create a menu where each menu item has a name and an associated action (which is a function or lambda that is executed when the menu item is selected). `MenuBuilder` acts as a builder pattern to create a list of `MenuItem` objects.

Let's break the code down further, starting with this line:

```
private val items = mutableListOf<MenuItem>()
```

Here, we define items, and we can notice several things:

- `items` is a `mutableList` that stores the `MenuItem` objects added through calls to the `item` function.
- This list is `private`, meaning it's not accessible outside the `MenuBuilder` class, ensuring that only the class methods can modify it.
- The list is also initialized as an empty mutable list, which will store all the `MenuItem` objects added by the user.

Now let's go with the first function:

```
fun item(name: String, action: () -> Unit) {
    items.add(MenuItem(name, action))
}
```

The parameter `name` parameter is a string representing the name or label of the menu item (e.g., "Option 1, Section 1, etc."), while the `action` parameter is a lambda (or function) that is executed when the menu item is selected. The type of the action is `() -> Unit`, which means that it is a function that takes no parameters and does not return any value (remember that `Unit` is the equivalent of `void` in Java and Kotlin). In summary, the function creates a new `MenuItem` object using these parameters and adds it to the list of items.

Now let's look at the second function:

```
fun build(): List<MenuItem> {
    return items.toList()
}
```

The `build()` function is used to finalize the building process of the menu. It returns an immutable list (`List<MenuItem>`) that contains all the `MenuItem` objects added using the `item` function. Since it converts the `items` list into a read-only list using `toList()`, it ensures that the returned list cannot be modified from outside.

We then need to add a `data` class that holds a name and an action (a lambda function):

```
data class MenuItem(val name: String, val action: () -> Unit)
```

The focus on `buildMenu` is critical to understanding how the power of higher-order functions and lambdas is used:

```
fun buildMenu(init: (MenuBuilder) -> Unit): List<MenuItem> {
    val builder = MenuBuilder()
    init(builder)
    return builder.build()
}
```

The purpose of `buildMenu` is to dynamically create a menu using a `MenuBuilder` object that is initialized within the function. It allows the user to declaratively define menu items and their associated actions and returns an immutable list of `MenuItem` that represents the constructed menu.

The `init` parameter is a lambda (or anonymous function) that takes an object of type `MenuBuilder` as an argument. This means that the `init` lambda must receive a `MenuBuilder` object and execute some code with it (such as adding items to the menu). The code block passed to `init` can then use that `MenuBuilder` to invoke functions such as `item` and add items to the menu.

We need to understand this line:

```
init(builder)
```

This is where we call the `init` lambda, passing it the `builder` object. This means that any code that the user defines in the lambda block will now have access to the `builder` object, allowing them to add items to the menu using `builder.item(...)`.

Now we are going to run the next code, which will create a menu with three options:

- Option 1
- Option 2
- Exit

This is the code:

```
fun main() {
    val menu = buildMenu { builder ->
        builder.item("Option 1") { println("Option 1") }
        builder.item("Option 2") { println("Option 2") }
        builder.item("Exit") { println("Exit") }
    }
    menu.forEachIndexed { index, item ->
        println("${index + 1}. ${item.name}")
```

```
    }
    menu[0].action()
}
```

Let's break down this code to understand it further.

The `main` function is where we do the execution. We start with this:

```
val menu = buildMenu { builder ->
```

Here, we are calling the `buildMenu` function, which is a higher-order function designed to build a menu using a `MenuBuilder` object. This function takes a lambda argument, which receives `MenuBuilder` and uses it to define the menu items.

Inside the lambda, the `builder` object is the one used to add items to the menu.

Now we add items with this line:

```
builder.item("Option 1") { println("Option 1") }
```

Here, we are using the builder's `item` method (which is an instance of `MenuBuilder`) to add a menu item. The `item` method takes two parameters:

- `name`: The name of the item (in this case, `"Option 1"`).
- `action`: A lambda representing the action to be executed when this item is selected. In this case, the action is to print "`You selected option 1"` when the item is selected.

We do the same with `Option 2` and `Exit` too.

After all the items are added to `MenuBuilder`, the lambda completes its execution. At this point, the execution flow continues in the `buildMenu` function, which then calls `builder.build()`. This method converts the mutable list of items into an immutable list and returns it as the menu.

Let's now print the menu items in a numbered list. This can be achieved with the following:

```
menu.forEachIndexed { index, item ->
    println("${index + 1}. ${item.name}")
}
```

The code block iterates through the `MenuItem` list called `menu` using `forEachIndexed`. This function allows us to access both the index (the position of the item in the list) and the item itself. Then, during the iteration, inside the block, `println` is used to print each menu item's name to the console, preceded by its option number in the format "`1. Option 1"`, "`2. Option 2"`, "`3. Exit"`. This ensures that the menu items are displayed in an orderly and user-friendly manner.

Now for the last line of code:

```
menu[0].action()
```

Here, we are simulating that the user selects the first option in the menu (index 0 in the list). Since `menu[0]` is the first `MenuItem` ("`Option 1`"), this code executes the action associated with that item, which is to print "`You selected option 1`".

- `menu[0]` accesses the first item in the menu list.
- `.action()` calls the lambda that was associated with this item when the menu was constructed. This lambda prints the corresponding message.

This example clearly demonstrates how Kotlin leverages the power of lambdas and higher-order functions to create a flexible and dynamic menu-building system. Now, to better understand this approach, it's helpful to explore how lambdas and higher-order functions work together, and why they're so valuable in this context.

Here, we see the use of lambdas:

```
builder.item("Option 1") {
    println("You selected option 1")
}
```

In this code snippet, the lambda is the action that will be executed when the `"Option 1"` item is selected. The use of lambdas is crucial here because it allows you to easily and directly define the behavior of each menu item without the need to create separate functions for each action. This not only makes the code cleaner but also improves its readability and flexibility.

In this example, there are several instances where higher-order functions are used, but the most notable one is the `item` method within the `MenuBuilder` class:

```
fun item(name: String, action: () -> Unit) {
    items.add(MenuItem(name, action))
}
```

The `item` function qualifies as a higher-order function because it takes a lambda (`action: () -> Unit`) as a parameter. This lambda represents the behavior that will be executed when a menu item is selected. By combining both the name of the item and its associated action, this function enables the menu to be built declaratively.

The fact that `item` is a higher-order function allows the calling code to pass different functions (lambdas) for each menu item, providing great flexibility. Each item can have its own custom action without needing to overload the code with multiple methods.

In the exercise, we used many higher-order functions and lambdas, so we are going to separate concepts, see the differences and similarities, and see how they are related. This is the most important part of this topic. For this reason, we are explaining higher-order functions again, but with the aim of clearing up very specific doubts.

Here are the key features of lambda:

- A lambda is an anonymous function.
- It is an unnamed function that can be treated as a value.
- It is a concise way of writing functions that can be passed as arguments.
- It represents an executable block of code.

A lambda itself is not a higher-order function. Instead, lambdas are usually arguments passed into higher-order functions. The higher-order function is the one that accepts (or returns) a lambda.

The features of a **higher-order function** are as follows:

- It is a function that accepts other functions as parameters and/or returns functions
- It can manipulate other functions.
- It is a broader concept that describes the behavior of a function.
- It defines a feature of the function, not its syntax.

Relationship between lambdas and higher-order functions

Lambdas, which are anonymous functions (functions without a name), play a crucial role when used as arguments to higher-order functions. In Kotlin, they are especially useful for writing short and concise code, as they eliminate the need for a formal function declaration. This makes them ideal for scenarios where you need to pass small pieces of functionality directly into another function, enhancing readability and reducing boilerplate.

In Kotlin, lambdas are commonly used as arguments to higher-order functions, such as `map`, `filter`, and `reduce`, which accept functions as parameters and apply those functions to collections or values.

```
val names = listOf("Jose", "Noemi", "Viena", "Dimas")
val uppercasedNames = names.map { it.uppercase() }
println(uppercasedNames)
```

The `names` list is a list of lowercase names, `map` is a higher-order function that applies a transformation to each element in the list, and the `{ it.uppercase() }` lambda takes each name in `names` and converts it to uppercase. The result, stored in `uppercasedNames`, is a new list where each name is uppercase.

Simple lambda (not a higher-order function)

Before exploring more advanced uses of lambdas, let's start with a very simple example. A lambda can be thought of as a short block of code that can be assigned to a variable and executed later, similar to an anonymous function. This makes them useful when you want to define small pieces of behavior without creating a full function.

```
val suma = { x: Int, y: Int -> x + y }
```

In this case, `{ x: Int, y: Int -> x + y }` is a lambda that takes two parameters and returns their sum:

- **Lambda parameters**: `x: Int` and `y: Int`: These are the parameters of the lambda, both of type `Int`. When you call this lambda, you must pass two integer values for `x` and `y`.
- **Lambda body**: `x + y`: After the parameters and the `->` operator, we have the body of the lambda, which in this case is simply `x + y`. This is the value that the lambda returns.

The lambda takes `x` and `y`, performs the addition operation, and returns the result.

Higher-order functions

A higher-order function is a function that can receive another function (or a lambda) as a parameter, or return one as a result. This makes them extremely powerful for creating flexible and reusable code.

Here is a simple example:

```
fun operate(a: Int, b: Int, operation: (Int, Int) -> Int): Int {
    return operation(a, b)
}
```

This code defines a function called `operate` that takes three parameters and returns an integer value. The `operate` function is an example of a higher-order function because one of its parameters, `operation`, is a lambda (or function) that is passed as an argument.

This first line defines a function called `operate` that takes three parameters:

- `a: Int`: An integer (`Int`) representing the first operand.
- `b: Int`: Another integer representing the second operand.
- `operation: (Int, Int) -> Int`: This is a function or lambda type parameter that receives two integers and returns one integer. It specifies that the third parameter of `operate` is a function that takes two integers as input and returns one integer as a result.

Inside `operate`, the `operation` function is called by passing `a` and `b` as arguments. What this line does is apply the `operation` function to the values of `a` and `b` and return the result of this operation.

Using a lambda with a higher-order function

So far, we have seen lambdas on their own and also how a higher-order function can be defined. The next step is to see how they work together. By passing a lambda as an argument to a higher-order function, we can define custom behavior in a very concise way, without needing to declare a separate function.

Here's an example:

```
val result = operate(10, 1) { x, y -> x + y }
```

This code uses the `operate` function, which takes two numbers and a lambda as parameters, to calculate the result of adding 10 and 1.

First, let's call the `operate` function. The `operate` function is called with three arguments:

- `10`: the first number, which is the value of a.
- 1: the second number, which is the value of b.
- `{ x, y -> x + y }`: A lambda representing the operation to be performed between a and b. In this case, the lambda takes two parameters (x and y) and returns their sum (`x + y`).

The `{ x, y -> x + y }` lambda is an anonymous function that takes two parameters (**x** and y) and returns their sum. In this example, x corresponds to the first number (`10`) and y to the second number (`1`).

This is an example of how Kotlin allows the use of lambdas and higher-order functions to perform flexible operations.

With the examples we have seen and the code explanations, we can summarize as follows: lambdas are anonymous functions, and higher-order functions are functions that operate with other functions.

The goal of lambdas is to create concise functions, and for higher-order functions, it is the manipulation of functions.

A lambda can or cannot be a higher-order function. For it to be one, it needs to receive functions. A lambda is a way or form of writing a function, while a higher-order function is a feature of a function. Many lambdas are not higher-order functions, and it is not a problem. We can also say it in another way: that a lambda is the only way of writing (syntax) an anonymous function, while a higher-order function is a function that operates with other functions, regardless of how it is written.

With that, we now understand lambdas and higher-order functions. Now let's move on to see how this combination of higher-order functions, lambdas, and receivers allows for writing more expressive and simplified code, providing a powerful way to customize runtime behavior.

Receivers

The concept of a receiver, as it exists in Kotlin, does not have a direct equivalent in Java. In Kotlin, a receiver is an object that provides a specific context within a function or lambda, allowing us to interact with its properties and methods directly, without needing to explicitly reference it (e.g., using `this`).

It is important to note, however, that you can only interact with the properties and methods that are available at the correct access level. While the syntax may look as if the function is defined inside the class, a receiver (such as in extension functions) is essentially just syntax sugar and does not grant access to private members.

In Java, this concept is not directly available. While you can achieve similar behavior using methods or passing objects explicitly, Java lacks the syntactic sugar provided by Kotlin's receivers. For example, in Kotlin, we can define extension functions or use lambdas with receivers, where the receiver becomes the implicit context within the block of code. This allows for more concise and readable code, as we can interact with the receiver object seamlessly within the function or lambda.

A receiver in Kotlin establishes a context when we define it. By defining a receiver within a lambda or a function, the receiver can be accessed as if it were within the object. This helps us to avoid explicit references; therefore, we will have cleaner and less repetitive code, meaning we will be able to access the methods and properties as we normally do in objects, but without needing to use the name of the object or the word `this`.

Receivers in Kotlin are a versatile feature that can be used in multiple contexts, such as the following:

- Extension functions
- Lambdas with receivers
- Scope functions
- Property delegates
- DSL builders
- Extension properties
- Objects with receivers
- Inline functions
- Interfaces
- Type aliases

The concept of receivers allows us to define a specific context within a function or lambda, enabling direct access to the properties and methods of an object without explicitly referencing it. This principle remains consistent across various contexts in Kotlin, making it unnecessary to redefine the concept for every use case.

In this chapter, we will focus on two key contexts where receivers are particularly useful: lambdas and in extension functions. These examples will demonstrate how receivers enhance readability and flexibility in Kotlin code.

To explain the concept of a receiver further, it is an object on which methods can be called and properties accessed within the body of a function, as if the function were a method of that object. A receiver allows us to interact with the object directly, often without explicitly referencing its name. For example, we commonly use the keyword `this` to refer to the current object in a context, but a receiver allows us to achieve this seamlessly, often without even needing this.

As mentioned earlier, receivers can be implemented in different elements, but for the purposes of this chapter, we will focus on extension functions and lambdas to demonstrate their practical applications.

Extension function with a receiver

In *Chapter 4*, we already explained the extension function. Now we are going to recap the concept. This time, we will understand it further, while introducing its relationship with receivers.

To illustrate this, here is an extension function:

```
fun String.addAsterisk(): String {
    return "$this*"
}
```

Let's break down the elements of this code, taking advantage of the fact that there is little code to see the details in depth:

- `fun`: This is a keyword indicating that we are declaring a function. This is the start of any function in Kotlin.
- `String.`: This is the receiver type. The dot (`.`) indicates that we are creating an extension, meaning that this function will be available to any `String` object. In this case, `String` becomes `this` inside the function.
- `addAsterisk`:
    - This is the name of the function.
    - It follows Kotlin naming conventions (camelCase).
    - It describes the action that the function performs.
- `()`:
    - Empty parentheses indicate that the function takes no additional parameters.
    - They could include parameters if necessary: (`count: Int`).
- `String`:
    - This is the return type of the function.
    - It indicates that the function will return a `String`.
    - In Kotlin, it is explicit, although it could be inferred
- `{...}`:
    - This is the code block that defines the behavior of the function.
    - It contains the logic of the function.
- `return "$this*"`:
    - `return` indicates the value that the function will return.
    - `this` refers to `String` on which the function is called.
    - The `$` operator allows string interpolation.
    - The asterisk is concatenated at the end.

With the code, we are now going to execute the extension function that we made:

```
fun main(){
    print("Hello".addAsterisk())
}
```

Inside the `main` classic function, we are going to print the string `"Hello"`. To do this, we apply the function that we previously defined. This function simply adds an asterisk to the string. We then use print to display the result, showing the text string with the asterisk added.

The receiver is `String`, since this function is being defined as an extension of the `String` class. This means that the object on which `addAsterisk` is called is treated as the receiver within the function.

The receiver type in this case is `String`, which means this function can only be called on objects of type `String`. So, by defining the function as `fun String.addAsterisk()`, we ensure that it is an extension function specifically for strings.

Let's analyze this code:

```
fun main(){
    print("Hello".addAsterisk().addAsterisk().addAsterisk())
}
```

Each call to `addAsterisk` returns a new `String`. Since the function does not modify the original `String` (strings in Kotlin are immutable), a new value with the added asterisk is produced each time.

The value returned by `addAsterisk` is a string, which allows the function to be applied repeatedly to the result of each call. The ability to chain `.addAsterisk()` three times (or more) is because of the following:

- Each call returns a new string.
- This allows the function to be applied repeatedly on the result of each call, adding an additional asterisk each time.

So, to summarize, extension functions with a receiver in Kotlin allow you to extend existing types without modifying them, provide clear and concise syntax, and maintain the context of the original object using `this`.

Lambda with a receiver

Now we are going to explore how to use a lambda with a receiver. To do this, we will revisit the code from the beginning of the chapter, where we worked with higher-order functions and lambdas. This time, we will focus on adapting the previously defined lambda to include a receiver.

In the initial code, we have this:

```
class MenuBuilder {
    private val items = mutableListOf<MenuItem>()
    fun item(name: String, action: () -> Unit) {
        items.add(MenuItem(name, action))
    }
    fun build(): List<MenuItem> {
        return items.toList()
    }
}
```

We don't need to make any changes to this code since we are only defining `MenuBuilder`. This is the code we mentioned:

```
data class MenuItem(val name: String, val action: () -> Unit)
```

The `data` class also remains the same, since it is not where we are going to have an impact either on lambda or with the receiver.

There is the `buildMenu` function implemented using only a lambda:

```
fun buildMenu(init: (MenuBuilder) -> Unit): List<MenuItem> {
    val builder = MenuBuilder()
    init(builder)
    return builder.build()
}
```

Now comes the part where we have to make changes to go from lambda to using lambda and a receiver:

```
fun buildMenu(init: MenuBuilder.() -> Unit): List<MenuItem> {
    val builder = MenuBuilder()
    init(builder)
    return builder.build()
```

Modified `buildMenu` signature: We changed the type of the `init` lambda in `buildMenu` from `(MenuBuilder) -> Unit` to `MenuBuilder.() -> Unit`. Instead of passing `builder` as an argument, we call `init` directly on `builder`, allowing `MenuBuilder` to be the receiver within the lambda:

```
// Before
fun buildMenu(init: (MenuBuilder) -> Unit): List<MenuItem>
// After
fun buildMenu(init: MenuBuilder.() -> Unit): List<MenuItem>
```

As you can see, instead of passing `builder` as an argument to `init`, we now call `init` directly on `builder`:

```
// Before
init(builder)
// After
builder.init()
```

Inside `main`, we can now add menu items directly, without having to refer to `builder` explicitly:

```
val menu = buildMenu {
    item("Option 1") { println("Option 1") }
    item("Option 2") { println("Option 2") }
    item("Exit") { println("Exit") }
}
```

Since `MenuBuilder` is the receiver of the lambda, we can call `item` directly instead of `builder.item`. By removing the need to explicitly refer to `builder`, the code inside `buildMenu` is more readable and more concise.

We could use it, for example, for **Domain-Specific Languages (DSLs)**. This structure is more friendly for the creation of DSLs, which is one of the main applications of receiver lambdas in Kotlin. This change makes the use of `buildMenu` more idiomatic in Kotlin and takes advantage of the capabilities of receiver lambdas to make the code more expressive and easier to read.

This code exemplifies three fundamental best practices in modern software design:

- First, immutability is implemented intelligently. Although a mutable list is used internally to build the menu efficiently (`MutableList`), the external exposure is immutable, ensuring that once the menu is built, its state cannot be modified by external code.
- Second, encapsulation is achieved by hiding implementation details through a private list and exposing only the necessary methods to interact with the menu, maintaining a clear and well-defined public API.

- Third, extensibility is achieved through a flexible structure that allows new functionalities to be easily added without modifying existing code, following the open/closed principle – the code is open for extension but closed for modification. For example, new menu item types or additional behaviors could be added without needing to change the base `builder` structure.

This implementation of the `buildMenu` function demonstrates the power of modern Kotlin design through several key aspects:

- The effective use of lambda receivers enables a natural and intuitive syntax, while the clean DSL implementation provides a declarative way to build menus that is both readable and maintainable.
- The well-structured builder pattern demonstrates a thoughtful approach to object construction, allowing for step-by-step menu creation with a fluent interface.
- Clear separation of responsibilities is achieved by distinct components handling their specific tasks – `MenuBuilder` manages construction, `MenuItem` holds the data, and the `buildMenu` function orchestrates the process.
- It leverages Kotlin best practices such as smart use of receivers, immutable data structures, and extension functions, resulting in a robust and flexible solution that can be easily extended or modified as needs evolve. To summarize, in this section, we explored receivers in Kotlin, a feature that allows for direct interaction with an object's properties and methods without explicit references. Unlike Java, which lacks this concept, Kotlin's receiver enables a context where you can work directly within an object's scope in functions or lambdas, avoiding repetitive code and improving readability.

Receivers in Kotlin enhance versatility and can be used in various contexts, including **extension functions** and **lambdas with receivers** – the two main areas of focus in this chapter. Extension functions use a receiver to add functionality to existing types without modifying them, maintaining context with this. For instance, a function to add an asterisk to a string demonstrates how extension functions treat the object (in this case, `String`) as the receiver.

This section also covered **lambdas with receivers**, which combine higher-order functions and receivers, allowing access to an object's properties and methods directly within the lambda. By transforming a function's lambda parameter to use a receiver, we enable a cleaner, more declarative syntax, which is especially useful for creating DSLs. This approach not only enhances readability and conciseness but also aligns with Kotlin's idiomatic style, making code expressive and easier to understand.

To summarize, in this section, we explored receivers in Kotlin, a feature that allows for direct interaction with an object's properties and methods without explicit references. Unlike Java, which lacks this concept, Kotlin's receiver enables a context where you can work directly within an object's scope in functions or lambdas, avoiding repetitive code and improving readability.

In the next section, we'll focus on the idea of collections in the context of lambdas. We'll explore how lambdas can be used to manipulate collections, making operations such as filtering, mapping, and reducing more concise and expressive. This will lay the foundation for understanding how Kotlin leverages functional programming to simplify data processing. By focusing on practical examples, we'll demonstrate the power and flexibility of lambdas when working with collections, preparing us for a deeper dive into collections and sequences in the next chapter.

Collections

Finally, we are going to see some code examples where we will begin to deal with a very popular concept: collections. It is important to clarify that, in the next chapter, we are going to work with collections and sequences, but in this part, where we will take a look at collections in the context of lambda, we want to explain with some code examples some details that will allow us to reinforce the lambda concept and continue to understand other concepts in this chapter of the book.

Kotlin leverages functional programming through its collections, and these operations are driven by the use of lambdas. Learning to use lambdas in the context of collections allows developers to get used to writing more functional code, which is a key concept in Kotlin.

Including collections in a chapter about lambdas makes a lot of sense because, in Kotlin, collections and lambdas are closely linked in the context of functional programming.

Collections in Java versus Kotlin

One of the fundamental differences between Java and Kotlin when it comes to handling collections lies in how they approach mutability.

In Java, all collections are inherently mutable, meaning that any code that has a reference to a collection can modify its contents. For example, when you pass `List` to a method in Java, that method always has the ability to modify the list, adding or removing elements, which can lead to unintended side effects and make code less predictable.

Kotlin, on the other hand, introduces a clear and explicit distinction between mutable and immutable collections. This separation is directly reflected in the type system, where `List` represents an immutable (read-only) collection and `MutableList` represents a collection that can be modified.

This distinction is not just conceptual but is supported by the compiler: attempting to modify an immutable collection will result in a compilation error, not a runtime error. This feature of Kotlin promotes a safer and more predictable design, as it makes the developer's intent explicit on whether a collection should be modifiable or not.

The difference becomes even more apparent in everyday practice. When working in Kotlin, you must make a conscious decision about the mutability of your collections. By default, factory functions such as `listOf()` create immutable collections, while `mutableListOf()` is used when you specifically need a collection that can be modified. This clarity in code intent not only improves security but also makes code easier to understand and maintain, as immutability by default reduces the chance of bugs related to unintentional modifications of collections.

This explicit distinction of mutability in Kotlin reflects a more modern design philosophy that favors immutability by default, which is especially valuable in concurrent programming and long-term code maintenance. While in Java you would need to use additional constructs such as `Collections.unmodifiableList()` to achieve immutability, in Kotlin, this feature is built into the language naturally and efficiently. These are the options (immutables and mutables) we have available:

```
// Inmutables
interface Collection<out E>
interface List<out E>
interface Set<out E>
interface Map<K, out V>

// Mutables
interface MutableCollection<E>
interface MutableList<E>
interface MutableSet<E>
interface MutableMap<K, V>
```

Immutable interfaces in Kotlin allow only read operations on the collection data. It is not possible to add, remove, or modify elements directly. Let's look at these interfaces:

- `Collection<out E>`: Represents a generic collection of elements, where `E` is the type of the elements. out indicates that `E` is covariant, meaning it can be used as a return type but not as a parameter type. This ensures that the collection can only be safely used for read operations.

- `List<out E>`: An ordered list of elements, similar to List in Java, that allows index access. It only allows elements to be read and the order of the elements to be maintained, but does not allow them to be altered.
- `Set<out E>`: A collection of single elements in no particular order. Like `List`, it does not allow elements to be modified or new elements to be added.
- `Map<K, out V>`: A collection of key-value pairs, where `K` is the type of the key and the `V` is the type of the value. `Map` only allows access to the pairs without altering them. Since it is immutable, key-value pairs cannot be added or removed once it is created.

Mutable interfaces extend immutable ones and allow for read and write operations. This means that we can add, remove, or modify elements in the collection. Let's look at these interfaces:

- `MutableCollection<E>`: Allows you to add and remove elements in a generic collection. It does not have the out modifier, so `E` is invariant, allowing both the reading and modification of elements.
- `MutableList<E>`: It is a list that allows modification operations. In addition to reading elements by their index, it allows you to add, remove, and update elements in specific positions.
- `MutableSet<E>`: It is a set that allows you to add and remove elements, while maintaining the restriction of not allowing duplicate elements. It allows you to modify the collection after its creation.
- `MutableMap<K, V>`: It is a collection of key-value pairs where entries can be added, modified, or deleted. This allows you to update the value associated with a specific key, add new keys and values, or delete existing pairs.

Now let's take a look at an example of mutability and immutability in collections:

```
// Example of using an mimmutable list
val immutableList: List<String> = listOf("Viena", "Noemi", "Jose")
// immutableList.add("Fabiola")  // Error: unable to add item

// Example of using a mutable list
val mutableList: MutableList<String> = mutableListOf("Viena", "Noemi",
"Jose")
mutableList.add("Fabiola")  // it works: You can add a new item
println(mutableList)  // Output: [Viena, Noemi, Jose, Fabiola]
```

These two types of lists offer different levels of control over data, and choosing between them depends on the specific needs of your application. Using immutable lists by default and switching to mutable lists only when necessary is a best practice to keep your code clean and robust.

Kotlin has a clear goal: promoting immutability. So, as a practice, it makes code safer by avoiding unwanted side effects and hard-to-track bugs. By separating interfaces, Kotlin makes it easier to distinguish when data is being manipulated in a mutable or an immutable way, helping to avoid accidental modifications to data.

Operations with collections

Kotlin's basic operations on collections represent the foundation of how we manipulate and access data stored in these structures. Unlike Java, Kotlin provides a more concise and expressive syntax for these operations, allowing for more readable and maintainable code. When we talk about basic operations, we are referring to those actions that we perform frequently, such as accessing elements, checking their existence, or determining the size of the collection.

Accessing elements in Kotlin can be done in multiple ways, each designed for different use cases. The most direct way is through the indexing operator `[]`, similar to Java, but Kotlin adds extension functions that make the code safer and more expressive. For example, `first()` and `last()` provide direct access to the first and last elements respectively, while `firstOrNull()` and `lastOrNull()` offer a safe way to handle empty collections by returning `null` instead of throwing an exception.

Note

Since Java 21, sequenced collections offer some of the functionality mentioned here, such as `first()` and `last()`. It also introduced adding and removing sequences.

Kotlin offers a set of elegant and expressive operations for working with collections. Functions such as `contains()` make it simple to check whether an element exists in a collection, while `isEmpty()` and `isNotEmpty()` provide intuitive ways to verify whether a collection has elements. These functions are cleaner and more direct compared to the approaches often used in Java, such as checking whether the size of a collection is zero or calling the `contains()` method from the collection interface. Moreover, functions such as `containsAll()` allow you to check for the presence of multiple elements in a single operation, streamlining these common tasks. Handling the size and capacity of collections is done through the `size` property, which is more concise than Java's `size()` method. This property is immutable in read-only collections, which helps keep the collection state consistent. For mutable collections, the size is automatically updated with modification operations, always maintaining a consistent state.

Let's look at a practical example that illustrates these basic operations:

```
val numbers = listOf(1, 2, 3, 4, 5)
// Element access
val firstNumber = numbers.first()       // 1
val lastNumber = numbers.last()         // 5
val thirdNumber = numbers[2]            // 3
val safeFirst = numbers.firstOrNull()   // 1 (null if list is empty)
```

We are creating an immutable list called `numbers` with values 1, 2, 3, 4, and 5. Being an immutable list, we cannot add or remove elements after its creation.

The `first()` function returns the first element of the list. In this case, `firstNumber` will be equal to 1. The `last()` function returns the last element of the list. In this case, `lastNumber` will be 5, the last element of the numbers.

We can access a specific element in the list by using its index in square brackets. In this case, `thirdNumber` will be 3, since index 2 corresponds to the third element in the list (indexes in Kotlin start at 0). The `firstOrNull()` function returns the first element of the list or `null` if the list is empty. This method is useful when you are not sure whether the list has any elements and you want to avoid an exception. Here, `safeFirst` will be 1, the first element of numbers, but if the list were empty, `safeFirst` would be `null`.

In short:

- `first()`: Returns the first element of the list
- `last()`: Returns the last element of the list
- `[index]`: Accesses an element at the specified position
- `firstOrNull()`: Returns the first element or `null` if the list is empty

These functions allow you to easily and safely access elements of a list in Kotlin.

Now let's look at some verification operations:

```
// Verification
val contains = list.contains(3) // true
val isEmpty = list.isEmpty() // false
```

The `contains()` function checks whether a specific element is present in the list. In this case, `list.contains(3)` returns `true` if the value 3 is in the list, and `false` if it is not.

The `isEmpty()` function checks whether the list contains no elements. It returns `true` if the list is empty and `false` if it has at least one element.

These verification functions are useful for validating the contents and status of a list before performing further operations.

Let's move on to some more example code. In the following code, we will demonstrate the use of three common functional operations in Kotlin applied to lists: `map`, `filter`, and `flatMap`. These functions allows you to transform, filter, and flatten lists in a declarative and concise way:

```
val numbers = listOf(10, 20, 30, 40, 50)
// Map - transforms each element by multiplying it by 2
val doubled = numbers.map { it * 2 } // [20, 40, 60, 80, 100]
// Filter - filters elements larger than 25
val filteredNumbers = numbers.filter { it > 25 } // [30, 40, 50]
// FlatMap - flattens and transforms, using a list of lists based on
`numbers`
val nested = numbers.map { listOf(it, it + 5) } // [[10, 15], [20, 25],
[30, 35], [40, 45], [50, 55]]
val flattened = nested.flatMap { it } // [10, 15, 20, 25, 30, 35, 40, 45,
50, 55]
```

Let's look at the operations:

- `map`: Transforms each element individually. In this case, the `map` operator `{ it * 2 }` multiplies each element of the numbers by 2. This turns the list into `[20, 40, 60, 80, 100]`.
- `filter`: Selects elements based on a condition. In our example, instead of filtering out only even numbers (which in this case would include all numbers), we change the condition to select only numbers greater than 25. This results in `[30, 40, 50]`.
- `flatMap`: Transforms each element in a list and then flattens all the lists into one. Here, in `nested`, each number in `numbers` becomes a sublist containing the current number and that current number plus 5. For example, `10` becomes `[10, 15]`, `20` becomes `[20, 25]`, and so on. So, `nested` becomes `[[10, 15], [20, 25], [30, 35], [40, 45], [50, 55]]`. Then `flatMap { it }` flattens `nested` into a single list, `flattened`, containing `[10, 15, 20, 25, 30, 35, 40, 45, 50, 55]`.

These are important points to remember:

- `map`: Transforms each element individually.
- `filter`: Selects elements based on a condition.

- `flatMap`: Transforms each element in a list and then flattens all the lists into one.
- The key difference between `map` and `flatMap`:
  - `map`: Returns a list of the same size as the original.
  - `flatMap`: Can return a list of a different size as it flattens the lists into one resultant list.

The order of operations can affect both performance and the final result, so it is important to consider the most efficient sequence depending on the use case.

Collections and lambdas

As we initially mentioned, we want to talk about collections in the context of lambdas, so we are going to show several pieces of code where we will address the topic to explain the details that we consider important. Let's start with this code:

```
val immutableList: List<String> = listOf("Viena", "Noemi", "Jose")

// Lambda operations on immutable list
val namesWithA = immutableList.filter { it.contains('a') }
println("Names with 'a': $namesWithA")
```

Here, the `filter` function takes a lambda as a parameter and creates a new list with the elements that meet a specific condition. In this case, the `{ it.contains('a') }` lambda checks whether each name (represented by `it`) contains the letter `'a'`.

Then, the `namesWithA` variable will store the result of this operation, which will be a list with the names that include the letter `'a'`. In `immutableList`, the only name that contains the letter `'a'` is `"Viena"`, so `namesWithA` will have the value `["Viena"]`.

Finally, `println` prints the result to the console:

```
Names with 'a': [Viena]
```

Let's continue with this code:

```
val upperNames = immutableList.map { it.uppercase() }
println("Uppercase names: $upperNames")

val nameLengths = immutableList.map { "${it}: ${it.length} characters" }
println("Name length: $nameLengths")
```

As far as `upperNames` is concerned, the `map` function applies the `{ it.uppercase() }` lambda to each element in the list. It represents each name in the list (`"Viena", "Noemi", "Jose"`).

`uppercase()` converts each name to uppercase. `upperNames` will be a list containing each name in uppercase.

In this case, `upperNames` will be [“VIENA", “NOEMI", “JOSE"].

The `println("UpperNames: $upperNames")` line will print names in capital letters:

```
Uppercase names: [VIENA, NOEMI, JOSE]
```

What do we gather from `nameLengths`:

- Again, `map` applies a lambda to each element of the list, this time to create a string that includes the name and its length.
- The `{ "${it}: ${it.length} characters" }` lambda builds a string for each name:
    - `${it}` represents the name itself.
    - `${it.length}` represents the length of the name, calculated using the `length` property

`nameLengths` will be a list of strings describing the name and its length.

In this case, `nameLengths` will be `[Viena: 5 characters, Noemi: 5 characters, Jose: 4 characters]`.

The `println("Name length: $nameLengths")` line will print the following:

```
Name length: [Viena: 5 characters, Noemi: 5 characters, Jose: 4
characters]
```

Let's play with `mutableList`. This is the code:

```
// Mutable list
val mutableList: MutableList<String> = mutableListOf("Viena", "Noemi",
"Jose")
mutableList.add("Fabiola")
// Operations with lambda in mutable list
val sortedNames = mutableList.sortedBy { it.length }
println("Names sorted by length: $sortedNames")
```

Let's break this code down:

- Here, `mutableList` – a mutable list of type `String` – is declared, which initially contains the names `"Viena"`, `"Noemi"`, and `"Jose"`. Being a mutable list, elements can be added, removed, or modified.
- The `add` function allows adding `"Fabiola"` to `mutableList`. After this operation, `mutableList` contains: `["Viena", "Noemi", "Jose", "Fabiola"]`.
- Then the `sortedBy` function allows you to sort the elements of `mutableList` according to a specific criterion provided by a lambda. In this case, the `{ it.length }` lambda indicates that the list should be sorted according to the length of each name (`it.length`). `sortedBy` returns a new sorted list, leaving the original `mutableList` unchanged.
- `sortedNames` will contain the names of `mutableList` sorted by length, from shortest to longest. The result will be `["Jose", "Viena", "Noemi", "Fabiola"]`.

In summary, we can say the following:

- `mutableList` allows you to modify its content. `"Fabiola"` is added using `add`.
- Operation with `sortedBy`: Using an `{ it.length }` lambda, the names are sorted by their length.
- Result: The `sortedBy` operation returns a new list, `sortedNames`, with the names sorted by length, leaving the original list unchanged.

This example demonstrates how Kotlin allows you to sort lists declaratively using `sortedBy` together with a lambda to specify the sort order.

Now we are going to show an example in which we will do more advanced or complex things. This is the code:

```
// Combining multiple operations
val processedNames = mutableList
    .filter { it.length > 4 }
    .map { it.uppercase() }
    .sortedBy { it }
println("Processed Names: $processedNames")
```

In this example, the `filter` function selects the elements of `mutableList` that meet a condition. In this case, the `{ it.length > 4 }` lambda filters out names whose length is greater than 4 characters.

If `mutableList` contains the names `["Viena", "Noemi", "Jose", "Fabiola"]`, `filter` will select `["Viena", "Noemi", "Fabiola"]` because `"Jose"` is only 4 characters long.

After filtering, the `map` function is applied, which transforms each element of the resulting list. The `{ it.uppercase() }` lambda converts each name to uppercase. The result of `map` will be `["VIENA", "NOEMI", "FABIOLA"]`.

Then, `sortedBy` is applied, which sorts the elements in alphabetical order. The `{ it }` lambda indicates that the value of each element will be used directly for sorting.

Finally, the resulting list, `processedNames`, will be sorted as `[FABIOLA, NOEMI, VIENA]`. The `println("Processed Names: $processedNames")` line will print it like so:

```
Processed Names: [FABIOLA, NOEMI, VIENA]
```

We can note the following:

- Filtering (`filter`): Selects only names with more than 4 characters.
- Transformation (`map`): Converts each name to uppercase.
- Ordering (`sortedBy`): Sorts the resulting names in alphabetical order.

Here's an overview of how lambdas get involved:

- Each lambda – (`{ it.length > 4 }`, `{ it.uppercase() }`, and `{ it }`) – defines a specific operation on the elements of the list.
- `filter` uses a lambda to select elements based on a condition.
- `map` uses a lambda to transform each element.
- `sortedBy` uses a lambda to determine how to sort the elements.

By chaining these operations together, each step receives a transformed list as constructed in the lambda from the previous step.

Together, lambdas allow us to concisely and clearly express how we want to manipulate the elements of the list, without needing to write complex loops or conditions. This makes the code more readable and focused on the goal of each transformation.

Lambdas and collections in Kotlin represent one of the most powerful synergies in the language. When we look at the previous code, we can see how this combination transforms operations that would be complex and verbose in Java into concise and expressive expressions in Kotlin.

The combination of lambdas and collections in Kotlin represents a quantum leap in how we express data transformations. Not only does it make code more concise and less error-prone, but it also makes it more expressive and maintainable. This synergy demonstrates Kotlin's commitment to expressiveness and code safety, providing powerful tools that make development more productive and enjoyable.

For developers coming from Java, this combination represents a new way of thinking about data processing, moving away from traditional imperative loops towards a more functional and declarative style. The result is code that is easier to write, read, and maintain, while maintaining familiarity with fundamental collection concepts.

Summary

In this chapter, we explored one of Kotlin's most powerful and expressive features: lambda expressions. These allow you to take a functional programming approach, simplifying complex operations and making it easier to write concise, readable code. First, we delved into higher-order functions to reinforce the concept of functions that can accept other functions as parameters or return them, which lays the groundwork for advanced techniques in Kotlin.

We also introduced the concept of receivers in lambdas and functions, which provide a cleaner, more declarative way to extend functions and directly access an object's properties and methods, without needing to explicitly refer to it. This feature, which does not exist in Java, improves code flexibility and readability, allowing operations to be integrated more naturally into the flow of code.

Finally, we applied these concepts in the context of collections, where lambdas excel at operations such as filtering, mapping, and data reduction. Kotlin makes it easy to process data structures with a functional approach, making code not only efficient but also more expressive and readable. Through examples of `map`, `filter`, and `flatMap`, we demonstrated how collections and lambdas in Kotlin simplify data transformations, providing powerful, declarative tools that outperform traditional control structures in Java.

This chapter was essential to understanding how Kotlin brings functional programming to a practical and applicable level. You learned how lambdas allow for writing more expressive and maintainable code, simplifying common data manipulation tasks. Furthermore, the use of receivers, in combination with higher-order functions, opens the door to new ways of structuring code, making it more intuitive and less error-prone.

In the next chapter, we'll explore in depth how to handle and optimize data processing in Kotlin. We'll learn how to choose between collections and sequences based on performance needs, addressing issues of lazy evaluation and how each choice affects memory usage and code efficiency. This approach will expand the functional foundations covered in this chapter, offering advanced tools for managing and processing large volumes of data.

10

Collections and Sequences

Building on our exploration of lambda expressions in the previous chapter, this chapter invites you to dive into the dynamic world of Kotlin's collections and sequences. At its core, a collection is more than just a container for data – it's a powerful, functional tool that lets you transform and process data with clarity and efficiency. Sequences take this a step further by introducing lazy evaluation, enabling more efficient operations on large datasets or complex pipelines.

In this chapter, we will begin by exploring what collections and sequences truly are and why they are essential in Kotlin. We'll examine key collection functions – such as `filter`, `fold`, `groupBy`, and others – comparing their succinct, declarative style in Kotlin with the more verbose approaches often seen in Java. This side-by-side comparison not only reinforces your understanding of functional programming but also highlights how Kotlin's design promotes immutability, readability, and safe data handling.

Next, we will turn our focus to sequences and their lazy evaluation model. Unlike Java Streams, which create intermediate collections for each operation, Kotlin sequences process elements one at a time through the entire chain of operations. This approach not only reduces memory overhead but also makes sequences reusable, offering practical advantages when working with extensive data transformations.

Lastly, we'll address interoperability between Java and Kotlin collections – a crucial aspect for developers transitioning from Java or working in mixed-language projects. Through practical examples, you'll learn how Kotlin seamlessly integrates with Java's collection framework, how mutability and nullability are managed, and about strategies to avoid common pitfalls.

Whether your goal is to simplify data transformations, improve performance with lazy processing, or smoothly integrate with existing Java code, this chapter will equip you with the insights and techniques to harness the full potential of Kotlin's data-handling capabilities. Let's embark on this journey to elevate your code to a new level of expressiveness and efficiency.

In this chapter, we're going to cover the following main topics:

- Collections functions
- Sequences
- Interoperability between Java and Kotlin collections

Technical requirements

To begin, you can use any text editor or **Integrated Development Environment** (**IDE**) of your choice with the Java language, but it is certain that some extra configurations will have to be done; that is why IntelliJ IDEA **Community Edition** (**CE**) is recommended. This tool already comes with everything you need to work with both Java and Kotlin. The list of requirements for this chapter is as follows:

- Java JDK 17 or higher
- IntelliJ IDEA CE
- Kotlin 1.x or 2.x

The code used in the chapters can be found in the book's accompanying GitHub repository: `https://github.com/PacktPublishing/Kotlin-for-Java-Developers`.

Collections functions

In the previous chapter, we dipped our toes into collections while exploring lambda expressions, laying the groundwork for a functional programming approach. In this section, we'll take a closer look at collection functions – powerful methods such as `filter`, `map`, `fold`, and `groupBy` that enable you to manipulate data with clarity and efficiency.

These functions are more than just tools; they embody a declarative way of thinking about data processing. Instead of describing how to iterate over elements, you specify what transformation or filtering you need, making your code more readable and maintainable. This is especially important in modern software development, where concise and expressive code can significantly improve productivity and reduce errors.

To provide a practical context, we will begin by comparing how Java and Kotlin handle common operations such as filtering. This not only highlights Kotlin's streamlined syntax but also reinforces the connection with the lambda expressions discussed earlier. By understanding both the underlying concepts and the language-specific implementations, you will appreciate the advantages Kotlin brings to data manipulation.

Let's explore these collection functions in depth and see how they build on the concepts we introduced in the previous chapter.

filter

First, we will show the code of how it is done in Java and mention the differences. In this example, we are going to filter a list and we will keep the even numbers. It is a fairly simple example, but it will help us concentrate only on the comparison between Java and Kotlin. This is the code on how to use `filter` in Java:

```
List<Integer> numbers = Arrays.asList(1, 2, 3, 4, 5); List<Integer>
evenNumbers = numbers.stream().filter(n -> n % 2 == 0).collect(Collectors.
toList());
```

The Java code uses the Stream API to filter a list of integers and keep only the even numbers. Let's break it down and explain it step by step. We use the Stream API in Java because it makes it easy to work with collections of data using a functional, declarative, and efficient approach.

We will use Streams since we remember that, instead of writing how to process the data (a `for` or `while` loop), with Streams we can describe what to do.

This simplifies the code, making it easier to read and understand, especially in complex operations. In other words, we can say that we are already "improving" it by trying to make it simple.

```
List<Integer> numbers = Arrays.asList(1, 2, 3, 4, 5);
```

`List<Integer>` declares that `numbers` is a list of integers (`Integer`) and `Arrays.asList(1, 2, 3, 4, 5)` creates an immutable list (not modifiable in size) with the numbers from 1 to 5:

```
List<Integer> evenNumbers = numbers.stream()
```

`stream()` converts the `numbers` list into a stream. A stream is a sequence of data that allows functional operations (such as `filter`, `map`, etc.) to be performed in a declarative manner.

It does not modify the original list but rather creates a new data stream to process.

```
.filter(n -> n % 2 == 0)
```

`filter` applies a filtering criterion to each element in the flow.

`n -> n % 2 == 0`: This is a lambda expression that takes each `n` element and checks whether the remainder of the division by 2 is equal to 0. If this condition is true, the number `n` passes the filter and is included in the resulting stream. If it is false, the number is discarded.

```
.collect(Collectors.toList());
```

`collect` converts the resulting stream into a collection.

`Collectors.toList()` specifies that we want the final result to be a list. After this operation, we get a new list containing only even numbers.

In all fairness, `collect(Collectors.toList())` can be abbreviated to just `toList()`. We mentioned the long form here because there are many more `Collectors` (you can even create your own). Specifying Collector makes it obvious that this is a termination operation.

The original list numbers are still [1, 2, 3, 4, 5]. The new `evenNumbers` list contains only [2, 4], which are the even numbers.

Let's remember that we use Streams because it is a way to optimize what we want to do using Java. Now, let's see the advantages of doing it this way.

The Stream API allows you to do chain operations, such as `filter`, `map`, or `reduce`, without the need for complex structures.

If necessary, we can use parallel `Stream()` instead of `stream()` to process large amounts of data in parallel.

We prefer to say, "what to do" (filter even numbers) rather than "how to do it" (like a `for`, `while` loop).

Of course, we can do it in Java without Streams. This code does not need much explanation:

```
List<Integer> evenNumbers = new ArrayList<>();
for (Integer n : numbers) {
    if (n % 2 == 0) {
        evenNumbers.add(n);
    }
}
```

Let's see what the code for this same exercise looks like, but with Kotlin:

```
val numbers = listOf(1, 2, 3, 4, 5)
val evenNumbers = numbers.filter { it % 2 == 0 }
```

In the first line, we see `listOf(1, 2, 3, 4, 5)`, which creates an immutable list containing the numbers 1 through 5. In Kotlin, `listOf` generates a list that cannot be modified, promoting a functional and type-safe design.

In the second line, we are using `filter`, which is a function of the Collections API in Kotlin that takes a predicate (a condition) as a parameter.

It returns a new list containing only the elements of the original list that satisfy the predicate.

- `{ it % 2 == 0 }`: This is the predicate used by the `filter` function.
- `it`: This is an implicit reference to each element in the list. In this case, it refers to each number in the `numbers` list.

The result would be the same in both Java and Kotlin; we only get the even numbers from the list. We could also do it imperatively, but it would not make sense since the code would be longer. That is why, when we talk about this exercise in Java and Kotlin, in the case of Java, we use Streams so that it is as equal as possible, and thus we're able to directly compare the languages. But it can be done imperatively in both languages, although the code would be much longer.

Let's review the characteristics of Kotlin compared to what we already saw in Java, highlighting both the similarities and the advantages Kotlin brings:

Commonalities with Java Streams

- **Inmutability**: Both Kotlin and Java Streams express *what to do* (e.g., filter even elements) rather than *how to do it* (such as iterating over the elements).
- **Declarativity**: Both Kotlin and Java Streams express *what to do* (e.g., filter even elements) rather than *how to do it* (such as iterating over the elements).

Kotlin-specific advantages

- **Conciseness**: Filtering a list can be done in a single line, without additional structures such as loops or verbose Stream syntax.
- **Simplicity of conversion**: In Kotlin, converting the result to a list only requires calling `toList()`, whereas in Java Streams you typically need to use `Collectors.toList()`.

- **Integration with extension functions**: Operations such as `filter`, `map`, and `take` are available directly on collections, making the syntax more natural and expressive.

It is worth noting the difference in data processing compared to the Stream API in Java. Streams in Java are lazy and execute only when a terminal operation is called, without creating intermediate collections at each step. By contrast, operations on Kotlin collections are eager and create intermediate results, while Kotlin sequences provide the same kind of lazy, pipeline-based processing as Java Streams.

fold

For our next example, we will use `fold`. In Java, we did not have this operation until version 22. The `fold` operation is used to accumulate values from a collection, using an initial accumulator and a function. In Kotlin, `fold` is part of the collections API. In Java, a similar effect is achieved using the reduce method of Streams, but it may require additional steps.

The example is an exercise in which we want to add the elements of a list with an initial accumulator of 10.

This is the Java code:

```
import java.util.Arrays;
import java.util.List;

public class FoldExample {
    public static void main(String[] args) {
        List<Integer> numbers = Arrays.asList(1, 2, 3, 4, 5);

        int initial = 10;
        int sum = numbers.stream()
            .reduce(initial, (acc, num) -> acc + num);

        System.out.println(sum);
    }
}
```

We know that `Arrays.asList(1, 2, 3, 4, 5)` creates a list with numbers.

```
stream().reduce(initial, (acc, num) -> acc + num):
```

`reduce` is the closest equivalent to `fold` in Java.

It starts with an accumulator value (`initial = 10`).

On each element of the list, it applies the operation (`acc + num`) and updates the accumulator with the new result.

The result would then be the sum of 10 + 1 + 2 + 3 + 4 + 5 = 25.

Now let's see the Kotlin code to do the same exercise:

```
val numbers = listOf(1, 2, 3, 4, 5)
val sum = numbers.fold(10) { acc, num ->
    acc + num
}
println(sum)
```

We know `listOf(1, 2, 3, 4, 5)` creates an immutable list of numbers.

```
fold(10):
```

It then starts the operation with an initial accumulator of 10.

```
Lambda { acc, num -> acc + num }:
```

`acc` is the value accumulated so far.

`num` is the current element of the list.

The operation returns the accumulated result (`acc + num`) for the next iteration.

Now that we've seen the two options, we can see that in Kotlin, the `fold` function is more expressive, compact, and specifically designed for this type of operation.

In Java, although `reduce` can achieve the same thing, the code is longer and less intuitive due to the nature of the Stream API. This shows how Kotlin is optimized for a cleaner and more direct functional approach.

We can clearly see that the code in Kotlin is reduced, and also the simplicity of reading it.

GroupBy

Let's do one more example with this dynamic of comparing Kotlin and Java. This is the Java code:

```
import java.util.*;
import java.util.stream.Collectors;
class Product {
    String name;
```

```
    String category;
    double price;
}
```

First, we define a product class. Within this class, we put three properties: `name`, `category`, and `price`. All of this we can use as information about the product we are going to create.

Let's add a constructor for the product. This is the code:

```
public Product(String name, String category, double price) {
    this.name = name;
    this.category = category;
    this.price = price;
}
```

Now we see that we have to receive three arguments for the constructor, and thus assign the value to the `name`, `category`, and `price` properties.

We add the setter and getter of each of the properties. This is the code:

```
    public String getName() {
        return name;
    }
     public void setName(String name) {
        this.name = name;
    }
     public String getCategory() {
        return category;
    }
     public void setCategory(String category) {
        this.category = category;
    }
    public double getPrice() {
        return price;
    }
    public void setPrice(double price) {
        this.price = price;
    }
}
```

Let's see how to start the exercise. In the function, we are going to create the list of products:

```
public class Main {
public static void main(String[] args) {
    List<Product> products = Arrays.asList(
        new Product("Kotlin Master", "Books", 90.0),
        new Product("Phone", "Electronics", 1500.0),
        new Product("Shoes", "Clothing", 120.0),
        new Product("Jacket", "Clothing", 150.0),
        new Product("Book", "Books", 30.0)
    );
}
```

In the previous code, we created five products: two books, one telephone, and two items considered clothing. The following code uses the Stream API in Java to group a list of products by category and calculate the total prices in each category:

```
        Map<String, Double> totalsByCategory = products.stream()
            .collect(Collectors.groupingBy(
                Product::getCategory,
                Collectors.summingDouble(Product::getPrice)
            ));

        System.out.println(totalsByCategory);
```

- `stream()`: Converts the list of products into a stream. A stream allows functional operations such a grouping, filtering, transformation, and so on, to be performed on the list of data.
- `Collectors.groupingBy`: Groups the items in the stream by a key. Next, we can see that we have `Product::getCategory`. This is a reference to the `getCategory()` method of the `Product` class. This indicates that the items should be grouped by the `category` property.
- `Intermediate result`: A map where the key is the category and the value is a list of products in that category.
- `Collectors.summingDouble`: This is a reducer (reduction operation) that calculates the sum of values extracted from each group.
- `Product::getPrice`: This is a reference to the `getPrice()` method of the `Product` class. This indicates that the price of each product should be extracted for summing.

- `.collect`: This is the terminal operation that transforms the flow into a map. Here, the result is a map (`Map<String, Double>`) where:
    - The key is the category (`String`).
    - The value is the total price (`Double`).

Here's the code flow summary:

- Input: A list of `Product` objects with `category` and `price` properties.
- Process:
    - Group the products by the category property using `groupingBy`.
    - Calculate the total prices for each category using `summingDouble`.
- Output: A map (`Map<String, Double>`) with the categories as keys and the price totals as values.

This code is useful in applications such as inventory systems, financial analysis, or categorized data processing. It is a perfect example of the power of the Stream API in Java to manipulate and transform collections of data in a functional and declarative way.

Now, let's see this same exercise in Kotlin:

```
data class Product(val name: String, val category: String, val price:
Double)
fun main() {
    val products = listOf(
        Product("Kotlin Master", "Books", 90.0),
        Product("Phone", "Electronics", 800.0),
        Product("Shoes", "Clothing", 120.0),
        Product("Jacket", "Clothing", 150.0),
        Product("Book", "Books", 30.0)
    )

    val totalsByCategory = products.groupBy { it.category }
        .mapValues { (_, items) -> items.sumOf { it.price } }
    println(totalsByCategory)
}
```

We define the product class with its three properties in the first line of code. We create the product list. We will only detail the last part, since the first one was quite easy to read:

```
val totalsByCategory = products.groupBy { it.category }
    .mapValues { (_, items) -> items.sumOf { it.price } }
```

Let's break down the preceding code snippet:

- `groupBy { it.category }`: Groups products by the `category` property.
- `mapValues { (_, items) -> items.sumOf { it.price } }`: Take each group of products (`items`) and calculate the total price (`sumOf`). The underscore (_) is used here to ignore the map key, since only the values (`items`) are relevant for this operation.

Kotlin lets you write concise, declarative code with its expressive collections API. In contrast, Java Streams, while powerful, need more setup and tend to be more verbose, which can make the code harder to read and maintain.

Partition, sortedBy, associateBy, maxBy/minBy

To wrap up our discussion on collection functions, we'll now present an extended exercise that showcases additional functions without comparing them to Java. Since we covered the differences already in previous sections, we will focus solely on exploring more collection functions in Kotlin. Let's begin with a familiar example from previous chapters by defining a `Book` data class:

```
data class Book(
    val title: String,
    val author: String,
    val genre: String,
    val year: Int,
    val rating: Double,
    val pages: Int
)
```

The code is quite simple and does not require explanation. We will continue creating the list of book objects. This is the code:

```
val books = listOf(
    Book("The Pragmatic Programmer", "Dave Thomas", "Programming", 1999,
4.8, 320),
    Book("Clean Code", "Robert Martin", "Programming", 2008, 4.7, 464),
    Book("Design Patterns", "Gang of Four", "Programming", 1994, 4.6,
395),
```

```
    Book("Refactoring", "Martin Fowler", "Programming", 1999, 4.7, 431),
    Book("Domain-Driven Design", "Eric Evans", "Programming", 2003, 4.5,
560)
)
```

partition

Let's discuss our first function – `partition`. It's a function in the Kotlin Collections API that splits a list into two lists based on a predicate (a boolean condition). This is the code:

```
val (longBooks, shortBooks) = books.partition { it.pages > 400 }
println("Long books: ${longBooks.map { it.title }}")
```

It takes a lambda as an argument. In this case, the condition is { `it.pages > 400` }, which checks if a book has more than 400 pages.

We'll use the `books` list, which is the original list of books.

- `partition` returns a pair of lists:
    - The first list contains the elements that meet the condition (`it.pages > 400`).
    - The second list contains the elements that don't meet the condition.
- `val (longBooks, shortBooks)` directly extracts the two lists from the books List.
- `longBooks`: List of books with more than 400 pages.
- `shortBooks`: List of books with 400 pages or less.
- `longBooks.map { it.title }`: Converts the `longBooks` list into a new list containing only the titles of the books.
- `map` transforms each element of the `list (it)` into the value of its `title` property.

This approach has the following advantages:

- **Conciseness and readability:** Destructured assignment makes the code easy to read.
- **Clear functionality:** Partition splits the list without the need for loops or complex structures.
- **Expressive transformation:** The `map` function allows you to easily transform books into their titles.

The code uses `partition` to sort books into long and short ones based on their page count and then extracts the titles of the long books for display. It's an idiomatic example of Kotlin taking advantage of the high-level features of its collections API to work with data in a declarative and efficient manner.

sortedBy

Now we will use `sortedBy`. In this Kotlin code example, we will sort a list of books by the year of publication and then print the titles of the books along with their years in a friendly format. This is the code:

```
val booksByYear = books.sortedBy { it.year }
println("Books sorted by year: ${booksByYear.map { "${it.title} (${it.
year})" }}")
```

- `sortedBy { it.year }`: Sort books by year.
- `books`: This is the original list of books. Each element is assumed to be an object with `title` and `year` properties.
- `sortedBy`:
    - This is a Kotlin Collections API function that sorts the elements of a list by a criterion.
    - It receives a lambda as an argument. In this case, the criterion is `{it.year}`, which takes the value of the `year` property of each book.

The result is a new list called `booksByYear`, where books are sorted by their year of publication in ascending order.

- `map { "${it.title} (${it.year})" }`:
    - Transforms each item in the list into something new.
    - In this case, it transforms each book (`it`) into a string that combines its title (`it.title`) and its year (`it.year`), in the format `Title (Year)`.

After `map`, we are left with a list of strings with the desired format.

- Books sorted by year `${}`: Use interpolation to insert the result of `booksByYear.map { ... }` into the string.

Finally, it displays the message with the book titles sorted by year and formatted.

The entire sorting and transformation process is done in just a few lines, without the need for additional structures such as loops. `sortedBy` and `map` clearly express the intent of the code: sorting and formatting. The original `books` list is not modified; a new `booksByYear` list is created with the sorted data.

This Kotlin code demonstrates how to use `sortedBy` to sort collections efficiently and map transform data into a print-friendly format. It's an idiomatic and declarative approach that highlights Kotlin's expressiveness.

associateBy

Let's create code that uses the `associateBy` function to transform a list of books into a map where the key is the author and the value is the corresponding book. Let's break down and explain how this code works step by step:

```
val booksByAuthor = books.associateBy { it.author }
println("Books by author: ${booksByAuthor.keys}")
```

The first thing we'll mention is that `associateBy` creates a map.

- `books`: This is a list of objects (in this case, books). Each object has, presumably, an `author` property and others, such as `title` or `year`.
- `associateBy`:
    - This is a function in the Kotlin Collections API that transforms a list into a map.
    - It takes a lambda that specifies how to generate the keys of the map.
    - In this case, the key is `it.author` (i.e., the author of each book).
    - By default behavior, the value stored in the map is the entire object (in this case, the book).

  As a result, we see that a map is created where:

    - `Key` is the author of each book.
    - `Value` is the corresponding book object.

We could ask ourselves the following: What happens if there are repeated authors? `associateBy` overwrites the value in case there are duplicate keys. This means that if there are multiple books by the same author, only the last book found in the list will be kept.

How can you avoid overwriting?

If you want each author to have a list of books, you can use `groupBy` instead of `associateBy`:

```
val booksByAuthor = books.groupBy { it.author }
```

This approach will generate a map where:

- The key is still the author
- The value is a list of books by the author

The code uses `associateBy` to create a map where each author is associated with a single book. It then prints the authors' names as keys to the map. This approach is useful for turning a list into a quick, searchable map, but if you need to handle multiple books per author, it would be better to use `groupBy`.

maxBy/minBy

Let's move on to the last function we'll look at for now. In the following code, we want to find the largest book (i.e., the book with the largest number of pages) from a list of books and then print its title and number of pages. Here's the code:

```
val longestBook = books.maxBy { it.pages }
println("Longest book: ${longestBook.title} (${longestBook.pages} pages)")
```

Let's go through the different functions in the code:

- `books`: This is a list of `Book` objects. Each book has properties such as `title`, `pages`, and so on.
- `maxBy { it.pages }`: This function finds the element in the list that has the maximum value according to the specified criteria.
- `it.pages`: The property that is evaluated to determine which one has the most pages.
- `Return`: Returns the book with the most pages.

A question that may arise is what happens if the list is empty? If the `books` list is empty, `maxBy` will return `null`. In this case, we can handle the `null` value using a simple `null` check before accessing its properties:

```
val longestBook = books.maxBy { it.pages }
if (longestBook != null) {
    println("Longest book: ${longestBook.title} (${longestBook.pages}
pages)")
```

```
} else {
    println("There are no books in the list.")
}
```

As we can see, it is important when using some of the functions to have knowledge of the particularities of how we can rely on Kotlin to perform certain actions. In short, `maxBy` is a function of the Kotlin Collections API that finds the element with the maximum value according to a specified criterion.

In this section, we examined Kotlin's `Collections` functions – demonstrating operations such as `filter`, `fold`, `groupBy`, `associateBy`, and `maxBy` – and highlighted how Kotlin's concise, expressive approach simplifies tasks such as filtering even numbers, summing with an accumulator, grouping products, and identifying maximum values compared to Java's more verbose Stream API. With these insights, you're now equipped to write cleaner, more maintainable code, paving the way for our next topic.

We will now transition from collections to sequences, focusing on their lazy evaluation and performance benefits. You'll learn when to use sequences over collections to optimize data processing, particularly with large datasets or complex transformations, and how sequences can be a powerful alternative to `Collections`.

Sequences

Sequences in Kotlin represent a significant evolution in collection handling, especially for developers coming from Java. While Java 8+ introduced Streams as a way to process collections in a lazy manner, Kotlin refined this concept with sequences, offering a more elegant and efficient alternative.

Lazy evaluation is at the heart of sequences. This means that operations are not executed immediately when they are declared, but only when they are needed. For a Java developer, this is similar to how Streams work. The main difference is in how elements are processed: Java Streams can batch or buffer elements depending on the operation (e.g., `sorted` or `distinct` may need to see multiple elements), while Kotlin sequences consistently process each element through the entire chain of operations before moving on to the next.

For example, when you filter and transform a collection in Java using Streams, each intermediate operation creates a new temporary collection. In contrast, Kotlin processes an element through all operations before moving on to the next, significantly reducing memory usage and improving performance, especially on large collections.

In addition to efficiency, sequences offer a more intuitive and concise syntax. While Java requires the use of Collectors and specific methods for terminal operations, Kotlin simplifies this with natural extension functions. This simplicity does not sacrifice power: sequences maintain all the capabilities of Streams but present them in a more accessible way.

Another significant advantage is reusability. Unlike Java Streams, which can only be consumed once, sequences can be reused multiple times. This eliminates a common point of failure in Java, where developers try to reuse an already consumed stream.

Let's compare how Java and Kotlin perform a functional operation on a list of books to achieve the following:

- Filter books with more than 300 pages
- Get their titles
- Take only the first 3 results
- Convert the final result into a list of titles

Have a look at the Java code:

```
List<Book> books = getBooks();
Stream<String> titleStream = books.stream()
    .filter(book -> book.getPages() > 300)
    .map(Book::getTitle)
    .limit(3)
.toList();
```

Let's try to understand the code:

- `getBooks()`: Gets the list of books.
- `books.stream()`: Converts the list of books into a stream, allowing functional operations such as filtering and mapping.
- `filter(book -> book.getPages() > 300)`:
    - Filters out books with more than 300 pages.
    - Only books that meet this condition move on to the next step.
- `map(Book::getTitle)`: Transforms the stream of books into a stream of strings, where each string is the title of the book.
- `limit(3)`: Limits the stream to the first 3 elements resulting from filtering and mapping.
- `collect(Collectors.toList())`: Converts the resulting stream into a list.

The result of this code would be a titles list containing the titles of the first 3 books with more than 300 pages.

Let's look at the equivalent code in Kotlin:

```
val books = getBooks()
val titles = books.asSequence()
    .filter { it.pages > 300 }
    .map { it.title }
    .take(3)
    .toList()
```

Let's try to understand the preceding code:

- `getBooks()`: Gets the list of books.
- `books.asSequence()`: Converts the list of books into a sequence, which allows processing the elements in a lazy way (lazy evaluation).
- `filter { it.pages > 300 }`: Filters books with more than 300 pages. Books that do not meet the condition do not go to the next step.
- `map { it.title }`: Transforms the sequence of books into a sequence of strings, where each string is the title of the book.
- `take(3)`: Limits the sequence to the first 3 elements resulting from filtering and mapping.
- `toList()`: Converts the resulting sequence into a list.

The result would be the same: a titles list that will contain the titles of the first 3 books with more than 300 pages.

In Java, Streams are created with `stream()` and use lazy evaluation, meaning that intermediate operations such as `filter`, `map`, and `limit` are not executed until a terminal operation is invoked (e.g., `collect`, `forEach`). While powerful, they often require more verbose syntax and additional utilities such as `Collector` to transform results into collections.

In contrast, Kotlin uses sequences, which are generated with `asSequence()` and use lazy evaluation, processing elements only when necessary. This allows for a more concise and expressive syntax, with similar methods such as `filter`, `map`, and `take`, and a simple list conversion using `toList()`. Kotlin, therefore, offers a cleaner and more efficient approach for long pipelines or large amounts of data.

Lazy evaluation

We will compare Streams and sequences again. Let's do that with Java code first:

```
// Java - Stream processing with multiple filters

List<Book> result = books.stream()
    .filter(predicate1.and(predicate2)) // Combine conditions into one
predicate
    .toList(); // or collect(Collectors.toList()) for Java <16
```

Here's how things play out in the Kotlin code:

```
// Kotlin - Process element by element
books.asSequence()
.filter { predicate1 } // Do not create intermediate collection
.filter { predicate2 } // Do not create intermediate collection
.toList()
```

In Java, stream operations such as `filter()` do not create intermediate collections. Instead, each element is pulled through the pipeline one by one. Combining conditions with `pedicate.and()` results in a more concise and efficient expression.

When working with data streams, one important difference between Java Streams and Kotlin sequences lies in their design and usage patterns – not in how they handle intermediate collections.

Both Java Streams and Kotlin sequences process data lazily, element by element, without creating intermediate collections for operations such as `filter` or `map`. Instead, each element flows through the entire pipeline before moving on to the next. This lazy evaluation makes both approaches efficient for large datasets.

However, Kotlin sequences tend to integrate more seamlessly with Kotlin's collection APIs and lambdas with receivers, making them feel more natural in idiomatic Kotlin code. Meanwhile, Java Streams often rely on static method calls and can be slightly more verbose.

The following example demonstrates how Kotlin sequences can be used to build efficient and readable pipelines, particularly when working with transformations and filters on large datasets.

Code reuse

Let's talk about another difference between Streams and sequences: Streams cannot be reused, while sequences can be. Let's explain it step by step. We'll start with the Java code:

```
Stream<Book> stream = books.stream().filter(predicate);
stream.forEach(System.out::println);
stream.forEach(System.out::println); // Throws exception
```

Let's try and understand this code:

- `Stream<Book>`:
    - A Stream in Java is a structure that allows functional operations to be performed on a collection.
    - Once a Stream is consumed (for example, with `forEach`), it cannot be reused. This is because Streams are designed for one-time processing, and after a terminal operation, they are marked as consumed.
- First iteration: `stream.forEach(System.out::println)`:
    - Iterates over the elements of the Stream and prints them.
    - After this terminal operation (`forEach`), the Stream is consumed.
- Second iteration:
    - `stream.forEach(System.out::println)`: Tries to iterate again, but throws an exception: "`java.lang.IllegalStateException`: stream has already been operated upon or closed".

The most important thing to remember is that this happens because Java Streams are not reusable once consumed.

Now, let's see what happens in a similar case using Kotlin. This is the code:

```
val sequence = books.asSequence().filter { predicate }
sequence.forEach { println(it) }
sequence.forEach { println(it) } // Works correctly
```

We will explain in the same way, but now in Kotlin code.

- `asSequence`:
    - Converts the `books` collection into a sequence in Kotlin.
    - Sequences are structures designed to perform lazy evaluation, which means that the data is processed element by element and on demand.
- First iteration:
    - `sequence.forEach { println(it) }`:
        - Iterates over the elements of the sequence, applying the filter and then printing them.
        - Since the sequence processes the elements lazily, it does not store a consumed state after this operation.
- Second iteration:
    - `sequence.forEach { println(it) }`:
        - Iterates over the elements again from the beginning, applying the same operations.
        - Sequences in Kotlin can be reused because processing happens dynamically at each iteration.

Streams in Java are designed for one-time processing, meaning they cannot be reused; if you try to iterate over an already consumed Stream, an exception is thrown. They are evaluated lazily: intermediate operations are not executed until a terminal operation is invoked.

In contrast, sequences in Kotlin are also lazy by design, processing elements one by one only when necessary. Unlike Streams, a sequence can typically be iterated multiple times without throwing exceptions (as long as it is not backed by a one-time resource such as an Iterator). This makes sequences more convenient and expressive for long pipelines or when reuse is required.

The preceding example highlighted the reusability advantage of sequences in Kotlin, a feature that makes them more versatile compared to Java Streams. Now, let's take a look at terminal operations.

Terminal operations

Terminal operations are operations performed at the end of a data pipeline, such as a Stream in Java or a sequence in Kotlin. These operations trigger the processing of all the elements in the stream or sequence – using them to produce a final result – and, as a result, the Stream or sequence is exhausted and cannot be reused for further processing.

Let's see common examples of terminal operations in Java:

```
long count = books.stream().count(); // Total number of books
```

`count()`: Returns the number of elements in the stream:

```
Optional<Book> firstBook = books.stream().findFirst();
```

`findFirst()`: Finds the first element in the stream:

```
List<Book> bookList = books.stream().collect(Collectors.toList());
```

`collect(Collectors.toList())`: Converts the stream to a list.

Now let's see how these operations would work in Kotlin. Here is the code:

```
val count = books.asSequence().count() // Total number of books
```

`count()`: Returns the number of elements in the sequence:

```
val firstBook = books.asSequence().firstOrNull()
```

`firstOrNull()`: Finds the first element of the sequence, or returns null if it is empty:

```
val bookList = books.asSequence().toList()
```

`toList()`: Converts the sequence to a list.

The terminal operation triggers all processing in the order defined in the pipeline.

Terminal operations are crucial in processing Streams in Java and sequences in Kotlin, as they mark the end of the pipeline and consume the stream or sequence. In the case of Java Streams, once a terminal operation is executed, the Stream is consumed and cannot be reused. On the other hand, sequences in Kotlin allow data to be processed and then reused in new pipelines, offering greater flexibility.

These operations always produce a final result, which can vary depending on the purpose. For example, they can return a single value such as `count` or `sum`, generate a `collection`, such as with `toList` or collect, or simply perform a side effect, such as printing the elements with `forEach`. Their main purpose is to transform the stream or sequence into something tangible or useful.

Another key aspect of terminal operations is that they trigger the execution of all intermediate operations previously defined in the pipeline, such as `filter` or `map`. Until a terminal operation is invoked, these intermediate operations are not executed, especially in the case of sequences, where evaluation is lazy.

Finally, terminal operations end the processing of the pipeline. This means that, once executed, no more operations can be added to the stream (in Java) or to the processed sequence. This behavior ensures that the pipeline has a clear end, producing the expected result after applying all the defined transformations.

Advantages of sequences over Streams

Kotlin sequences have several advantages over Java Streams, making them more convenient and powerful in many use cases. One of the most obvious differences is Kotlin's more concise syntax. Thanks to higher-order functions and Kotlin's ability to work with lambdas natively, operations with sequences require less code and are more readable than their equivalents in Java Streams, where verbosity can be a disadvantage.

Another big advantage is that sequences in Kotlin can be converted to collections more directly. In Java Streams, when you want to transform a stream into a collection, you usually need to rely on the `Collector` utility (e.g. `Collectors.toList()`); in Kotlin, it is enough to call `toList()`, which simplifies the conversion. Additionally, sequences benefit from the intuitive extension functions offered by Kotlin, such as `filter`, `map`, and `take`, which are built naturally into the language and allow for more expressive and consistent usage.

Sequences also have better integration with the Kotlin type system, allowing them to take advantage of advanced features such as nullability interoperability. For example, while Streams return an Optional when working with possible null values, sequences simply use the Kotlin type system, returning null directly. This eliminates the need to handle additional containers such as `Optional`, and improves readability and data flow handling.

Here's when to use sequences:

- When you are working with large collections
- When you are working with chained operations
- When lazy processing is required
- When you need an infinite generation of elements

Here's when *not* to use sequences:

- When you're working with small collections
- When you're working with simple operations
- When you need parallelism (use `Collections` instead)

Another major advantage of using sequences is that it is simpler to create them as compared to Streams. Sequences can be easily generated from existing collections with `asSequence()` or through functions such as `generateSequence`. In contrast, Streams require explicit calls to `stream()` or `Stream.of()`, which can be less intuitive for developers unfamiliar with the Java API.

In this section, we explored Kotlin sequences and their advantages over Java Streams, noting how lazy evaluation, efficient memory usage, and intuitive syntax – supported by Kotlin's robust type system – enable more streamlined functional programming. We also discussed scenarios where sequences outperform collections, especially with large datasets and complex pipelines. With this foundation in place, we will now transition to interoperability between Java and Kotlin collections, examining practical examples and techniques that bridge both ecosystems to maximize their strengths in mixed-language environments.

Interoperability between Java and Kotlin collections

In this section, we will discuss the interoperability between Java and Kotlin collections. While we now understand the differences and similarities between the two languages, you might still have questions about how to work with mutable versus immutable collections, handle nullability, or convert collections between the languages. We'll address these concerns and explore practical examples that demonstrate seamless integration in mixed-language environments.

First, we will talk about how Kotlin automatically handles the conversation between Java and Kotlin collections. When a Java method expects a Java collection, you can pass a Kotlin collection and vice versa.

Remember that since Kotlin is designed to be fully compatible with the Java ecosystem, this means that you can use Java collections in your Kotlin code.

Another important consideration is understanding the differences in mutability and nullability. While Java treats all collections as mutable and allows nulls, Kotlin makes these distinctions explicit in its type system. This provides greater compile-time safety but requires special attention when working with existing Java code. Let's try and understand this better through the following code examples.

Using Java collections in Kotlin

Let's take a look at how to use a Java collection in Kotlin. The behavior of each collection – such as whether it's mutable or immutable and what operations are available – depends on the specific type you receive. Java collections map directly to their Kotlin equivalents, like so:

Java Type	Kotlin Type
`java.util.List`	`kotlin.collections.List`
`java.util.Set`	`kotlin.collections.Set`
`java.util.Map`	`kotlin.collections.Map`

Let's see in code how we would use a Java list in Kotlin. This is the code of a Java file:

```
public class JavaBookRepository {
    public List<Book> getJavaBooks() {
        List<Book> books = new ArrayList<>();
        books.add(new Book("Clean Code", "Robert Martin", 2008));
        books.add(new Book("Design Patterns", "Gang of Four", 1994));
        return books;
    }
}
```

Let's try and understand the preceding code:

- `List<Book>`: Uses Java's `List` interface (part of the `java.util` package) to store a list of books.
- The `getJavaBooks` method:
    - Creates and returns a list of books (`ArrayList`) with two initial elements:
        - "*Clean Code*" by Robert Martin, published in 2008
        - "*Design Patterns*" by Gang of Four, published in 1994

Now we will go through the Kotlin code that demonstrates how to use a collection from Java (in this case, a list of books) and how to interact with it, either using Java's own methods or by converting it to a native Kotlin collection:

```
// Kotlin file
// Using Java collection in Kotlin
val javaRepo = JavaBookRepository()
val javaBooks: java.util.List<Book> = javaRepo.getJavaBooks()
```

```
// We can use Java methods
javaBooks.add(Book("Refactoring", "Martin Fowler", 1999))

// Or convert to Kotlin collection
val kotlinBooks: List<Book> = javaBooks
// We can also convert to Kotlin MutableList
val mutableKotlinBooks: MutableList<Book> = javaBooks.toMutableList()
```

Let's try to understand the preceding code:

- `JavaBookRepository`:
    - It is a class written in Java that contains the `getJavaBooks` method, which returns a list of books.
    - In this step, an instance of this class is created to access its methods from Kotlin.
- `javaRepo.getJavaBooks()`:
    - Calls the `getJavaBooks` method of the `JavaBookRepository` class, which returns a list of books (`java.util.List<Book>`).
    - Although it is not mandatory to specify the type in Kotlin, it is explicitly stated here that `javaBooks` is a Java list (`java.util.List`), to highlight that this is a Java collection and not a native Kotlin one.

Now we will see how to use Java methods.

- `add`:
    - This is a method provided by the Java `List` interface.
    - It allows you to add a new book (`Book`) to the list.

We create two `Book` objects of class `Book` with the title `"Refactoring"`, the author `"Martin Fowler"`, and the year `1999`, and then add them to the `javaBooks` list.

There is also the possibility to convert the Java list to a Kotlin collection. In this step, the Java list (`java.util.List<Book>`) is assigned to a Kotlin variable of type `List<Book>`:

```
javaBooks.add(Book("Refactoring", "Martin Fowler", 1999))
```

Although it looks like an automatic conversion occurs, in reality, Kotlin simply treats the Java list as if it were a Kotlin collection.

If our code looked like the following:

```
kotlinBooks.add(Book("New Book", "Author", 2023)) // Error: `add` is not
available on a Kotlin `List`
```

It would be considered an error, because `kotlinBooks` is an immutable list in Kotlin. `List` in Kotlin is immutable by design. Even though it comes from a Java list (which is mutable), assigning it as `List` in Kotlin makes it immutable.

At last, we have the following:

```
val mutableKotlinBooks: MutableList<Book> = javaBooks.toMutableList()
```

When converting a Java `List` to Kotlin, it is interpreted as a `MutableList` by default. This means that you can still modify its contents – for example:

```
val mutableKotlinBooks: MutableList<Book> = javaBooks
```

In Kotlin, however, there is a clear distinction between mutable (`MutableList`) and read-only (`List`) collections, which helps reduce errors related to accidental modifications.

Using Kotlin collections instead of Java collections makes your code more idiomatic and compatible with the rest of the Kotlin ecosystem.

Once converted, you can use all the advanced Kotlin functions, such as `filter`, `map`, or `sorted`.

Using Kotlin collections in Java

Now we will do the same exercise but in reverse – using Kotlin collections in Java. First, we will write the definition of the `Book` class and the method, but we will use them in the Java programming language:

```
// Kotlin file: Books.kt
data class Book(
    val title: String,
    val author: String,
    val year: Int
)

// Function that creates and returns a Kotlin list
fun getKotlinBooks(): List<Book> {
    return listOf(
        Book("Clean Code", "Robert Martin", 2008),
```

```
        Book("Design Patterns", "Gang of Four", 1994)
    )
}
```

As we can see, we have a `data` class in Kotlin that is designed to store data in a concise way, with three properties.

Next, we see that we defined `getKotlinBooks()`, and it uses the `listOf` function to create an immutable list of books.

This means that no items can be added, removed, or modified after the list is created.

Now, let's see how to use this Kotlin code from Java. This is the code:

```
// Java file: JavaBooksHandler.java
public class JavaBooksHandler {
    public void handleBooks() {
        // Using Kotlin List in Java
        List<Book> books = BooksKt.getKotlinBooks();

        // We can use List normally in Java
        System.out.println("First book: " + books.get(0));

        // Trying to modify the List will cause error
        books.add(new Book("Refactoring", "Martin Fowler", 1999)); //
UnsupportedOperationException
    }
}
```

This code demonstrates how to interact with a Kotlin immutable list from Java, highlighting the interoperability between both languages and some important behaviors when using Kotlin collections in Java.

- `BooksKt.getKotlinBooks()`: This is a function defined in Kotlin (in the `Books.kt` file) that returns an immutable list of books (`List<Book>`). In Java, all functions defined in a Kotlin file are exposed as static methods of a class automatically generated by the Kotlin compiler. By convention, the name of this class is the name of the Kotlin file followed by `Kt` (in this case, `Books.kt`).

- `List<Book>`: Although in Kotlin the list is immutable (`List<Book>`), when used in Java, it appears as a `java.util.List`, but with restricted behavior.

The list returned by this function is immutable in Kotlin, but in Java, it is interpreted as `java.util.List` (which is normally mutable in Java).

When we are printing the following:

```
System.out.println("First book: " + books.get(0));
```

We can access the list elements using the standard `java.util.List` methods such as get. This works normally, since the read operation does not violate immutability.

But we're going to observe something unexpected in this line of Java code:

```
books.add(new Book("Refactoring", "Martin Fowler", 1999)); //
UnsupportedOperationException
```

Although the list appears to be `java.util.List`, it is actually an immutable list generated by Kotlin. Trying to modify it (e.g. adding an item) will throw an exception at runtime.

Kotlin uses immutable implementations under the hood (such as `java.util.Collections.unmodifiableList`) to ensure immutability.

In Java, there is no distinction between mutable and immutable lists at the type level, so `books.add(...)` compiles, but fails at runtime.

We could take two recommendations to avoid these kinds of errors:

- Do not modify lists returned by Kotlin.
- Treat any Kotlin list as if it were strictly immutable.

If you need a mutable list, create a copy. Another option would be to create a mutable list explicitly.

This code highlights the interoperability between Kotlin and Java, showing how Kotlin guarantees immutability even when its collections are used in Java. However, due to the differences in the design of collections between the two languages, it is important to be aware of possible exceptions such as `UnsupportedOperationException`. To avoid problems, we should treat lists returned from Kotlin as immutable or explicitly convert them to mutable lists if we need to modify them in Java.

Summary

In this chapter, we explored the essential concepts of *Collections and Sequences* in Kotlin and compared them with their Java counterparts. You learned about key collection functions such as `filter`, `fold`, `groupBy`, and `maxBy`, along with their concise and expressive implementations in Kotlin. We discussed the advantages of Kotlin collections, including their immutability, declarative syntax, and functional programming capabilities, which simplify complex data manipulation tasks.

In addition, we delved into sequences and their lazy evaluation model, which optimizes memory usage and processing for large datasets or long pipelines. By comparing sequences to Java Streams, we highlighted their superior syntax, reusability, and integration with Kotlin's type system. These comparisons equipped you with the knowledge to choose between collections and sequences depending on performance needs and application context.

Finally, we addressed the interoperability between Java and Kotlin collections, demonstrating how Kotlin seamlessly integrates with Java's collection framework. You saw practical examples of using Java collections in Kotlin and vice versa, gaining insight into potential pitfalls, such as handling mutability and immutability, and learning strategies to bridge the gap between the two ecosystems effectively.

This information is invaluable for developers transitioning from Java to Kotlin or working in mixed-language environments. It ensures that their applications can leverage the strengths of both languages while maintaining compatibility and efficiency.

In the next chapter, we shift our focus to Kotlin coroutines – a powerful tool for writing asynchronous, non-blocking code. You'll learn what coroutines are, how they differ from traditional threading models, and how to effectively manage concurrency, timeouts, and cancellations to build efficient, responsive applications.

Part 4

Coroutines, Testing and DSLs

In this part, you will explore Kotlin's coroutines, testing capabilities, and the power of **domain-specific languages (DSLs)**, all essential for building efficient, reliable, and expressive applications. You will begin with an introduction to coroutines, learning how they provide a structured and lightweight approach to concurrency. Next, you will dive into the differences between synchronous and asynchronous execution, handling exceptions, and managing coroutine cancellation for robust error handling. You will then examine key coroutine concepts such as Job, Scope, and Context, which allow precise control over coroutine execution and lifecycle management. Afterward, you will focus on Kotlin's testing ecosystem, with an emphasis on JUnit for unit testing, while also reviewing the advantages and disadvantages of MockK and Kotest as alternative testing solutions. Finally, you will learn how to design and implement internal DSLs in Kotlin, leveraging features such as lambdas with receivers and extension functions to create expressive, type-safe, and domain-focused code.

This part has the following chapters:

11

Coroutines

In this chapter, we will explore one of Kotlin's most powerful and transformative features – **coroutines**. Designed to simplify and enhance asynchronous programming, coroutines allow developers to write non-blocking, concurrent code with ease and clarity. By offering a structured and intuitive approach to handling tasks such as API calls, database operations, and UI updates, coroutines have become a cornerstone for modern Kotlin development.

Unlike traditional approaches to asynchronous programming, such as threads and callbacks, coroutines eliminate complexity by providing a way to write asynchronous code that looks and behaves like synchronous code. This chapter introduces you to the fundamentals of coroutines, teaching you how to avoid issues with callbacks and enabling you to manage concurrency gracefully and efficiently.

Kotlin's coroutines framework is built on top of lightweight threads, providing developers with the tools to execute tasks in parallel, handle timeouts and cancellations, and switch between different execution contexts. Throughout this chapter, we will uncover how coroutines work, why they are an improvement over traditional concurrency models, and how to leverage them to build robust and responsive applications.

We will start by understanding what coroutines are and how they differ from threads and other concurrency mechanisms. Next, we will dive into the implementation of coroutines, learning about coroutine builders such as `launch` and `async`, as well as the importance of suspending functions in asynchronous workflows. We will then explore strategies for managing timeouts and cancellations, ensuring our applications remain efficient and responsive under various conditions. Finally, we will tackle the advanced concepts of context and scope, which are essential for organizing and managing coroutine life cycles effectively.

By the end of this chapter, you will have a comprehensive understanding of Kotlin coroutines, enabling you to write clean, maintainable, and high-performing asynchronous code. Whether you're developing Android applications, server-side services, or any system requiring concurrent operations, mastering coroutines will empower you to tackle complex challenges with confidence and precision.

We're going to cover the following topics:

- What is a coroutine?
- Coroutine implementation
- Timeouts and cancellations
- Contexts and scope

Technical requirements

You can use any text editor or **Integrated Development Environment (IDE)** of your choice with the Java language. We recommend IntelliJ IDEA **Community Edition (CE)**. This tool already comes with everything you need to work with both Java and Kotlin. The software requirements for this chapter, with required versions, are as follows:

- Java JDK 17 or higher
- IntelliJ IDEA CE
- Kotlin 1.x or 2.x

The code used in the chapters can be found in the book's accompanying GitHub repository: `https://github.com/PacktPublishing/Kotlin-for-Java-Developers`.

What is a coroutine?

To simplify what a coroutine is, let's first look at the official definition: "*A coroutine is an instance of a suspendable computation.*" While technically accurate, it may seem too abstract. Instead, let's break it down with a practical and relatable analogy.

Imagine you are dining at a restaurant. A waiter comes to your table, takes your food order, and heads to the kitchen to pass the order on to the chefs. Now, imagine the waiter stays in the kitchen, doing nothing but waiting for your food to be prepared. This would be inefficient, as the waiter could be serving drinks, attending to other tables, or bringing bread to your table while the food is being cooked.

A smarter approach is for the waiter to leave the instructions with the kitchen staff and return to attend to other customers or tasks. Once your food is ready, the kitchen would alert the waiter, who would promptly bring the dishes to your table.

This efficiency is exactly how **coroutines** operate. In programming, there's a "main thread" (like the waiter), which handles primary tasks (like serving the diners in our analogy). However, certain tasks (such as cooking the food) can take an unknown amount of time. These tasks are better handled asynchronously, without blocking the main thread.

The restaurant analogy

To make the concept of coroutines easier to grasp, let's stick with the restaurant analogy. This comparison helps illustrate how asynchronous tasks and concurrency work in Kotlin using coroutines:

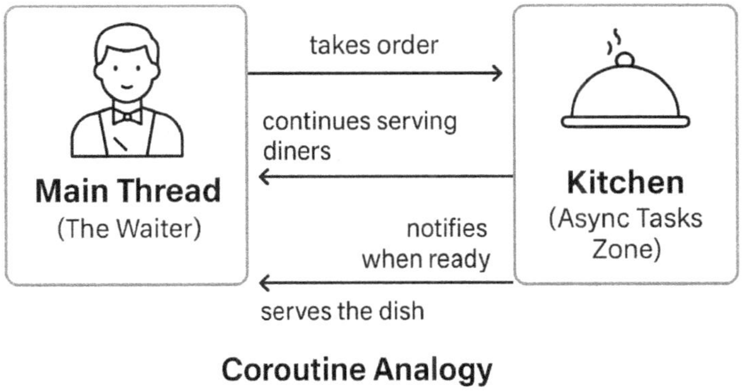

Figure 11.1 – Restaurant analogy for coroutines

Let's try to understand this analogy:

1. **Main thread as the waiter**: The main thread is responsible for visible and interactive tasks (like serving diners). It shouldn't be blocked (or stuck in the kitchen).
2. **Asynchronous tasks as the kitchen**: Some operations, like fetching data from the internet or reading from a database, are similar to cooking food in the kitchen. These tasks can take time and don't need the waiter (the main thread) to stand idle while waiting for them to finish.
3. **Coroutines as the waiter's delegation**: The waiter can delegate tasks such as food preparation to the kitchen while continuing to handle other responsibilities (serving drinks, taking new orders). Similarly, coroutines allow you to "pause" tasks and resume them later without stopping the main thread.

4. **Concurrent coroutines for multiple tasks**: Just as a waiter can manage multiple orders at once, you can create multiple coroutines to handle different tasks simultaneously. For instance, one chef can prepare appetizers, another can handle main courses, and yet another can prepare desserts – all while the waiter continues serving diners.

In programming terms

Kotlin simplifies asynchronous programming, but it doesn't include heavy low-level APIs in its standard library. Instead, it provides just enough tools for libraries, such as `kotlinx.coroutines`, to build powerful coroutine-based utilities. Unlike some other languages, Kotlin doesn't treat `async` and `await` as keywords or include them directly in the language. Instead, it uses suspending functions, which make asynchronous code safer and easier to use compared to traditional approaches such as futures or promises.

To better understand how coroutines work, let's map their behavior to real-world and programming concepts. This helps clarify how Kotlin approaches asynchronous programming in a more intuitive way:

- **Main thread**: The core execution thread that interacts with users (like serving diners).
- **Coroutine**: A lightweight task that runs asynchronously and can be paused and resumed without blocking the main thread.
- **Suspension**: Like the waiter leaving instructions in the kitchen, a coroutine can "pause" its execution, allowing the main thread to continue working until the task is complete.

The `kotlinx.coroutines` library, developed by JetBrains, is a feature-rich library that provides high-level tools for working with coroutines. It includes useful functions such as `launch` and `async`, which simplify working with background tasks.

Explanation of coroutines for a Java programmer

It's important to know that Java does not have coroutines. However, there are many ways we can achieve the results that coroutines achieve, and it is very likely that those of you who know Java might know some of these ways.

While there are projects such as Project Loom and Quasar that attempt to bring coroutine-like behavior to Java, they require third-party dependencies and are not yet widely adopted in the Java ecosystem.

Java thread handling was enhanced with virtual threads in version 21. They are a more lightweight threading model. Yet, virtual threads and coroutines serve different purposes. Virtual threads are primarily used for high-throughput, I/O-bound server applications based on a thread-per-request model. Coroutines, on the other hand, are typically used for various asynchronous tasks.

Note that it is perfectly possible for a coroutine to use a virtual thread to execute its tasks, especially if these tasks include blocking I/O operations.

In this section, we explored the fundamental concept of coroutines, learning how they provide a powerful and efficient alternative to traditional asynchronous programming models such as threads, futures, and promises. Using the analogy of a waiter in a restaurant, we visualized how coroutines delegate long-running tasks to the background while keeping the main thread free to handle interactive or essential tasks. Key characteristics of coroutines, such as their non-blocking nature, ease of readability, and lightweight execution, were highlighted as significant advantages over Java's concurrency options. For Java developers, the comparison to traditional tools such as threads and futures underlined the simplicity and efficiency that coroutines bring to the table.

In the next section, we will dive deeper into the practical aspects of working with coroutines. You'll learn how to create and manage coroutines using coroutine builders and suspending functions, setting the foundation for writing clean and effective asynchronous code in Kotlin. Let's begin our hands-on journey into coroutine implementation!

Coroutine implementation

Now let's see how to implement coroutines in a Kotlin project. For this, we'll start from scratch. First, we'll do something very simple; we can consider it the "`Hello World`" of coroutines. Then we'll increase the difficulty of the example and show other features.

We will start by adding the possibility of using coroutines in our project, and for that, we will add the dependency.

One thing to note is that using `kotlinx.coroutines` has become a convention in the Kotlin community, making it easier to collaborate and understand code.

We don't recommend trying to memorize the versions, since over time, these change, and they change faster than you can imagine. It is more important to know what the official `kotlinx.coroutines` repository is. GitHub is a reliable source to obtain information about the latest versions and news: `https://github.com/Kotlin/kotlinx.coroutines`.

In general terms, we can say that we need to add the coroutines dependency. We can find it in our `build.gradle.kts` file, and the configuration would be something like this:

```
dependencies {
testImplementation(kotlin("test"))
implementation("org.jetbrains.kotlinx:kotlinx-coroutines-core:1.8.0")
}
```

For coroutines, we add the one reference to `kotlinx 1.8.0`, which is enough for what we will do in this chapter. Now, in our first contact with coroutines, we are going to write `Hello World`. This will be our starting point for this entire chapter. This is the code:

```
import kotlinx.coroutines.delay
import kotlinx.coroutines.launch
import kotlinx.coroutines.runBlocking

fun main() = runBlocking {
    launch {
        delay(1000L)
        println("Kotlin World! ")
    }
    println("Hello")
}
```

The imports come from the `kotlinx.coroutines` package, which contains the main tools for working with coroutines in Kotlin:

- `delay`: A function that suspends the execution of a coroutine for a specific time (in milliseconds) without blocking the thread.
- `launch`: A function that starts a new coroutine in parallel with the existing execution.
- `runBlocking`: A function that runs a blocking coroutine, useful for simple examples or tests where we want to block the main thread until the inner coroutines finish.

The imports should be familiar. The first part that is noticeably different from basic "`Hello World`" code is the following:

```
fun main() = runBlocking {
```

The `runBlocking` instruction is used here to allow `main` to run as a coroutine. It blocks the main thread until all coroutines within its block finish executing.

This ensures that the program does not terminate before the coroutines finish.

Let's look at the `launch` instruction:

```
launch {
    delay(1000L)
    println("Kotlin World!")
}
```

`launch` creates a new coroutine. This coroutine runs concurrently with the rest of the code inside `runBlocking`.

Inside this coroutine, we have `delay(1000L)`, which suspends the coroutine for 1 second (1,000 milliseconds) without blocking the thread. This means that the main thread is free to perform other tasks in the meantime, and after one second, it prints `"Kotlin World!"`.

Finally, we have the last instruction:

```
println("Hello")
```

Since the coroutine does not block the thread, this message is printed before the coroutine finishes its task.

Summarizing the flow, we can describe it as follows:

1. The main function is executed and enters the `runBlocking` block.
2. Inside `runBlocking`, the following occurs:
    a. A coroutine is launched with `launch`.
    b. Execution continues without waiting for the coroutine to finish, so `println("Hello")` is executed immediately.
3. In the meantime, the coroutine executes `delay(1000L)`, which suspends the coroutine for one second.
4. After the delay, it prints `"Kotlin World!"`.
5. The program waits inside `runBlocking` until all coroutines inside its block finish. Only then does `runBlocking` complete and the program terminates.

After executing the code, we see the following as a result:

```
Hello
Kotlin World!
```

The reason we started with `Hello World` is simple – we are studying the simplest possible case to show how coroutines allow concurrent tasks (such as waiting a second) to be expressed without blocking the entire scope of execution. In this example, `runBlocking` blocks the main thread until all coroutines inside complete, but the coroutine launched with `launch` runs concurrently within that scope.

Compared to a traditional threading approach, this is more efficient and easier to read.

We introduced the concepts of `delay` and `launch` in a simple context. Now we will look at another example. We will simulate a restaurant scenario to demonstrate how coroutines handle asynchronous tasks.

We want to demonstrate how to perform multiple tasks simultaneously

We are going to show how not to block the main thread while waiting for long-running tasks. We will illustrate coordination between different asynchronous operations, something similar to what we mentioned about the waiter and the restaurant. This is the new code:

```
import kotlinx.coroutines.*
fun main() = runBlocking {
    println("Taking order...")

    // Coroutine 1: Preparing food in the kitchen
    val food = async { prepareFood() }

    // Coroutine 2: Serving drinks
    serveDrinks()

    // Wait for food to be ready and serve it
    println("Food is ready: ${food.await()}")
}

suspend fun prepareFood(): String {
    delay(3000) // Simulate food preparation
    return "Delicious meal"
}

fun serveDrinks() {
    println("Serving drinks to the table...")
}
```

The `runBlocking` block represents the main thread where primary actions (such as interacting with diners) occur. As mentioned before, the `runBlocking` instruction is a function that runs a block of code as a blocking coroutine. This means that the program will not end until all the code inside this block finishes. In this example, it represents the main thread, which acts as the waiter handling multiple tasks.

```
println("Taking order...")
```

The preceding line of code is printed immediately on the main thread (representing the waiter).

```
val food = async { prepareFood() }
```

`async` launches a new coroutine to execute the `prepareFood()` function concurrently.

`async` is a function that returns a `Deferred` object, which is like a "future" in Java. This object can be awaited or revisited later to get the results of the operation.

In this case, it represents the cook who starts preparing the food in the background.

Let us look at the `prepareFood` function:

```
suspend fun prepareFood(): String {
    delay(3000) // Simulate food preparation
    return "Delicious meal"
}
```

The `prepareFood` function is a suspended function, meaning that it can pause its execution and later resume exactly where it left off, without blocking the underlying thread while it is waiting. However, a `suspend` function can only be called from another `suspend` function or within a coroutine. It is also important to note that while the thread is not blocked, the coroutine that invokes `prepareFood` will remain suspended until the function resumes.

`delay(3000)` simulates a meal preparation time of three seconds. During this time, the coroutine is suspended, allowing the main thread to do other tasks.

After the delay, it returns `Delicious meal`.

While the food is being prepared (the async coroutine is suspended), the main thread continues to execute this function:

```
serveDrinks()
```

It prints the message `Serving drinks to the table...`.

Here, the waiter (main thread) serves drinks while waiting for the cook to finish the food:

```
println("Food is ready: ${food.await()}")
```

`food.await()` pauses execution at this point until the `prepareFood()` coroutine finishes and returns its result.

Once `prepareFood()` returns `Delicious meal`, the main thread prints the following:

```
Food is ready: Delicious meal
```

This is how the flow goes:

- `runBlocking` starts the main block.
- The waiter takes the order and starts serving the drinks.
- Meanwhile, the cook (coroutine) prepares the food in the background.
- After three seconds, the food is ready and the waiter serves it.

Returning to our analogy, we've already seen the following:

- `Waiter`: This is the main thread that organizes tasks. It can serve drinks and handle other orders without getting stuck waiting for the food to be ready.
- `Cook`: This is a coroutine that works independently in the background, preparing the food.
- `async` and `await`: `async` starts the cook's work and `await` makes sure the waiter waits for the result before serving the food.
- `delay`: This simulates the time it takes the cook to prepare the food.

This is what we see after running the program:

```
Taking order...
Serving drinks to the table...
Food is ready: Delicious meal
```

The main goal of this exercise was to demonstrate how coroutines allow you to do several things "at the same time" efficiently, just like a good waiter in a restaurant.

We are going to show another example that simulates loading book data from an API using coroutines in Kotlin. The repository (`BookRepository`) has a suspended function that simulates a two-second delay before returning the book data. In the `BookScreen` class, `withContext(Dispatchers.IO)` is used to execute the task in a context suitable for I/O operations, displaying success or error messages depending on the result. This demonstrates how to handle asynchronous tasks in an efficient and readable way. But we will build it in parts.

```
import kotlinx.coroutines.*
// Simulate a repository that fetches book data
class BookRepository {
    // Simulate an API call to fetch a book
    suspend fun fetchBookFromApi(bookId: String): Book {
        delay(2000) // Simulate network response time
        return Book(bookId, "Clean Code", "Robert C. Martin")
    }
}
```

`BookRepository` has a `suspend` function, `fetchBookFromApi`, which simulates calling an API to get the data for a book.

It uses `delay(2000)` to represent a two-second network delay, and then returns a `Book` object as the result.

We add this code, which defines the class that the `fetchBookFromApi` function returns:

```
data class Book(
    val id: String,
    val title: String,
    val author: String
)
```

`Book` is a data class that represents information about a book, with properties such as `id`, `title`, and `author`.

```
class BookScreen {
    private val repository = BookRepository()
    fun loadBookData() = runBlocking {
    try {
        println(" Loading book information...")
        // Send the request in a coroutine
        val book = withContext(Dispatchers.IO) {
            repository.fetchBookFromApi("9780132350884")
}
```

`BookScreen` defines the `loadBookData` method, which uses `runBlocking` to handle loading book data within a coroutine.

The loadBookData method uses withContext(Dispatchers.IO) to perform the book-fetching task in a context optimized for I/O operations.

Finally, we define main, which will allow us to execute the code:

```
fun main() {
    val screen = BookScreen()
    screen.loadBookData()
}
```

In the main function, you simply create an instance of BookScreen and call the loadBookData method to start the process.

Summarizing the program flow, this would be as follows:

- It prints "Loading book information..."
- It waits two seconds, simulating the API response.
- If everything goes well, it prints "Book loaded: Clean Code by Robert C. Martin".
- If an error occurs, it prints "Error loading book information: ..."

Let's take a closer look at what's happening in this exercise. We've successfully used runBlocking and withContext to run the task asynchronously and on a separate thread (Dispatchers.IO), which is ideal for I/O tasks such as API calls.

This approach is ideal for I/O tasks such as API calls because it allows us to perform these operations without blocking the main thread.

By offloading the work to a different dispatcher, we ensure that time-consuming operations (such as reading from a database, writing to a file, or calling an external API) don't freeze the UI or other critical processes. In Kotlin coroutines, Dispatchers.IO is specifically optimized for these types of tasks, giving us efficient and responsive code even when dealing with slow or unpredictable external systems.

We have included a try-catch block to catch possible exceptions that may occur during the API call, which is a good practice to make your code more robust.

Simulating API response time with a delay is useful to understand the behavior of coroutines in real-world scenarios.

In this section, we introduced the foundational ideas behind coroutines in Kotlin, focusing on how they enable writing asynchronous, non-blocking code that remains readable and efficient.

We illustrated real-world analogies and scenarios to highlight how coroutines support structured concurrency and safe context switching, making them a powerful tool for managing concurrent tasks in modern applications.

It's important to clarify when to use these different coroutine builders:

- `runBlocking` is typically used to bridge blocking and non-blocking code, for example, in tests or the `main` function of a small program. It blocks the current thread until its coroutine body finishes executing.
- In contrast, using coroutine builders such as `launch` or `async` within an existing coroutine scope, combined with context switching (`withContext`), lets you run asynchronous code without blocking any thread, ensuring better performance and responsiveness.

It is important to note, however, that coroutines are not magical. If you call blocking operations inside a `suspend` function – for example, using `Thread.sleep()` or synchronous I/O calls such as JDBC – you will still block the underlying thread. To fully benefit from coroutines, blocking calls should be replaced with non-blocking equivalents whenever possible.

So, while `runBlocking` is useful in specific entry points, using structured concurrency with `launch`, `async`, and `withContext` is preferred in production code to handle tasks concurrently and safely without halting your program's execution.

Now that we have a solid understanding of how to implement and use coroutines effectively, the next section will introduce timeouts and cancellations. You'll learn how to gracefully handle scenarios where tasks take too long or need to be interrupted, ensuring your applications remain responsive and efficient under various conditions. Let's continue exploring how Kotlin coroutines can simplify even the most complex asynchronous workflows!

Timeouts and cancellations

Now we will see two important elements that are good to know about in coroutines: timeouts and cancellations. Timeouts are time limits that you set for an operation. If the operation takes longer than the specified time, it is automatically cancelled.

A simple way to describe them using examples of daily activities would be as follows:

- Ordering a pizza and getting the notice: "If it doesn't arrive in 30 minutes, we cancel the order and refund you".
- When an ATM cancels the operation if we don't respond within a certain time.

Cancellations, as their name suggests, allow us to stop a coroutine in the middle of its execution. Let's look at a couple of examples:

- Canceling a download in progress.
- Canceling a bank transfer before it is completed.

Thinking of timeouts and cancellations as elements that we can use, we could easily give some situations where we could use them:

- API calls that should not take too long.
- File downloads that can be cancelled.
- Database operations with a time limit.
- Background processes that can be cancelled by the user.

Taking our previous example of books as a basis, we are now going to modify it to have both cancellation and timeouts.

The definitions of `BookRepository` and `Book` remain the same; we just add more time to `Delay`. Before, we had `2000`, but we will change the value to `3000`. We increased the time period to later; we set a time limit of two seconds and allowed three seconds to execute it (the timeout):

```
class BookRepository {
    // Simulates an API call to get a book
    suspend fun fetchBookFromApi(bookId: String): Book {
        delay(3000) // Simulates network response time
        return Book(bookId, "Clean Code", "Robert C. Martin")
    }
}
data class Book(
    val id: String,
    val title: String,
    val author: String
)
```

Now we will change `launch` to make it look like this:

```
val job = launch {
    try {
        println(" Loading book information...")
```

```
        // Set a timeout for the operation
        val book = withTimeout(2000) { // 2 second timeout
            repository.fetchBookFromApi("9780132350884")
        }

        println(" Book loaded: ${book.title} by ${book.author}")
    } catch (e: TimeoutCancellationException) {
        println(" Timeout exceeded when loading book.")
    } catch (e: Exception) {
        println(" Error loading book information: ${e.message}")
    }
}
```

We set a time limit of 2,000 milliseconds to complete the `fetchBookFromApi` operation. If the task does not finish within this time, `TimeoutCancellationException` is thrown. This mechanism is essential in applications where it is critical to avoid long blockages and ensure fast responses.

In this statement, we can see that the approach uses `job`, as declared with `launch`, to handle the execution of the coroutine:

```
val job = launch {
```

This allows the job to be explicitly cancelled if necessary, providing flexibility to stop execution in specific situations. For example, the job could be cancelled with a call to `job.cancelAndJoin()` if the task is detected to be no longer relevant or if an external event occurs.

Exception handling is a key part of this approach:

```
} catch (e: TimeoutCancellationException) {
println(" Timeout exceeded when loading book.")
```

These last lines demonstrate how to handle scenarios where the time limit is exceeded, ensuring that the system can respond appropriately without crashing. Other exceptions are also handled to catch generic errors during execution.

While this approach is powerful, it adds complexity to the code. It requires explicitly handling both the job and exceptions, which may be unnecessary for simple tasks. However, in cases where strict time limits or precise cancellations are needed, this structure proves invaluable.

Outside of `loadBookData`, we will also modify the code in the following way:

```
// Change: Cancel the job after 4 seconds
delay(4000)
println(" Canceling the loading of the book...")
job.cancelAndJoin() // Cancel the job and wait for it to finish
println("Task cancelled.")
```

Notice that we have introduced a delay of 4,000 milliseconds and manual cancellation. Also notice that we use a job to cancel the task explicitly with `job.cancelAndJoin()`.

The cancellation and timeout scenario introduces a more controlled approach to handling asynchronous tasks in Kotlin. Using `launch` and `withTimeout`, a time limit is set for the execution of an operation.

This ensures that the task does not exceed the time we decide, throwing an exception (`TimeoutCancellationException`) if the time runs out. Also, by encapsulating the logic in a job, the task can be cancelled explicitly when necessary, optimizing resources and allowing better management of multiple concurrent tasks.

This example we developed includes robust exception handling to differentiate between a timeout and other errors. In summary, this model is ideal for applications where time limits and cancellation of irrelevant or delayed tasks are required, although it adds a bit more complexity to the code.

This section emphasized the importance of timeouts and cancellations in effective coroutine management. By enforcing time limits and enabling controlled interruption of tasks, Kotlin coroutines provide mechanisms to keep applications responsive and resilient, especially when dealing with potentially long-running operations.

We also introduced the concept of cancellations, allowing tasks to be stopped explicitly when they are no longer needed. By leveraging the job object, we illustrated how to manage and cancel ongoing tasks using `job.cancelAndJoin()`, ensuring efficient resource management. Additionally, we incorporated robust exception handling to distinguish between timeout-specific issues (`TimeoutCancellationException`) and other errors, adding resilience to our code.

By combining these techniques, we showed how to handle asynchronous tasks in a controlled and efficient manner, enabling developers to create responsive applications that gracefully handle delays and interruptions. This approach is particularly useful in scenarios involving API calls, file downloads, or user-cancelled operations, providing flexibility and reliability.

Next, we'll explore contexts and scopes, diving deeper into how coroutines manage their execution environments and life cycle. You'll learn about coroutine dispatchers, structured concurrency, and how to properly manage coroutine life cycles to maintain clean, predictable, and efficient code. Let's continue building our understanding of Kotlin coroutines with these advanced concepts!

Contexts and scope

Context and scope are fundamental concepts in the world of Kotlin coroutines and play a crucial role in managing their life cycle and behavior.

A context in Kotlin coroutines is like a container that groups key information about how and where a coroutine will run. This context includes the following:

- **Dispatcher**: Defines which thread or thread group the coroutine will run on, as follows:
    - `Dispatchers.IO` for I/O operations (such as working with files or network calls).
    - `Dispatchers.Main` for updating the UI.
- **Job**: Represents the specific task the coroutine performs. It also allows you to cancel it or monitor its progress.
- **Other attributes**: Can include things such as the following:
    - `CoroutineName`: A useful identifier to distinguish coroutines.
    - `NonCancellable`: Indicates that the coroutine should not be cancelled, even if its parent or associated scope is.

In addition, you can put custom elements into the coroutine context, such as an **Mapped Diagnostic Context** (**MDC**) for logging. It is also important to remember that thread-local variables are not effective with coroutines, since a coroutine may resume on a different thread. If you need thread-local-like behavior, you should use `ThreadContextElement` to propagate context across suspensions.

In short, a coroutine's context sets up its execution environment: it defines where it runs, how it interacts with other processes, and what rules it should follow while working. It's like giving the coroutine a roadmap and tools to get it to perform its task correctly.

The code for `BookRepository` and `Book` remains the same; we don't have to make any changes.

The changes start with the `BookScreen` code. We add the scope as follows:

```
class BookScreen {
    private val repository = BookRepository()
    private val scope = CoroutineScope(Dispatchers.Main + Job())
```

`CoroutineScope` is used, which automatically encapsulates the context and the associated job. With this change, instead of the previously temporary scope used with `runBlocking`, now there is a permanent scope with `CoroutineScope(Dispatchers.Main + Job())`.

This makes it easier to manage related tasks, allowing all coroutines associated with the scope to be cancelled with a single call (`scope.cancel()`).

We need better organization for larger applications or those with multiple coroutines.

Let's make some changes in the structure:

```
fun loadBookDetails(bookId: String) {
    scope.launch {
    withContext(Dispatchers.IO) {
        // code here
        }
    }
}
```

We notice with these changes that a specific scope is defined at the class level and dispatchers are explicitly specified. In addition, we are now handling specific execution contexts, and we are going to allow global cancellation of all coroutines.

Regarding the execution context, we can also say that with the previous code, dispatchers were not specified, and now we are indicating one, `dispatchers.IO`, for input and output operations.

We also need to change `val book`. It should look like this:

```
val book = withTimeout(3000) {
    // Set a timeout of 3 seconds
    withContext(Dispatchers.IO) {
        // Run the task in the I/O Dispatcher
        repository.fetchBookFromApi(bookId)
    }
}
```

We add this `function(cancelAllTasks)` after `loadBookDetails`:

```
fun cancelAllTasks() {
    scope.cancel() // Cancels all coroutines in the Scope
    println("All tasks were cancelled.")
}
```

We centralize canceling all active coroutines of the scope with `scope.cancel()` in the `cancelAllTasks()` method.

The main code part now looks like this:

```
fun main() {
    val screen = BookScreen()
    // Start loading book details
    screen.loadBookDetails("1")

    // Simulate task cancellation after 5 seconds
    runBlocking {
        delay(5000)
        screen.cancelAllTasks()
    }
}
```

With the `loadBookDetails` instruction, we will start loading the book details to display them. With the second part, `runBlocking`, we would be simulating the cancellation of tasks after five seconds.

So, let's get to the differences:

- **Life cycle management**:
    - `runBlocking` blocks the main thread until all the internal coroutines complete. It's useful for testing or small examples, but it's not ideal for real applications because it freezes the main thread while it waits. The problem is that the thread is blocked, which affects performance if there are more concurrent tasks.
    - Using `CoroutineScope` acts as a container that allows you to manage all the coroutines created within it. This is ideal for real-world applications because it allows you to manage the life cycle of multiple coroutines in a centralized manner.
    - We can see that in the code, we can now cancel all related coroutines at once using `scope.cancel()`. This is useful in situations where, for example, a user leaves a screen in a mobile app.

- **Dispatchers:**
    - Before the changes, no dispatcher was specified. All code runs in the default context of `runBlocking`. This meant that tasks such as `fetchBookFromApi` run on the same thread as `runBlocking`. This can be problematic if you are doing intensive tasks, such as API calls or database access, because they might block the main thread.
    - By implementing `Dispatchers.IO`, we take advantage of the fact that it is designed for I/O tasks, such as network calls. This ensures that these tasks are executed in a thread optimized for operations of this type, without blocking the main thread.
    - So, we clearly separate the network tasks (in `Dispatchers.IO`) from the UI-related tasks (in `Dispatchers.Main`).
- **Cancellation of coroutines:**
    - Previously, we cancelled manually with `job.cancelAndJoin()`. This stops the specific coroutine and waits for all resources to be released. This is effective but requires you to control each job individually. Switching to `scope.cancel()` stops all coroutines associated with `CoroutineScope`. This is cleaner and more scalable, especially if you have multiple related tasks.
- **Separation of contexts:**
    - Initially, there was no explicit separation of contexts. All operations, such as API calls and result handling, are executed in the same thread. With the changes, the contexts were separated clearly, as we can see:

    ```
    withContext(Dispatchers.IO) { repository.
    fetchBookFromApi(bookId)
    }
    ```

Networking code (API call) runs in `Dispatchers.IO`, while the rest of the code (e.g., printing to the console) can run in `Dispatchers.Main`. This improves performance and keeps the UI smooth.

In summary, the final code represents a more mature and professional implementation of coroutine handling in Kotlin, where each operation is executed in the most appropriate context: the UI in the main dispatcher and network operations in the I/O dispatcher. This approach not only optimizes the use of system resources but also provides a clearer and more maintainable structure, where responsibilities are well defined and separated. Operation cancellation is handled more robustly through a shared scope, allowing for efficient coroutine life cycle management.

Furthermore, this implementation pattern better reflects real-world practices in app development, especially on Android, where it is crucial to properly handle execution contexts and component life cycles. By using `CoroutineScope` defined at the class level along with specific dispatchers, you achieve more predictable and maintainable code, which can scale better as your app grows and becomes more complex.

Summary

In this chapter, we delved into Kotlin coroutines, one of the most transformative features of the language for handling asynchronous programming. Here is a summary of what we've learned.

We started by demystifying coroutines through relatable analogies, such as a waiter in a restaurant. This helped visualize how coroutines enable concurrent, non-blocking tasks while keeping the main thread free for interactive operations.

We introduced coroutine builders such as `launch` and `runBlocking`, along with suspending functions such as `delay`. Through practical examples such as "`Hello World`" and the restaurant scenario, we showcased how to create and manage coroutines effectively.

We explored the critical concepts of setting time limits (`withTimeout`) and manually canceling tasks (`job.cancelAndJoin`). These mechanisms ensure efficient resource usage and help handle long-running tasks gracefully, as seen in the book-fetching example.

Finally, we covered how `CoroutineScope` and dispatchers are used to manage execution contexts and life cycles. We demonstrated how separating contexts (e.g., `Dispatchers.IO` for network calls and `Dispatchers.Main` for UI updates) improves application performance and maintainability. We also highlighted the importance of structured concurrency, enabling efficient cancellation and life cycle management for related tasks.

This chapter provided a robust foundation for understanding and applying Kotlin coroutines, a game-changing feature that simplifies asynchronous programming. By transitioning from basic examples to real-world scenarios, you now understand how coroutines enhance concurrency, improve code readability, and make resource management more efficient. These concepts are critical for developing scalable and responsive applications, whether for Android, server-side, or other Kotlin-based projects.

In the next chapter, we will build upon what you've learned by comparing synchronous and asynchronous programming models. You'll dive deeper into suspending functions to handle asynchronous operations cleanly, explore channels for communication between coroutines, and understand how to manage exceptions in asynchronous workflows. These advanced topics will equip you with the tools to write efficient, safe, and elegant asynchronous code, preparing you for complex application development challenges.

12

Synchronous and Asynchronous Programming

Modern programming demands efficient and responsive applications that can handle multiple tasks simultaneously without compromising the user experience. In this chapter, we'll dive into one of the most fundamental and powerful aspects of Kotlin: asynchronous programming.

We'll start by exploring the essential difference between synchronous and asynchronous programming, laying a solid foundation for understanding how Kotlin handles concurrent operations. We'll see how synchronous code, while intuitive, can limit the performance of our applications in scenarios involving slow or resource-intensive operations.

We'll then dive into suspended functions, a distinctive feature of Kotlin that allows you to write asynchronous code in an elegant and maintainable way. These functions are the cornerstone of concurrency handling in Kotlin, allowing us to write asynchronous code that looks and behaves like synchronous code.

The chapter also covers channels, a powerful concept for communication between different pieces of asynchronous code. Channels provide a safe and efficient way to transmit streams of values between coroutines, allowing for the implementation of complex communication and synchronization patterns.

Finally, we'll cover exception handling in the asynchronous context, a critical aspect that significantly differentiates it from traditional error handling. We'll learn how to effectively handle and propagate errors in asynchronous applications, ensuring that our code is robust and resilient.

By the end of this chapter, you'll have the tools necessary to write efficient and elegant asynchronous code in Kotlin, preparing you to develop modern applications that can effectively handle multiple tasks while maintaining a great user experience.

We're going to cover the following main topics:

- Synchronous and asynchronous
- Suspending functions
- Channels
- Exception handling

Technical requirements

To begin, you can use any text editor or **Integrated Development Environment** (**IDE**) you choose with the Java language. We recommend the IntelliJ IDEA **Community Edition** (**CE**) IDE. This tool already comes with everything you need to work with both Java and Kotlin. The list of requirements for this chapter is as follows:

- Java JDK 17 or higher
- IntelliJ IDEA CE
- Kotlin 1.x or 2.x

The code used in the chapters can be found in the book's accompanying GitHub repository: `https://github.com/PacktPublishing/Kotlin-for-Java-Developers`.

Synchronous and asynchronous

Before diving into code, it's important to understand the fundamental difference between synchronous and asynchronous execution. In synchronous programming, tasks are performed one after another, and each step waits for the previous one to complete. In contrast, asynchronous programming allows tasks to run independently or in parallel, enabling a program to remain responsive while waiting for slower operations, such as network or database calls.

In this section, we'll explore these concepts through practical Kotlin examples. We'll see how Kotlin handles both synchronous and asynchronous execution.

What is synchronous programming?

Synchronous programming is very easy to describe. It is the execution of instructions or tasks in a sequential manner, that is, we start at the beginning and finish at the end.

Let's imagine that we have three tasks:

- Task A
- Task B
- Task C

Using this approach, we want to execute these three tasks in that specific order in a program, since we need all three to "finish" the program.

In this situation, the first step would be to execute task A, but we have to wait for the completion of task A to advance to task B. Similarly, in this case, we have to wait for task B to complete to be able to advance to task C, and once task C is completed, only then can we say that we have completed the execution of our program.

We can then see in a practical way the advantages and disadvantages of asynchronous programming with this example.

These are the advantages of synchronous programming:

- Simplicity and clarity in the execution flow
- Easy to read and debug

While the disadvantages are as follows:

- Blocks the current thread, which can degrade performance.
- Not suitable for applications that require high scalability or many simultaneous operations (such as mobile or web applications with multiple users).

Let's do a code example to see how it would be used. We will use the waiter analogy from the previous chapter:

```
fun takeOrderSync(): String {
    Thread.sleep(3000) // Simulates the order preparation time
    return "Delicious Meal"
}

fun main() {
    println("Taking the order...")
    val order = takeOrderSync()
    println("Order served: $order")
}
```

💡 **Quick tip**: Enhance your coding experience with the **AI Code Explainer** and **Quick Copy** features. Open this book in the next-gen Packt Reader.

(1) Click the **Copy** button to quickly copy code into your coding environment.

(2) Click the **Explain** button to get the AI assistant to explain a block of code to you.

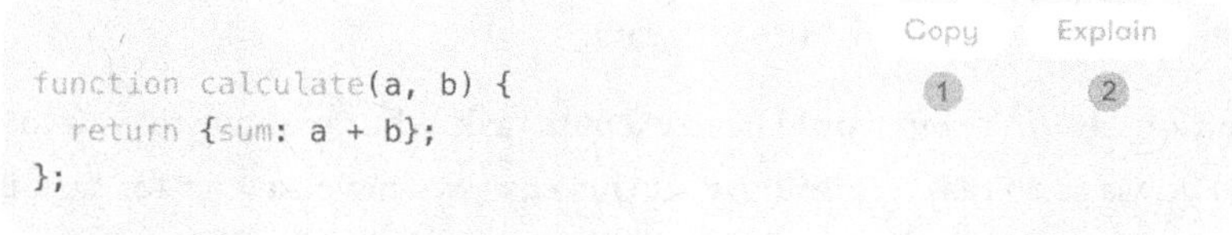

🔒 **The next-gen Packt Reader** is included for free with the purchase of this book. Scan the QR code OR go to `https://packtpub.com/unlock`, then use the search bar to find this book by name. Double-check the edition shown to make sure you get the right one.

Let's try to understand the code.

First, we have a function called `takeOrderSync`, which returns `String`, and we have a pause that we intentionally place to simulate the preparation of an order. Finally, we have `return`, where the string we indicated is returned.

Now we move on to the `main` function, which executes our code. We start with a print that helps us simulate the first step of the algorithm, which is simulating that we take an order.

The next instruction is the call to the `takeOrderSync` function, and we store what it returns in `Order`.

Finally, the last line only prints that we have served the order, with the value of what the order contains.

If we run this code, we will see this result:

```
Taking the order...
Order served: Delicious Meal
```

As we have mentioned earlier and now observed in the code, in a synchronous programming model, operations are processed one after another, following a set order. Each operation blocks the execution of the program until it is completed (the instruction that simulates the preparation of the order with `sleep (3000)`), which means that the thread of execution is left waiting while each task is carried out. This approach guarantees that a new operation is not started until the previous one has finished, thus ensuring a predictable and controlled workflow.

What is asynchronous programming?

Now let's look at asynchronous programming. Unlike synchronous programming, we can have tasks that run independently and do not block the main flow of the program. We can say that, in this way of working, we can start a task, and since we do not know when it will end, we can send it to the background, while other tasks are also still running. This allows our program not to freeze and thus be able to continue moving forward or interacting with the user, or other tasks, without problems.

Let's go to the code. In this example, we will do the same thing we did in the synchronous example, but now asynchronously:

```
fun takeOrderAsync(callback: (String) -> Unit) {
    Thread {
        try {
            Thread.sleep(3000) // Simulates the order preparation time
            callback("Delicious Meal")
        } catch (e: InterruptedException) {
            e.printStackTrace()
        }
    }.start()
}
fun main() {
    println("Taking the order...")
    takeOrderAsync { result ->
        println("Order served: $result")
    }
    println("Serving drinks while waiting...")
}
```

As we can see, the code does the same thing as the previous example, but we are going to explain some parts by line of code to make it clear where things are happening differently.

First, we define a function called `takeOrderAsync`, where we place a callback. Then the `takeOrderAsync` function receives a parameter called `callback`, which is a lambda function with a `String` argument and a return value (`Unit`).

A new thread is created with `Thread { ... }`, which allows the task to be executed asynchronously (without blocking the main thread). Within the thread, the `Thread.sleep(3000)` function pauses the current thread for 3 seconds to simulate a delay, such as the preparation time of an order.

When the "work" is finished, the callback is executed, passing the message `Delicious Meal`.

The thread starts its execution with `start()`.

Now we move on to the `main` block.

We can see how, first, "`Taking the order...`" is printed, making it look like the waiter is taking the order, then `takeOrderAsync` is called, which starts the simulation in a secondary thread.

While the thread waits for 3 seconds, the program continues to run.

The `({ result -> println("Order served: $result") })` callback will be executed once the order is "ready," printing the result (`"Order served: Delicious Meal"`).

While the child thread is paused, the main thread continues running and prints `Serving drinks while waiting....`

Let's describe the flow in general terms:

1. `Taking the order...` is printed.
2. The `takeOrderAsync` function starts a new thread, where the "order" takes 3 seconds to complete.
3. While the order is being processed, the main thread does not wait and continues executing the next line: `Serving drinks while waiting....`
4. After 3 seconds, the secondary thread finishes and calls the callback, printing `Order served: Delicious Meal`.

After running this code, we can see the following result:

```
Taking the order...
Serving drinks while waiting...
Order served: Delicious Meal
```

As we can see in this example, we are using asynchronous programming in Kotlin. The `takeOrderAsync` function uses an asynchronous operation with a separate thread, allowing the program to not block while waiting for the result.

The callback is invoked to print the result (`Order served: Delicious Meal`) when the job (preparing the order) is finished. Since the callback itself has a return type of `Unit`, it doesn't return any value to the caller; its only purpose here is to execute the printing.

This technique is useful when you want to handle tasks that take time without stopping the main execution of the program.

Just to have another point of comparison, and since we know about coroutines, we will use the same example of synchronous and asynchronous programming, but now with coroutines, which would be another way of doing it asynchronously, now using this feature of Kotlin. This is the code:

```
import kotlinx.coroutines.*

fun main() = runBlocking {
    println("Taking the order...")
     // We start a coroutine to simulate the preparation of the order
    takeOrderAsync { result ->
        println("Order served: $result")
    }

    println("Serving drinks while waiting...")
    delay(4000) // We wait to make sure the application does not finish
early
}

fun takeOrderAsync(callback: (String) -> Unit) {
    GlobalScope.launch {
    delay(3000) // Simulate the preparation time of the order without
blocking the main thread
    callback("Delicious Meal")
    }
}
```

Let's try to understand this code. As we already know, `runBlocking` in `main` serves to block the main thread until the coroutines have completed their tasks. It is necessary here so that the application does not terminate prematurely.

`GlobalScope.launch` in `takeOrderAsync` allows us to start a new coroutine globally, handling asynchronous execution without the need for manual threads.

The `delay(3000)` instruction simulates the waiting time (3 seconds) in a non-blocking manner, unlike `Thread.sleep`, which does block the current thread.

The `callback("Delicious Meal")` callback instruction, once the delay ends, is executed to notify that the order is ready.

After that, we only see one print instruction, `println("Serving drinks while waiting...")`, but we see that the program continues to run while the coroutine works in the background, simulating that the waiter is serving drinks.

Finally, we see that we have the `delay(4000)` instruction, which guarantees that the coroutine has enough time to finish its task before the main program ends.

The output is the following:

```
Taking the order...
Serving drinks while waiting...
Order served: Delicious Meal
```

If we compare the asynchronous version with the one using coroutines, we notice a few important differences.

In the coroutine version, we don't use `Thread` explicitly. Instead, coroutines manage the execution in a cleaner and more structured way. The `delay` function allows us to simulate asynchronous operations without blocking the main thread. And as we've already seen, coroutines are much lighter than regular threads and make asynchronous programming more straightforward.

The code is also cleaner and clearer – from reading it, we can notice the difference.

In this section, we explored the fundamental differences between synchronous and asynchronous programming. Through conceptual explanations and practical examples, we observed how synchronous programming processes tasks sequentially, ensuring simplicity but often causing performance bottlenecks. On the other hand, asynchronous programming enables tasks to execute independently, allowing the program to continue without waiting for lengthy operations, thus enhancing scalability and responsiveness.

We illustrated these concepts using examples based on the waiter analogy, showcasing both synchronous and asynchronous approaches. By introducing Kotlin coroutines as a modern solution for asynchronous programming, we demonstrated how they simplify code while maintaining efficiency and readability compared to traditional threading methods.

Now that we have a solid understanding of synchronous and asynchronous programming, it's time to delve deeper into one of Kotlin's most powerful features: **suspending functions**. These functions form the backbone of coroutines, enabling efficient asynchronous operations with a seamless, readable flow. In the next section, we will explore how to define and use suspending functions, as well as their role in real-world applications.

Suspending functions

Let's look at an important concept within asynchronous programming in Kotlin. We can say that they are the cornerstone that allows us to write asynchronous code in a sequential and easy-to-understand way, revolutionizing the way we handle operations that take time.

Suspending functions are functions that can suspend their execution without blocking the thread where it is running. In other words, we can say that it is a function that can pause execution at a certain point, free the thread for other tasks, and finally resume its execution later, which is likely to happen in a different thread.

We can identify a `suspend` function by how it is defined. These functions have the `suspend` modifier, which automatically makes them a `suspend` function.

Let's create an example with code:

```
import kotlinx.coroutines.*
// Suspendable function to take the order
suspend fun takeOrderSuspend(): String {
    delay(3000) // Simulates the preparation time of the order
    return "Delicious Meal"
}
fun main() = runBlocking {
    println("Taking the order...")

    // We call the suspendable function directly in the coroutine
    val order = takeOrderSuspend()
    println("Order served: $order")

    println("Serving drinks while waiting...")
}
```

Let's try to understand this code. We have a function we call `takeOrderSuspend`, and we use the reserved word `suspend`, which means that it can suspend its execution, like when we use `delay`. In this way, this eliminates the need for callbacks. At the end of this function, we return a `String`.

We now continue with the `main` function block. Notice that we are using `runBlocking`. Remember that this is to execute the coroutine code and wait for it to finish. This way, we ensure that the program does not end before completing the execution.

The program calls `takeOrderSuspend()` and waits for the result.

Once the function returns "`Delicious Meal`", the value is stored in the variable order. "`Order served: Delicious Meal`" is printed to show that the order is ready.

Finally, we have `println` about the drinks. This message indicates that the program is serving drinks while waiting for the order to be ready.

This message is executed after `takeOrderSuspend()` completes because `runBlocking` causes the thread to wait until the suspendable task finishes.

The flow looks like this:

1. `"Taking the order..."` is printed.
2. The `takeOrderSuspend()` function is called. The coroutine is suspended for 3 seconds with a delay.
3. In the meantime, the main thread is free, but since we are using `runBlocking`, it waits for the coroutine to finish.
4. After 3 seconds, `"Order served: Delicious Meal"` is printed.
5. Finally, `"Serving drinks while waiting..."` is printed.

If we run the code, we get this result, confirming what was mentioned:

```
Taking the order...
Order served: Delicious Meal
Serving drinks while waiting...
```

With what we have already seen, we can answer the following question: *What was the use of the suspending function?*

- Facilitates asynchronous code: It allows you to write cleaner and more readable code without "callback hell".
- Efficiency: It does not block the thread while waiting.
- Compatible with coroutines: It is the basis of the Kotlin concurrency model.

Suspending functions in Kotlin, defined with the `suspend` keyword, allow you to pause and resume the execution of a coroutine without blocking the main thread or consuming unnecessary resources. These functions are ideal for handling time-consuming tasks, such as network operations or timers. However, they can only be called from active coroutines or from other suspendable functions, ensuring a clean and efficient asynchronous flow.

Let's briefly look at some cases where we can apply the `suspend` function and a common case that we could encounter on a daily basis as programmers.

This is the code:

```
// API calls
suspend fun getProduct(id: String): Product {
    return withContext(Dispatchers.IO) {
    api.getProduct(id) // Simulates a call to get product data
    }
}
```

In this function, the goal is to get a product from a simulated external API.

The `withContext(Dispatchers.IO)` instruction executes the code block in the `Dispatchers.IO`, a thread pool optimized for input/output operations, such as network calls or file access.

`api.getProduct(id)` simulates getting the product from a server.

Let's see another example:

```
// Database operations
suspend fun saveProduct(product: Product) {
    withContext(Dispatchers.IO) {
    database.insert(product) // Simulates inserting the product into the
database
    }
}
```

In this function, the objective is to save a product in the simulated database.

With `withContext(Dispatchers.IO)`, we place the write operation in the database in the context optimized for input/output.

`database.insert(product)` is the instruction that inserts the product into the database.

Now we move on to a function that combines the two previous ones to perform a complete operation of updating an inventory. This is the code:

```
// Combination of operations
suspend fun updateInventory(id: String, newStock: Int) {
    val product = getProduct(id) // Gets the product from the API
    product.updateStock(newStock) // Updates the available quantity of the
product
    saveProduct(product) // Saves the updated product to the database
}
```

This is the flow of the example:

1. Call `updateInventory` with the product ID and the new stock.
2. Get the product from the API using `getProduct`.
3. Modify the stock quantity of the product.
4. Save the updated product in the database with `saveProduct`.

We use `Dispatchers.IO` for input/output operations (network and database) that are I/O intensive and can block the main thread if not handled properly.

`Dispatchers.IO` ensures that these tasks are executed in separate threads, optimizing the application and avoiding deadlocks.

Using suspendable functions in Kotlin allows you to write more efficient and readable code when handling long operations such as API calls or database access. These functions suspend their execution without blocking the main thread, freeing up resources for other tasks while waiting for their completion. Additionally, by maintaining a sequential logical structure, they make the program flow easier to understand, combining power and clarity in handling asynchronous tasks.

In this section, we explored one of Kotlin's most powerful features for asynchronous programming: suspending functions. These functions allow us to write code that looks and behaves like synchronous code while running asynchronously under the hood. By defining functions with the `suspend` keyword, we can handle long-running operations, such as API calls or database operations, without blocking the main thread or consuming unnecessary resources.

We demonstrated how suspending functions enable efficient and readable code through examples, such as retrieving and saving product data or combining multiple operations to update an inventory. These examples showcased how suspending functions leverage `Dispatchers.IO` to optimize input/output tasks and maintain a logical, sequential flow.

Suspending functions are foundational to Kotlin's concurrency model, making them essential for developers aiming to write scalable and maintainable applications. They bridge the gap between synchronous simplicity and asynchronous performance, ensuring that applications remain responsive while managing complex workflows.

Now that we understand how suspending functions streamline asynchronous programming in Kotlin, it's time to introduce another key component of concurrency: **channels**. Channels provide a powerful way to transfer data between coroutines safely and efficiently, enabling patterns such as producer-consumer workflows and pipelines. In the next section, we will dive into how channels work, their different types, and practical examples of how to integrate them into real-world applications. Let's continue exploring Kotlin's robust asynchronous programming capabilities!

Channels

Channels are a fundamental tool in Kotlin for communication between coroutines, offering a safe and efficient way to transfer streams of values between different pieces of asynchronous code.

Strictly speaking, we can say that the definition of a channel is a flow of data that is sent and received between different coroutines. We could define it in a simpler way, as a means by which coroutines can communicate.

Types of channels

We will start by describing the types of channels. For our examples, we will use the context of a delivery app.

Buffered channels

Buffered channels allow data to be temporarily stored in a buffer, decoupling the producer from the consumer. The buffer size is defined when the channel is created, allowing the producer to send multiple items without blocking, as long as the buffer is not full. The consumer, on the other hand, can process data at its own pace, drawing from the buffer as long as items are available, facilitating asynchronous coordination between both parties.

It is useful to us when there is a mismatch between the speed of the producer and the consumer. The advantage of using it is its flexibility and better handling of latency between tasks.

Let's see the code in pieces:

```
import kotlinx.coroutines.*
import kotlinx.coroutines.channels.Channel
```

The first lines are the imports. They are not very relevant, but we clarify that, unlike everything seen in this chapter, we are adding a new import. This import is the one referring to channels.

Here are the next lines:

```
fun main() = runBlocking {
    val ordersChannel = Channel<String>(3) // Buffer with capacity for 3
orders
```

A channel with a buffer capacity of 3 is created. It allows a producer (who sends data to the channel) and a consumer (who receives data from the channel) to work asynchronously.

The Buffer definition: If the producer sends more than 3 elements without the consumer processing them, the channel blocks the producer until the consumer frees up space.

Let's define the first launch. This is the code:

```
launch {
    val orders = listOf("Order 1", "Order 2", "Order 3", "Order 4", "Order
5")
    for (order in orders) {
        println("Sending: $order to the order system")
        ordersChannel.send(order) // Only blocks if the buffer is full
    }
    ordersChannel.close() // We close the channel after sending all the
orders
}
```

This part simulates sending orders to the channel.

Here is the flow:

1. Five orders are created in a list (Order 1 to Order 5).
2. Each order is sent to the channel using `ordersChannel.send(order)`. If the buffer is full (more than 3 unprocessed orders), this sending is blocked until the consumer processes at least one order.
3. When all orders are sent, the channel is closed with `ordersChannel.close()`, indicating that no more data will be sent.

Let's take a look at the second coroutine block:

```
launch {
    for (order in ordersChannel) {
    delay(1500) // Simulates the order processing
    println("Processing: $order in the kitchen")
    }
}
```

This block simulates the processing of orders. This is part of the same application as the producer coroutine. It represents the consumer coroutine that processes each order from the channel. Both producer and consumer coroutines run within the same `main` function to demonstrate how channels and buffers work together.

The flow would be as follows:

1. It uses a `for` loop to iterate over the orders in the channel.
2. Each order is processed with a delay of 1.5 seconds (`delay(1500)`), simulating the time needed to prepare it.
3. The loop ends automatically when the channel is closed and all orders have been processed.

After running this code, the output we would have would be something like this:

```
Sending: Order 1 to the ordering system
Sending: Order 2 to the ordering system
Sending: Order 3 to the ordering system
Processing: Order 1 in the kitchen
Sending: Order 4 to the ordering system
Processing: Order 2 in the kitchen
Sending: Order 5 to the ordering system
Processing: Order 3 in the kitchen
Processing: Order 4 in the kitchen
Processing: Order 5 in the kitchen
```

In general, we can observe the following:

- **Buffered channel:** A 3-item capacity channel is used, allowing up to 3 orders to be temporarily stored without blocking the producer.
- **Producer (order dispatch):** The producer simulates an ordering system that sends 5 orders to the channel.

  If the buffer is full, the sending is blocked until the consumer frees up space.

- **Consumer (order processing)**: The consumer simulates order processing in the kitchen, with a 1.5-second delay for each order, representing the time needed to prepare each order.

Here is the program flow:

- Orders are sent to the channel until the buffer is full.
- Orders are processed one by one as they become available in the channel.
- Once all orders are processed, the channel closes and the program ends.

Unbuffered channels

The unbuffered channels transfer data directly between the producer and consumer, ensuring strict synchronization: the producer waits until the consumer is ready to receive. Having no buffering capacity, they cannot have messages on hold, making them ideal for scenarios where both parties are perfectly synchronized and no buffering is required. They are simple and efficient in these specific cases, facilitating a direct flow of communication.

Let's see the same example but with unbuffered channels. We do not place the imports again, since they are the same. This is the code:

```
fun main() = runBlocking {
    val ordersChannel = Channel<String>() // Unbuffered channel
```

An unbuffered channel is created (`Channel<String>()`). This means that data is not buffered: the sender is blocked until the receiver is ready to process it.

Let's see the first `launch`:

```
launch {
    val orders = listOf("Order 1", "Order 2", "Order 3", "Order 4", "Order
5")
    for (order in orders) {
        println("Sending: $order to the order system")
        ordersChannel.send(order) // Blocks until the consumer receives
the order
    }
    ordersChannel.close() // Close the channel after sending all orders
}
```

In the previous code, we see a coroutine is launched that acts as the producer.

It creates a list of orders and sends them to the channel using `ordersChannel.send(order)`.

We have an **unbuffered behavior,** `val ordersChannel = Channel<String>()`, where if the consumer is not ready to receive an order, the sending is blocked until the consumer processes it.

Finally, the channel is closed with `ordersChannel.close()` to indicate that no more data will be sent.

Let's see the code for the consumer coroutine:

```
launch {
    for (order in ordersChannel) {
        delay(1500) // Simulates order processing
        println("Processing: $order in the kitchen")
    }
}
```

This is the other coroutine that acts as the consumer.

It uses a `for` loop to receive each order from the channel.

The **unbuffered behavior** can be seen where the coroutine blocks `for (order in ordersChannel)` until an order is available.

After receiving an order, it simulates processing with `delay(1500)` and displays a message on the console.

Here is the code flow:

1. The producer sends a request to the channel.
2. If the consumer is ready, it receives the request and processes it.
3. The consumer takes 1.5 seconds to process each request (`delay(1500)`), while the producer blocks and cannot send the next request until the consumer has received the current one (due to the unbuffered nature).
4. The channel closes when the producer finishes sending all requests, and the consumer terminates when it receives all data from the channel.

This is the example of the output, that is, what we see after executing the code:

```
Sending: Order 1 to the order system
Processing: Order 1 in the kitchen
Sending: Order 2 to the order system
Processing: Order 2 in the kitchen
Sending: Order 3 to the order system
Processing: Order 3 in the kitchen
Sending: Order 4 to the order system
Processing: Order 4 in the kitchen
Sending: Order 5 to the order system
Processing: Order 5 in the kitchen
```

We have unbuffered behavior, which means that each order is sent and received one at a time; there is no buffering. We have synchronized blocking: The producer cannot send a new order until the consumer receives the current one. We know that it is useful in strict synchronization scenarios: Ideal for situations where the producer and consumer must operate in a coordinated manner.

Rendezvous channels

A rendezvous channel is not a different channel in theory from the unbuffered channel that we just saw. We can say that *rendezvous* and *unbuffered* describe the same type of channel in Kotlin.

The origin of the term rendezvous comes from the ADA programming language used for concurrent programming; the name is in French and could be translated to something such as an appointment or meeting. The main idea is that two processes must meet to achieve communication, and above all, it is related to the issue of synchronization that must be achieved between the receiver and the sender.

Unbuffered can be said to be an easier term to understand for technical reasons, since the name implies that it is a channel that does not have a buffer, and this name is also quite common in telecommunications technologies, messages, and so on.

Although we are using the rendezvous channel here, it's helpful to explain it further in the context of synchronization. Synchronization is a general concept in programming that ensures different parts of a program coordinate their actions safely and predictably, just like how the rendezvous channel forces the producer and consumer to meet at exactly the same moment.

We could ask ourselves: Why do we have two names for the same concept?

We could use one or the other depending on the context – for example:

Unbuffered is a bit more technical since it describes what the name suggests: that we do not have the capacity for storage.

Rendezvous is a bit more conceptual since it describes how everything will behave, having a producer and a consumer synchronizing directly. In fact, we already saw that, by default, if we use `Channel()`, it is a rendezvous or unbuffered channel; if we wanted a buffer, we would have to specify it.

In fact, to refer to a rendezvous channel in code, we must explicitly use `Channel.RENDEZVOUS`.

In the code, we will see that they are identical since, in truth, the producer blocks `send` until the consumer calls are received and the consumer blocks receive until the producer calls `send`.

If you want to highlight the absence of buffering, "unbuffered" is appropriate. If you want to highlight the need for direct synchronization, "rendezvous" is more descriptive.

If we go back to the previous example that we used in unbuffered, and we want to somehow make rendezvous noticeable, the only thing that would change would be the following:

```
val ordersChannel = Channel<String>(Channel.RENDEZVOUS) // Unbuffered
channel
```

Here, it is explicitly specified that the channel has the `Channel.RENDEZVOUS` capability (unbuffered).

So, we already know the following:

- Direct synchronization: Every send operation is paired with a receive operation.
- If the producer tries to send a message and there is no consumer ready to receive it, it blocks until there is one.
- This ensures that there is no backlog of messages and that the transfer occurs in real time between producer and consumer.

In short, we can say, then, that *rendezvous* emphasizes the synchronization aspect and *unbuffered* emphasizes the technical feature.

Ticker channels

A ticker channel is a type that is also available. What a ticker does is emit values at regular intervals. In fact, it is a little different from what we have already seen, since it is not used to transmit or communicate directly between producer and consumer. It is more of a timer that will periodically emit values.

Let's see an example of a ticker channel. The import can be omitted again, since we will use the same imports from the last examples. For coroutines in general, we would only add the ticker import:

```
import kotlinx.coroutines.channels.ticker
```

Now let's look at the main code and the definition of the ticker channel:

```
fun main() = runBlocking {
    val tickerChannel = ticker(delayMillis = 1000, initialDelayMillis = 0)
// Generate a packet every 1 second
```

As we can see, this channel generates a "tick" every second. It represents the automatic generation of packets at regular intervals.

Let's see the first `launch`:

```
launch {
    repeat(5) { // Simulate the generation of 5 packets
        tickerChannel.receive() // Receive an event from the ticker
        println("Packet generated: ${System.currentTimeMillis()}")
    }
    tickerChannel.cancel() // Cancel the ticker after generating the
packets
}
```

Each time a ticker event is received, a packet is generated and the corresponding message is printed. After generating all five packets, the ticker is cancelled to prevent further event generation.

Let's look at the second coroutine, which simulates processing the packets separately from ticker events:

```
launch {
    delay(1500) // Simulate a small delay before starting to process
    repeat(5) { // Process the 5 packets
        println(" Processing packet: ${System.currentTimeMillis()}")
        delay(2000) // Simulates the time it takes to process each packet
    }
}
```

In this last part, we can see how the processing of the generated packets is simulated, each one with a delay of 2 seconds.

If we run the code, we will see a result like this:

```
Generated package: 1697645362345
Generated package: 1697645363345
Generated package: 1697645364345
Generated package: 1697645365345
Generated package: 1697645366345
Processing package: 1697645362345
Processing package: 1697645363345
Processing package: 1697645364345
Processing package: 1697645365345
Processing package: 1697645366345
```

With this, we confirm that a ticker channel allows for the periodic generation of packets automatically every second, simulating a constant source of work. While packets are being generated, another process can independently simulate processing them in parallel with some delay, demonstrating how generation and processing operations can coexist efficiently, even though they are not directly communicating via a shared channel in this example.

Pipeline

Now we will see a concept that is not a channel, but it is a concept closely related to channels in Kotlin, and it is not exclusive to this language either. Pipeline is a design pattern that allows data to be processed through a series of sequential stages, where each stage executes a specific instruction or operation and passes the result of this to the next stage; hence, it is sequential.

In general, as mentioned, Pipeline is a design pattern within programming. It is not Kotlin-based, so in other areas of computing, programming, operating systems, or software development, we will also find this concept embedded. The Linux operating system is based on pipelines, where you have a number of command-line tools. Each of them takes an input, performs some kind of operation on this input, and creates new output. This output is then the input for the next stage in a pipeline.

In Kotlin, technically, channels are the basis for the implementation of a pipeline. This is because they are used as pipes that connect different stages of the process. Each stage of the pipeline will produce and consume data using these channels, which in the end allows for concurrent and efficient operations.

Let's see a code example where we apply a pipeline. Let's start with parts:

```
import kotlinx.coroutines.*
import kotlinx.coroutines.channels.Channel
import kotlinx.coroutines.channels.ReceiveChannel
import kotlinx.coroutines.channels.produce
```

The imports in this example are `Channel`, `coroutines`, produce, and `Receivechannel`:

```
fun CoroutineScope.producePackets(): ReceiveChannel<String> = produce{
    val packets = listOf("Package 1", "Package 2", "Package 3", "Package
4", "Package 5")
    for (pack in packets) {
        println(Generating: $pack)
        send(pack)
        delay(1000) // Simulates time between packet generation
    }
}
```

This is what happens in the preceding code:

First, it generates a list of packets and sends them to the next step in the pipeline via a channel.

We use this to create a channel and generate data, then we see messages being printed, indicating that a packet is being generated.

Each packet is sent to the channel with `send(pack)`. We introduce `delay(1000)` to simulate the time it will take to generate each packet.

We define the following function:

```
fun CoroutineScope.processPackets(input: ReceiveChannel<String>):
ReceiveChannel<String> = produce {
    for (pack in input) {
        println(Processing: $pack)
        delay(1500) // Simulates processing time
        send($pack processed)
    }
}
```

In this code, we can see that packets are consumed from the channel generated by `producePackets`. Each packet is processed (simulated with `delay(1500)`).

It sends the processed packet to the next channel using `send`.

We also see that a message is printed when a packet is being processed and a label is added to the packet (denoted by "`processed`") before it is sent.

Now we go with the last function:

```
fun CoroutineScope.packResults(input: ReceiveChannel<String>):
ReceiveChannel<String> = produce {
    for (pack in input) {
    println(Packing: $pack)
    delay(1000) // Simulates packaging time
    send($pack packed and ready for shipping)
    }
}
```

Here, we receive the processed packets from `processPackets`. We simulate the packaging of the results with `delay(1000)`.

We send the final packet to the next channel.

We see that a message is printed indicating that the result is being packaged, and the final label "`packed and ready for shipping`" is added before sending it.

This is the code for the `main` function:

```
fun main() = runBlocking {
    // Step 1: Generate packets
    val packetChannel = producePackets()

    // Step 2: Process packets
    val processedPackets = processPackets(packetChannel)

    // Step 3: Package results
    val packaged = packResults(processedPackets)

    // Consume the final result
    for (result in packaged) {
        println(Final result: $result)
    }
    println(Pipeline complete.)
}
```

The pipeline is very evident here. You will notice in the code that when we call the function, we are passing the result of the previous execution.

These are the stages into which we can divide the pipeline:

- `producePackets`: Generates the initial packets and sends them through a channel.
- `processPackets`: Receives packets from the previous channel, processes them, and sends the results to another channel.
- `packResults`: Takes the processed packets, packages them, and sends the final results.

At the end, we see how we consume the result of the entire pipeline.

In a `for` loop, consume the results of the final pipeline (packaged) and remember that when using `runBlocking`, the program waits for all coroutines and pipelines to complete their work before ending.

Each stage sends data to the next step through pipelines, decoupling the processes. Stages operate in parallel, processing data as it becomes available and pipelines synchronize production and consumption, preventing one stage from overloading another.

This pattern is ideal for scenarios such as real-time data processing, workflows in distributed systems, or complex simulations.

In this section, we explored channels, a key tool for communication between coroutines in Kotlin. Channels provide a safe and efficient way to transfer data streams, enabling the decoupling of producers and consumers while maintaining concurrency. We covered different types of channels, such as buffered, unbuffered (or rendezvous), and ticker channels, using examples inspired by delivery systems to illustrate their usage and behavior:

- Buffered channels allow temporary data storage, facilitating coordination when producers and consumers operate at different speeds.
- Unbuffered channels (or rendezvous) ensure strict synchronization between producers and consumers, making them ideal for scenarios requiring real-time data transfer.
- Ticker channels periodically emit data, simulating constant workflows such as timed tasks or real-time updates.
- Lastly, we introduced pipelines, which utilize channels to process data in stages, demonstrating their use in building scalable and maintainable concurrent systems.

These examples showcased the flexibility and power of channels in handling complex workflows while ensuring efficient resource utilization and clean separation of concerns.

Now that we understand how to use channels for efficient communication between coroutines and implement advanced patterns such as Pipeline, it's essential to address potential pitfalls. The next section, *Exception handling*, will delve into techniques for making your asynchronous workflows more robust by managing errors gracefully.

Exception handling

To close this chapter, we are going to concentrate on exception handling and everything that it involves. We are going to see in code some appropriate options for the previous examples. We will break down how we can do all this in a better way, thinking about having better error control, detecting failures, and good recurring practices.

At the beginning, we have defined the imports for this code in general coroutines, `Channel`, `ReceiveChannel`, and `produce`:

```
import kotlinx.coroutines.*
import kotlinx.coroutines.channels.Channel
import kotlinx.coroutines.channels.ReceiveChannel
import kotlinx.coroutines.channels.produce
```

Next, we have the definition of `producePackets`. The only thing we do differently is adding `try/catch`. The objective is to be prepared in a basic way for an exception and show the error onscreen. Here, we can see how errors are handled and programmed, in `catch` that we have added and with the `throw` instruction:

```
fun CoroutineScope.producePackets(): ReceiveChannel<String> = produce {
    val packages = listOf("Packet 1", "Packet 2", "Packet 3", "Packet 4",
"Packet 5")
    for (pack in packages) {
        try {
            println(Generating: $pack)
            send(pack)
            delay(1000)
        } catch (e: Exception) {
            println(Error generating packet: ${e.message})
            throw e // Propagate the error
        }
    }
}
```

Next, we move on to the function that processes packets. In code and logic, it is similar, but again we add `try` with two options with `catch`. These are to handle timeouts and another to handle general errors. So, with this function, we have the ability to handle any situation – a general error and specifically one referring to timeout. This is the code:

```
fun CoroutineScope.processPackets(input: ReceiveChannel<String>):
ReceiveChannel<String> = produce {
    for (packet in input) {
        try {
            withTimeout(2000) { // 2 second timeout
                println(Processing: $packet)
                delay(1500)
                send("$packet processed")
            }
        } catch (e: TimeoutCancellationException) {
            println(Timeout processing $packet"
)
            throw e
        } catch (e: Exception) {
            println(Error processing packet: ${e.message})
            throw e
        }
    }
}
```

Finally, we go to the last function, the packaging. Here, we see that we can also add error handling and propagation. It is very similar to the previous ones that we already had in the first function that we mentioned. This is the code:

```
fun CoroutineScope.packagingResults(input: ReceiveChannel<String>):
ReceiveChannel<String> = produce {
    for (pack in input) {
        try {
            println(Packaging: $pack)
            delay(1000)
            send($pack packed and ready for shipping)
        } catch (e: Exception) {
            println(Error packaging package: ${e.message})
            throw e
```

```
            }
        }
    }
```

Now, let's look at and analyze the code that we would put in the `main` function. We will divide it into parts. Let's start with the first part. We create an exception handler to catch unhandled errors, and we also establish a scope for the coroutines with the default dispatcher. `CoroutineExceptionHandler` is defined to print the exception message.

This handler is added to `CoroutineScope`, meaning all coroutines launched within this scope will propagate their uncaught exceptions to the handler.

When using `CoroutinesExceptionHandler` we need to consider the behavior. If any coroutine throws an uncaught exception, the handler catches it – for example:

- If a coroutine in the `processPackets` stage times out or encounters an unexpected error that is not caught locally, the handler will print the error message.
- This ensures that unexpected failures do not crash the application or leave unhandled errors.

We use `CoroutineExceptionHandler` for global exception handling in applications with complex coroutine hierarchies or when we need to log errors in production systems.

It has limitations. For example, exceptions inside `throw` blocks are caught by `CoroutineExceptionHandler`, but exceptions inside `async` blocks need explicit handling because `async` returns a `Deferred` that encapsulates its exceptions.

After the explanation, let's see how we add it to our code:

```
fun main() = runBlocking {
// Global exception handler
    val exceptionHandler = CoroutineExceptionHandler { _, exception ->
    println(Error caught by CoroutineExceptionHandler: ${exception.
message})
    }
    // Creating the scope with the exception handler
val scope = CoroutineScope(Dispatchers.Default + exceptionHandler)
```

The second part is about the three channels. We see that this code fulfils the task of orchestrating a packet processing pipeline, handling exceptions, and ensuring the proper release of resources.

Three channels are created that represent the different stages of the pipeline:

- `packageChannel`: The channel that generates packets.
- `packagesProcessed`: The channel that processes the packets.
- `packaged`: The channel that packages the results.

Each channel operates within its own coroutine, started with `produce`, which allows handling the transmission of data between stages. This is the code:

```
try {
    val packageChannel = scope.producePackets()
    val = scope.processPackets(packageChannel)
    val packaged = scope.packagingResults(packagesProcessed)
```

In the next part, the data from the final channel is consumed (packaged), showing the processed and packaged results. The loop iterates until the channel closes and we have a message that confirms that the processing has concluded successfully. This is the code:

```
// Consume the final result
for (result in packaged) {
    println(Final result: $result)
}
println(Pipeline complete.)
```

We have the `catch` to capture any exception that occurs during the execution of the pipeline, and it will display a message with the error description. We will keep in mind that exceptions can be generated at any stage of the pipeline due to logical errors, communication problems, or data failures. This is the code:

```
} catch (e: Exception) {
    println(An error occurred in the pipeline: ${e.message})
```

The next block of code is the `finally` block, which is responsible for the cleanup and proper closing of resources. This is a block that is always executed, whether or not there are errors. With the `cancel` instruction, `CoroutineScope` is `Cancelled`, all the child coroutines within the scope are cancelled, and the associated resources are released, thus all the associated channels are automatically closed.

In other words, with the cancellation process, all the execution coroutines are stopped, and any pending operation is cancelled. We would then close the channels automatically and release all the resources used. This is the code:

```
} finally {
    println(Closing resources and channels.)
    scope.cancel() // Cancel all coroutines
}
```

In summary, in this last example, we have seen examples of different ways to handle exceptions. We saw the basic handling of exceptions with a simple `try/catch`. In the case of wanting to handle exceptions in the pipeline, it would be the same. We addressed the handling of specific timeouts and the possibility of handling multiple scenarios, where in one scenario, we were very specific, and with a timeout and in the same flow, we handled a general exception. In addition, we added `throw` to propagate the errors and allow the exception handler to capture them.

We also used a simplification of the cleanup, so we did not have to cancel each channel individually, and we did it all at once. With the scope, it was enough and all the coroutines were cancelled.

With this, we saw several elements to consider in order to apply them in a simple way.

Summary

In this chapter, we delved into the critical concepts of synchronous and asynchronous programming, emphasizing the strengths and challenges of each approach. We explored how Kotlin's coroutines, particularly suspending functions, transform asynchronous programming by enabling clean, sequential code that maintains non-blocking operations. By leveraging Kotlin's concurrency model, we demonstrated how to handle complex workflows efficiently.

We further expanded our understanding by introducing channels, a key mechanism for coroutine communication. Through practical examples, we showcased how buffered, unbuffered (or rendezvous), and ticker channels enable flexible and efficient data transfer. Additionally, we explored the Pipeline pattern, illustrating how channels support concurrent, staged processing of data streams, ensuring scalability and maintainability.

Finally, we addressed exception handling in asynchronous workflows, combining techniques such as `try/catch`, timeout handling, and `CoroutineExceptionHandler`. These strategies ensure that our applications remain robust and resilient, even in complex scenarios.

The concepts and techniques presented in this chapter are foundational for mastering Kotlin's asynchronous programming model. Understanding these principles is essential for building scalable, responsive, and maintainable applications that efficiently handle concurrent tasks.

In the next chapter, we will dive deeper into the coroutine ecosystem by exploring three cornerstone concepts: `Job`, `Scope`, and `Context`. These constructs provide a framework for managing coroutine lifecycles, scoping operations, and controlling execution contexts. Additionally, we will cover advanced exception handling techniques to ensure stability in your coroutine-based applications. Stay tuned to elevate your mastery of Kotlin's coroutine system!

13

Kotlin Testing

In this chapter, we will explore an essential aspect of software development: testing. Testing is the backbone of building reliable and maintainable software, and Kotlin offers a rich set of tools and frameworks to make testing efficient and intuitive. Whether you're writing unit tests to verify the smallest components of your code or integration tests to ensure different modules work harmoniously, Kotlin provides the flexibility to create high-quality tests tailored to your project's needs.

We will begin by diving into unit testing, the foundation of any testing strategy. You'll learn how to write tests that focus on individual components, ensuring they behave as expected in isolation. Through practical examples, you'll gain confidence in implementing unit tests and understanding their value in catching bugs early.

Next, we'll delve into integration testing, where we'll examine how different parts of an application interact. You'll see how to design and implement tests that ensure modules work seamlessly together, providing a critical layer of validation for your system's behavior in real-world scenarios.

Finally, we'll introduce testing frameworks that make testing in Kotlin a breeze. Frameworks such as JUnit and Kotest simplify the process of writing and managing tests, while also offering advanced features to make your tests more expressive and powerful. We'll discuss the strengths of each framework and how to choose the one that best fits your project.

In this chapter, we're going to cover the following main topics:

- Unit testing
- Integration testing
- Testing frameworks

Technical requirements

You can use any text editor or **Integrated Development Environment** (**IDE**) of your choice with the Java language. We recommend the IntelliJ IDEA **Community Edition** (**CE**) IDE. This tool already comes with everything you need to work with both Java and Kotlin.

The list of software requirements for this chapter is as follows:

- Java JDK 17 or higher
- IntelliJ IDEA CE
- Kotlin 1.x or 2.x

The code used in this chapter can be found in the book's accompanying GitHub repository: `https://github.com/PacktPublishing/Kotlin-for-Java-Developers`.

Unit testing

When we talk about unit testing, we are talking about the most basic but essential processes to ensure that our code works as we expect. Simply put, a unit test verifies that a specific piece of your code (such as a function or method) does what it's supposed to do, regardless of what's going on around it. It's like a magnifying glass that focuses on just one part of the code to make sure it's built well before integrating it with everything else.

For example, if you have a function that adds two numbers, your unit test will confirm that 2 + 3 always equals 5. It doesn't get complicated by external things, such as databases or services, because those distractions aren't part of its job.

The following are characteristics of unit testing:

- **Isolated**: Each test is independent and does not depend on another. This makes them reliable.
- **Fast**: Unit tests execute in milliseconds, which is ideal for running them every time you make a change to your code.
- **Deterministic**: Tests give the same result every time, if the code does not change.

Unit testing is an essential tool for any developer looking to create robust and reliable software. First, it helps you avoid unpleasant surprises by catching bugs before they reach production. This not only improves the quality of the final product but also reduces the costs associated with correcting problems later in development. Additionally, unit testing allows you to refactor with confidence. When you decide to restructure your code, having a solid set of tests ensures that any changes don't break existing functionality, acting as a safety net. Finally, unit tests serve as a form of living documentation. Each test details how your code should behave under certain conditions, making it not only easier for you to understand the system but also for other developers working on the project. Writing unit tests is not just good practice; it is an investment in the stability and maintainability of your software.

The following are quick tips for making useful unit tests:

- Give your tests clear names so it is obvious what they are checking.
- A test should focus on one thing.
- Use mocks when necessary, but don't abuse them. Keep tests simple and clear.

We are going to create our first unit test in Kotlin. We will start with a very simple example, as unit tests are typically straightforward functions or operations that perform only one task.

We can start with a new project without any existing code. Within the Kotlin directory, we are going to create a class.

We are going to call this class `Operations.kt`. This simple name allows us to understand that we are going to create operations within the class. This is the code:

```
class Operations(){
}
```

Now we are going to add an operation to our file; we will place an addition operation. This is the code:

```
class Operations(){
    fun sum(a:Int, b:Int): Int {
        return a + b
    }


}
```

In this code, we can see that we have an addition function in which we receive two values of the integer type. We are also indicating that it will return an integer, and within the function, we indicate that we will return the result of adding `a + b`.

If we wanted to have some code to execute, it would be like in any other class; we would just add the `main` function and place code inside it. In this case, we are just placing the main function as a reference; we will not place anything else as it is not necessary. The code looks as follows:

```
class Operations(){
    fun sum(a:Int, b:Int): Int {
        return a + b
    }
}

fun main(){
}
```

Now we are going to add the configurations necessary to have unit tests.

In the `build.gradle.kts` file (if you are using Gradle), we put this configuration:

```
plugins {
    kotlin("jvm") version "1.9.0"
}

dependencies {
    testImplementation("org.jetbrains.kotlin:kotlin-test")
    testImplementation("org.junit.jupiter:junit-jupiter:5.9.2")
}

tasks.test {
    useJUnitPlatform()
}
```

We know that the version of Kotlin (`jvm`) can vary. It depends on what we have installed. But in the `dependencies` section, notice that we are adding `kotlin-test` and `junit`, and in `tasks.test`, we add `useJUnitPlatform`.

This is only the case if we are using Gradle.

If we use Maven, we will have to use the POM file. This is what the `pom.xml` file would look like:

```
<dependencies>
    <dependency>
        <groupId>org.jetbrains.kotlin</groupId>
```

```
            <artifactId>kotlin-test-junit5</artifactId>
            <version>${kotlin.version}</version>
            <scope>test</scope>
        </dependency>
        <dependency>
            <groupId>org.junit.jupiter</groupId>
            <artifactId>junit-jupiter</artifactId>
            <version>5.9.2</version>
            <scope>test</scope>
        </dependency>
    </dependencies>
```

As we can see, the elements are actually the same and the configuration is similar to in Gradle.

Now we will briefly see what the basic directory structure of a project that contains unit tests is. Remember that we are starting from just having a Kotlin file; we are not referring to any specific architecture or configuration.

This is the structure:

```
src/
main/
kotlin/
Operations.kt
test/
kotlin/
OperationsTest.kt
```

This structure is important as it ensures that the build tool (Gradle or Maven) automatically recognizes the structure.

```
src/main/kotlin/Operations.kt
src/test/kotlin/OperationsTest.kt
```

First, we define the class using the `Test` convention after the name it refers to. The first import allows us to use the `Test` annotation to mark methods as test cases. The second import imports all the JUnit 5 assertion functions, such as `assertEquals` and `assertTrue`:

```
import org.junit.jupiter.api.Test
import org.junit.jupiter.api.Assertions.*
class OperationsTest {
}
```

So, we start with the declaration of the test class and then we create an instance of the class to be tested. In this case, we name it `testOperation`:

```
private val testOperation: Operations = Operations()
```

With `private`, we limit the scope of the `testOperation` variable to this test class, and `Operations()` calls the constructor of the `Operations` class. So, here, we create an instance of the `Operations` class to perform tests on its methods.

Now we define the method:

```
@Test
fun sum() {
    val expected = 10
    assertEquals(expected, testOperation.sum(5,5))
}
```

Let's explain the code point by point:

- `@Test`: Marks the method as a test case that will be executed by JUnit.
- `fun sum()`: This tests the behavior of the `sum` method of the `Operations` class.
- `val expected = 10`: This defines the expected result of the operation.
- `testOperation.sum(5,5)`: This calls the `sum` method of the `Operations` class, passing the values 5 and 5 as arguments.
- `assertEquals(expected, ...)`: This compares the expected value (`10`) with the actual value returned by `testOperation.sum(5,5)`. If they do not match, the test case fails.

When we run the code, we will see this as a result:

```
BUILD SUCCESSFUL in 1s
1 actionable task: 1 executed
> Task :compileKotlin UP-TO-DATE
> Task :compileJava NO-SOURCE
> Task :processResources NO-SOURCE
> Task :classes UP-TO-DATE
> Task :jar UP-TO-DATE
> Task :inspectClassesForKotlinIC UP-TO-DATE
> Task :processTestResources NO-SOURCE
> Task :compileTestKotlin
```

The test function was executed successfully. Now we are going to improve the code, and we are going to give some important recommendations. The code for the `Operations` class is the same; we are going to concentrate on improving the test:

```
class OperationsTest {
    private lateinit var operations: Operations
}
```

We start with the definition of the variable. We want it to have a clear name. Although by convention, sometimes it can simply have the word `test` as a prefix, there may be a need for it to have a clearer name, so we can use, for example, the name `operations`, thus making it clear that what we are testing in this case are operations.

Let's add this code after the variable:

```
@BeforeEach
fun setup() {
     operations = Operations()
}
```

The `BeforeEach` annotation allows us to run the following code before each test is executed. These instructions allow us to reinitialize the object before each test, avoiding side effects between tests. This approach is especially useful for tests that might modify the state of the object.

Now, let's look at the possible changes we can make to the test. This would be the new test code:

```
@Test
fun `sum of 5 and 5 should return 10`() {
// Given
    val expected = 10
// When
    val result = operations.sum(5, 5)

    // Then
    assertEquals(expected, result)

}
```

In the preceding code, we can see that we have a more descriptive test name, `sum of 5 and 5 should return 10`. Even though it is a longer name, we can see that it really clearly describes what test we are doing. This, of course, makes it easier for us to understand the purpose of the test without reading the code. So, it is very common to find names described as we just did in the code.

Furthermore, we can see that in this new code definition, we are using the `Given-When-Then` structure.

`Given-When-Then` is a very common way of structuring test cases in software development. It makes tests clearer and easier to understand. Although it is widely used in **Behavior-Driven Development (BDD)**, it also works very well to organize unit tests in a more orderly manner.

Each section that we are considering has a specific purpose. Let's go through them:

- Given/Arrange:
    - Prepares the test scenario
    - Initializes objects
    - Configures mocks
    - Defines inputs
- When/Act:
    - Executes the action to be tested
    - Generally a single operation
    - Invokes the method that we want to test
- Then/Assert:
    - Verifies the results
    - Contains the assertions
    - Verifies that the behavior is as expected

Another improvement we made was to separate the variable from the result:

```
val result = operations.sum(5, 5)
```

This makes debugging easier and improves the readability of the assertion. The preceding improvements transform test code into a superior version for several interconnected reasons: maintainability is increased because the clear, organized structure makes it easy to make future modifications without affecting other parts of the code; readability is improved by descriptive names and a Given-When-Then structure that clearly narrates the purpose of each test; robustness is increased by using practices such as BeforeEach that ensure a clean state before each test; debugging ease is enhanced by clearly separating each test step and storing intermediate results in explicit variables; and comprehension for other developers is improved because the code follows standard conventions and clearly communicates its intent, facilitating team collaboration and code review. All of these improvements work together to create tests that not only work correctly but are also easy to maintain and evolve over time.

Now we will see another example of unit testing. The example will reference the example of books that we use throughout this book. Let's see a simple example related to a book that can be sold at a certain discount. This is the base code of the `Book` class:

```
// Book.kt
class Book(
    val title: String,
    val price: Double
) {
    fun calculateDiscountedPrice(discountPercent: Int): Double {
        require(discountPercent in 0..100) { "Discount must be between 0 
and 100" }
        return price - (price * discountPercent / 100)
    }
}
```

Since we want to keep the example simple, we define only two properties, `title` and `price`.

They are read-only values (`val`), which means they cannot be changed once they are initialized.

The following is a brief explanation:

- `title`: A string that stores the title of the book.
- `price`: A decimal number that represents the price of the book.

Now we have the function to calculate the discount. First, we receive the `discountPercent` parameter, which represents the discount percentage to apply. It is an integer between 0 and 100.

The function validates that the `discountPercent` value is within the acceptable range (0 to 100) using `require`.

If the value is outside that range, it throws `IllegalArgumentException` with the message `Discount must be between 0 and 100`.

This ensures that an invalid discount is not applied.

Then we calculate the discounted price. This is done as follows:

- `price * discountPercent/100`: Calculates the discount based on the original price.
- `price - ...`: Subtracts the calculated discount from the original price, returning the final price.

Finally, we have the return value, which returns the final price (type `Double`) after applying the discount.

There are three important points to our example:

- **Robust validation**: Using `require` ensures that only valid values are processed.
- **Immutability**: `title` and `price` are immutable, which reduces errors and ensures consistency.
- **Flexibility**: The `calculateDiscountedPrice` function can handle any discount percentage within the specified range.

Now let's move on to the test. This is the code:

```
import org.junit.jupiter.api.Test
import org.junit.jupiter.api.Assertions.*
class BookTest {
    @Test
    fun `calculate 20 percent discount for a 100 dollar book`() {
        // Given
        val book = Book("Clean Code", 100.0)
        // When
        val discountedPrice = book.calculateDiscountedPrice(20)
        // Then
        assertEquals(80.0, discountedPrice)
    }
}
```

We make necessary imports that allow us to do the following:

- `@Test`: Mark the method as a unit test that will be executed by JUnit 5.
- `Assertions`: Provide methods such as `assertEquals` to verify that the results obtained from the test match the expected results.

We define `BookTest`, which is the class that contains the unit tests for the `Book` class. According to convention, the class name ends with `Test` to indicate that it is intended for testing.

We define our method and see that the name of the method clearly states what is being tested: `Calculate a 20% discount for a book that costs $100`.

A `Book` object is created with the title `Clean Code` and a price of $100.0. This is the preparation of the test environment.

The `calculateDiscountedPrice` method is called, which passes `20` as the discount percentage. This generates a discounted price that is stored in `discountedPrice`.

Verify that the calculated discounted price is exactly $80.0. If the result does not match, the test fails.

The test verifies only one specific case: a 20% discount applied to a book priced at $100.

This is a simple but effective case to validate that the discount formula in `calculateDiscountedPrice` works correctly.

If the `calculateDiscountedPrice` method does not correctly calculate the discount, the return value will not be `80.0`, and `assertEquals` will throw an error indicating that the test has failed.

The method name and code structure make the test easy to understand. Someone reading the test can quickly deduce what is being checked and why.

This is an example of a well-structured and clear unit test that follows best practices:

- It is specific and predictable.
- It has a descriptive name that explains exactly what is being tested.
- It verifies the behavior of a key function in a typical scenario.

This type of testing is crucial to ensure that functions work as expected, avoiding errors in production.

If we wanted to have a more complete test, we could add the following tests:

```
@Test
fun `no discount should return original price`() {
    // Given
    val discountPercent = 0
    // When
    val discountedPrice = book.calculateDiscountedPrice(discountPercent)
```

```
    // Then
    assertEquals(100.0, discountedPrice)
}
```

The preceding code is a test case that verifies that when no discount is applied (`discountPercent = 0`), the calculated price of a book remains the same as the original price. In the `Given` section, you set the initial context by indicating that the discount percentage is 0. In `When`, the `calculateDiscountedPrice` method of the `Book` object is called, passing the discount percentage as an argument. Finally, in `Then`, we verify with an assertion (`assertEquals`) that the calculated price is equal to `100.0`, which is the original expected price without a discount.

```
@Test
fun `full discount should return zero`() {
    // Given
    val discountPercent = 100
    // When
    val discountedPrice = book.calculateDiscountedPrice(discountPercent)
    // Then
    assertEquals(0.0, discountedPrice)
}
```

The previous code verifies that when a 100% discount is applied (`discountPercent = 100`), the calculated price of a book is equal to `0`. In the `Given` section, the discount percentage is defined as 100%. In `When`, the `calculateDiscountedPrice` method of the book object is called, passing this percentage as an argument. Finally, in `Then`, an assertion (`assertEquals`) is used to confirm that the discounted price is `0.0`, correctly reflecting a total discount of 100%.

```
@Test
fun `should throw exception when discount is negative`() {
    // When/Then
    assertThrows<IllegalArgumentException> {
        book.calculateDiscountedPrice(-1)
    }
}
```

The preceding code is from a test case that verifies that the `calculateDiscountedPrice` method throws an exception when a negative discount percentage is provided. In this case, the `When` and `Then` sections are combined, since the focus is on confirming that the method throws a specific exception (`IllegalArgumentException`). The test uses `assertThrows` to execute the method with an invalid value (-1) and ensures that the expected exception is thrown, thus validating the correct handling of invalid input in the code.

Finally, we have this test:

```
@Test
fun `should throw exception when discount is over 100`() {
// When/Then
    assertThrows<IllegalArgumentException> {
book.calculateDiscountedPrice(101)
    }
}
```

This test case verifies that the `calculateDiscountedPrice` method throws an exception when a discount percentage greater than 100 is provided, which is invalid. The `When` and `Then` sections are combined by `assertThrows`, which runs the method with an invalid value (`101`). The test ensures that a specific exception (`IllegalArgumentException`) is thrown, validating that the method correctly handles inputs outside the allowed range. This ensures the robustness of the code against invalid values.

The test coverage includes the following:

- Normal use case (20% discount)
- Case without discount (0%)
- Total discount case (100%)
- Negative input validation
- Input validation greater than 100

As we can see, when we devise tests, we must include all possible cases, even if they are obvious or simple, as this will allow us to have better code that is free of errors and problems in the future.

To finish this topic of unit testing, we will mention that there is the possibility that the test is parameterizable, which means that you can run the same test multiple times with different input values and expected results, without having to write the test code several times.

Using the example of the sum of two numbers as a reference, we are going to make it parameterizable. This is the code:

```
import org.junit.jupiter.api.Test
import org.junit.jupiter.params.ParameterizedTest
import org.junit.jupiter.params.provider.CsvSource
```

```
import org.junit.jupiter.api.Assertions.*

class OperationsTest {
    val testOperation = Operations()

    @ParameterizedTest
    @CsvSource(
        "5, 5, 10",
        "1, 2, 3",
        "0, 0, 0",
        "-1, 1, 0",
        "10, -5, 5"
    )
    fun sum(a: Int, b: Int, expected: Int) {
        assertEquals(expected, testOperation.sum(a, b))
    }
}
```

It uses `@ParameterizedTest` and `@CsvSource` to run multiple test cases with different input values without needing to write multiple functions. `@CsvSource` provides a list of number combinations (`a, b`) along with their expected results, allowing you to evaluate the `Operations` `sum` method with different values in a single test. JUnit takes each line from `@CsvSource` and automatically passes it to the `sum(a: Int, b: Int, expected: Int)` function, verifying with `assertEquals` that the returned result is as expected. This makes it easy to validate multiple scenarios without duplicating code.

The following are advantages of doing parameterizable tests:

- Cleaner, more maintainable code
- Easier to add new test cases
- Better visibility of the different scenarios you are testing
- Less repeated code

Next, we will move on to another type of test, but we will continue to rely on JUnit.

Integration testing

Integration testing is as important to the testing process as unit testing; it is responsible for verifying how different components of a system work together, ensuring that they work correctly when combined. Its scope includes testing entire business flows, validating interactions between systems, and ensuring that the integration of individual parts meets established requirements.

These are some of the typical components that are tested in this type of testing:

- Databases
- External services
- APIs
- Filesystems
- Network components

Differences between unit tests and integration tests

When writing automated tests, it's important to understand the different levels of testing and what each one is intended to verify. Two common types are unit tests and integration tests, and while they may seem similar at first glance, they serve very different purposes and involve different levels of complexity:

- **Complexity**: Integration tests are usually more complex to set up compared to unit tests. This is because they require the preparation of multiple components or systems that must work together. Additionally, they require more resources, such as databases, external services, or realistic test environments. For this reason, its execution tends to be slower and more demanding, both in time and computational capacity. On the other hand, unit tests are much simpler, since they test a single component in isolation. This makes them quick to run and easy to configure, making them an ideal tool for detecting small, specific errors in a piece of code.
- **Scope**: The scope of both tests also varies considerably. Unit tests focus on validating an individual component, verifying that it works correctly without depending on other elements of the system. This ensures that each part of the code serves its specific purpose independently. Instead, integration tests evaluate how multiple components interact with each other. They validate entire business flows and ensure that parts of the system work correctly together. This approach allows you to identify errors that may arise in the interaction between modules or services, something that unit tests cannot detect.

In summary, while unit tests focus on the internal functionality of the components, integration tests verify the correct communication and behavior of the system as a whole. Both types of testing are complementary and essential to guarantee software quality.

Let's see the benefits of integration tests:

- Detect integration problems
- Validate entire flows
- Ensure compatibility between components
- Find errors that unit tests cannot detect

Now let's look at some disadvantages:

- Longer execution time
- More complex configuration
- May be less stable
- Require more maintenance

Integration tests are typically organized in separate files from unit tests. Here is a common structure:

```
src/
main/
kotlin/
Book.kt
BookService.kt
BookRepository.kt
test/
kotlin/
unit/
BookTest.kt
integration/
BookServiceIntegrationTest.kt
```

Let's start with the domain classes. This refers to the classes that represent the business model and rules. This is the `Book.kt` code file:

```
data class Book( val id: String, val title: String, val price: Double, val
author: String, val isbn: String )
```

Reading it, we see that Book is a data class, which means that Kotlin automatically generates equals() and hashCode() to compare instances, toString() to print the object's contents in a readable way, and copy() to create copies of an object with modified values.

Each property is val, which means it is immutable.

Let's see the BookRepository.kt code:

```
interface BookRepository {
    suspend fun findById(id: String): Book?
    suspend fun save(book: Book): Book
}
```

This preview code defines an interface in Kotlin called BookRepository, which establishes the contract for interacting with a data source that stores Book.

The interface keyword defines an interface, meaning that this class only declares methods but does not implement their logic. Other classes must implement this interface and provide their own method definitions.

We have two declared methods: findById and save.

The first one searches for a book in the repository by its ID. It returns Book?. It returns a book if it finds one, or null if it does not exist. suspend indicates that this function is a suspend function, meaning that it can run inside a coroutine and make calls to asynchronous operations, such as querying a database or API.

The second method saves a book to the repository and returns the saved Book object. We see suspend again. As it is an operation that potentially interacts with a database or remote storage, the function is suspended so as not to block the main thread.

Now let's look at BootService.kt, which is the largest file of the three:

```
class BookService(private val repository: BookRepository) {
    suspend fun applyDiscount(bookId: String, discountPercent: Int): Book
{
        require(discountPercent in 0..100) { "Discount must be between 0
and 100" }
        val book = repository.findById(bookId)
        ?: throw NoSuchElementException("Book not found")
        val discountedPrice = book.price - (book.price * discountPercent /
100)
```

```
        return repository.save(Book(book.id, book.title, discountedPrice))
    }
}
```

This code defines a service called `BookService` that interacts with a repository (`BookRepository`) to apply a discount to a book.

It is a class that acts as the business logic layer. Your responsibility is to apply a discount to a workbook and delegate storage and retrieval operations to the repository. The class depends on an instance of `BookRepository`, which is injected via the constructor. This follows the principle of dependency injection, making it easier to test and code with flexibility.

The `applyDiscount` method indicates that it should be executed within a coroutine by `suspend`, since it interacts with suspended functions in the repository (`findById` and `save`).

It verifies that the discount percentage is within the valid range (0 to 100). If not, it throws `IllegalArgumentException` with the provided message.

`repository.findById(bookId)` finds the book in the repository using its ID. This method is suspended and must be executed inside a coroutine. With `?: throw NoSuchElementException`, if the book does not exist, it throws `NoSuchElementException` with the message `"Book not found"`. This ensures that no attempt is made to apply a discount to a non-existent book. `discountedPrice` calculates the final price after applying the discount.

Finally, let's look at the integration test code, starting with the imports for the `BookServiceIntegrationTest.kt` file:

```
// We import the libraries needed for the tests
import org.junit.jupiter.api.Test
import org.junit.jupiter.api.BeforeEach
import org.junit.jupiter.api.Assertions.*
// We import kotlinx.coroutines to handle suspended functions in tests
import kotlinx.coroutines.runTest
```

Now we create our integration class following the recommendations:

```
// We define the integration test class
class BookServiceIntegrationTest {
}
```

We will now see the code that will go inside it. Let's begin with the definition of the components that we are going to test:

```
// Variables for the components to be tested
private lateinit var bookRepository: BookRepository
private lateinit var bookService: BookService
private lateinit var testBook: Book
```

This is what these variables are for:

- `bookRepository`: Instance of the repository that simulates a database.
- `bookService`: Instance of the service that we are testing.
- `testBook`: A test book that will be used in the tests.

We use `lateinit` because in Kotlin, `val` variables must be initialized when declared. But since these depend on `@BeforeEach`, we use `lateinit var` to initialize them afterward.

Now we define a setup method:

```
@BeforeEach
fun setup() {
    bookRepository = TestBookRepository()
    bookService = BookService(bookRepository)

    testBook = Book("1", "Clean Code", 100.0)

    runTest {
        bookRepository.save(testBook)
    }
}
```

This `@BeforeEach` method is executed before each test to ensure that each test starts with a clean state. Let's analyze it line by line:

- A new test repository (`TestBookRepository`) is created.
- The `BookService` service is created using the repository.
- A test book (`testBook`) is created with ID `"1"` and a price of `100.0`.
- `testBook` is saved to the repository before each test using `runTest {}`.

Now let's look at the integration testing:

```
@Test
fun 'should apply discount to book price and persist changes '() = runTest
{
    // Given: We set up the test scenario
    val discountPercent = 20

    // When: We apply the discount
    val discountedBook = bookService.applyDiscount(testBook.id,
discountPercent)

    // Then: We verify that the discount was applied correctly
    assertEquals(80.0, discountedBook.price)

    // We also verify that the updated book was saved in the "database"
    val savedBook = bookRepository.findById(testBook.id)
    assertNotNull(savedBook)
    assertEquals(80.0, savedBook?.price)
}
```

In this method, we are testing that `BookService.applyDiscount()` correctly calculates the discounted price and saves the changes to the repository.

A 20% discount is defined, and the discount is applied using `applyDiscount()`. Then, it is verified that the new price is $80.0 (100 - 20% = 80). The book is then retrieved from the repository and it is verified that the updated price was saved.

We can add two basic integration tests as well, for example, in their corresponding file:

```
@Test
fun 'should throw exception when book not found'() = runTest {
    assertThrows<NoSuchElementException> {
        bookService.applyDiscount("non-existent-id", 20)
    }
}
```

This test is short but important; if `applyDiscount()` tries to modify a non-existent book, it should throw `NoSuchElementException`.

Let's add one more test:

```
@Test
fun 'should throw exception for invalid discount percentage '() = runTest
{
    assertThrows<IllegalArgumentException> {
        bookService.applyDiscount(testBook.id, 101)
    }
}
```

This last test checks whether the discount is greater than 100%. If it is, `require( discountPercent` in 0..100) should throw `IllegalArgumentException`.

To execute tests, it is simple, as with unit tests. Simply right-click on the `BookServiceIntegrationTest` class and select `Run 'BookServiceIntegrationTest'`. After running the test, if everything goes well, we should be able to see something like this:

```
BookServiceIntegrationTest
should apply discount to book price and persist changes() ✔
should throw exception when book not found() ✔
should throw exception for invalid discount percentage() ✔

Tests passed: 3
Tests failed: 0
Tests skipped: 0
```

We have to keep in mind that integration tests usually take longer than unit tests or may require additional configuration. They are also often run in a separate phase of the build cycle.

When a test has an error, the message will tell us how many errors it found. We will see something like this at the end:

```
java.lang.IllegalArgumentException: Price cannot be negative
at Book.<init>(Book.kt:5) at BookServiceIntegrationTest.
setup(BookServiceIntegrationTest.kt:20)
Test run finished after 1234 ms
[ 3 tests found ]
[2 tests successful]
[1 tests failed]
```

We can notice that the error message includes the following:

- Error type
- Error message
- Expected versus actual values
- Stack trace
- Exact location of the fault
- Summary of tests executed

Integration testing is essential to ensure that the various components of a system work together correctly. Unlike unit tests, which test isolated functions, integration tests verify entire business flows, ensuring that communication between services, databases, and other modules is stable and reliable. These tests help detect errors that could arise in the interaction between parts of the system, preventing failures in production and improving software quality.

While integration tests can be more complex and costly in terms of time and resources, their proper implementation significantly reduces the risk of critical failures. A balanced approach, combining unit tests with well-designed integration tests, allows for a robust system, ensuring not only the individual functionality of each component but also the stability and consistency of the system as a whole.

Testing frameworks

To finish this book, we will talk about some options that we want to offer as a starting point for anyone who wants to go deeper into testing with Kotlin. In this last part, we will briefly talk about the frameworks that are a viable option for testing, and we will explain the advantages, disadvantages, and scenarios where it is more convenient to use them.

We'll show a very short implementation of the frameworks that we will mention, and have a quick look at how they work. We will use two tests as a reference.

The tests are to verify the multiplication and divisibility of even numbers. The first test will evaluate whether the multiplication of two numbers (2 * 3) produces the expected result (6). The second test is a parameterized test, meaning it is run multiple times with different values provided in a list (`[2, 4, 6]`). On each run, it checks whether the given number is a multiple of 2 by checking that its remainder when divided by 2 is 0 (number % 2 == 0).

JUnit 5

We have already mentioned and used JUnit 5, so we don't have much more to say except that it is the most popular framework in both the Java and Kotlin ecosystems. The most recent version is 5, and it supports unit and integration tests.

The following are its main features:

- Support for unit and integration testing.
- Annotations such as `@Test`, `@BeforeEach`, `@AfterEach`, and `@DisplayName`.
- Allows parameterized tests with `@ParameterizedTest`.
- Integration with tools such as Gradle and Maven.
- Integration with frameworks such as Spring Boot and Testcontainers.

One disadvantage is that its syntax is less idiomatic in Kotlin. It has no native support for Kotlin DSL or functional styles. This is an example:

```
class SimpleTest {
    @Test
    fun `should multiply two numbers`() {
        assertEquals(6, 2 * 3)
    }
}
```

This code defines a simple unit test that checks the multiplication of two numbers. Inside the test function, 2 * 3 is calculated, and `assertEquals(6, 2 * 3)` is used to check that the result is 6. If the operation is correct, the test passes; otherwise, it fails.

Kotest

Previously known as KotlinTest, this is a testing framework designed specifically for Kotlin. For this reason, it offers a more idiomatic and flexible syntax compared to JUnit.

The main features of Kotest are as follows:

- Supports multiple testing styles (e.g., `FunSpec`, `BehaviorSpec`, `DescribeSpec`).
- Integration with Kotlin coroutines.
- Support for property-based testing with `PropTest`.
- Integration with other frameworks, such as MockK and Spring.
- Elegant and expressive DSL.
- Cleaner and more expressive code.

This is an example:

```
class MultiplicationTest : StringSpec({
    "should multiply two numbers" {
        2 * 3 shouldBe 6
    }
})
```

This code defines a unit test using `StringSpec`, a Kotest style that allows you to write tests more concisely. The test verifies that the multiplication of 2 * 3 equals 6 using `shouldBe`, a Kotest matcher that facilitates expressive assertions.

MockK

MockK is a mocking library designed specifically for Kotlin and allows us to create mocks and stubs and verify interactions in unit tests.

The main features of MockK are as follows:

- Idiomatic Kotlin syntax.
- Support for mocking objects, classes, extension functions, and coroutines.
- More expressive catches and checks (`verify { ... }`).
- Interaction verification with `verify`.
- Better integration with coroutines than Mockito.
- Integration with Kotest and JUnit.

As disadvantages, we can say that it is not very well known and the learning curve is a little longer. If you use Mockito in Java, you might find it easier, but even so, the learning curve is not that short.

This is an example:

```
class Calculator {
    fun multiply(a: Int, b: Int) = a * b
}
class MultiplicationTest : StringSpec({
    // Create calculator instance
    val calculator = mockk<Calculator>()

    // Test case
    "should multiply two numbers" {
        // Arrange - define what should happen when the mock is called
```

```
        every { calculator.multiply(2, 3) } returns 6

        // Act - call the mocked method
        val result = calculator.multiply(2, 3)

        // Assert - verify the result
        result shouldBe 6

        // Verify the mock was called
        verify(exactly = 1) { calculator.multiply(2, 3) }
    }
})
```

In this code, we are using MockK to simulate the behavior of the `Calculator` class, instead of using a real instance. A mock of `Calculator` is created and configured with `every { calculator.multiply(2, 3) } returns 6`, which means that when the `multiply(2, 3)` method is called, it will return 6 without performing the actual multiplication. The test then verifies that the result is as expected (6) with `shouldBe 6`, and uses `verify(exactly = 1) { calculator.multiply(2, 3) }` to make sure that the method was called once. This approach is useful for isolating tests and avoiding dependencies on real implementations.

With this, we have reviewed the three most widely used options, although we could have mentioned other options. This, however, is a good starting point for exploring the world of testing. Other tools that could be used are Testcontainers and Spek. The former is used more for integration with databases and normally requires more resources than those already mentioned. The latter is more for BDD-type tests and is not yet widely adopted in the industry, but it is growing little by little.

Summary

Throughout this chapter, we have explored the fundamental aspects of testing in Kotlin, covering unit testing and integration testing, and diving into the most powerful testing frameworks available. We started by understanding why unit testing is essential, not just for catching bugs but for enabling confident refactoring and serving as a form of real-time documentation.

We then moved on to integration testing, where we ensured that different components of an application work together seamlessly. Unlike unit tests, these allow us to detect issues that only arise when multiple modules interact, making them crucial for building robust, real-world applications.

Finally, we explored various testing frameworks that simplify the process, from the familiar JUnit 5 to the expressive Kotest and the specialized MockK for mocking dependencies. Each of these tools brings its own strengths, and you are now equipped to choose the right framework based on the needs of your project.

If there's one thing to take away from this chapter, it's that writing tests is not just about catching errors – it's about writing better, more maintainable code. With a solid testing strategy, you can confidently refactor, scale, and improve your applications without fear of breaking things.

You've come a long way in your Kotlin journey. We've explored Kotlin from the ground up, transitioning from a Java mindset to writing concise, expressive, and modern Kotlin code. Now, with testing as your safety net, you have everything you need to build reliable and scalable applications.

We sincerely appreciate the trust you've placed in this book. My goal was not just to teach Kotlin but to help you think in Kotlin, to embrace its idiomatic approach and feel confident applying it in real-world projects.

This might be the last chapter, but it's just the beginning of what you can build with Kotlin. Keep coding, keep testing, and, most importantly, keep growing as a developer.

14

Domain-Specific Languages in Kotlin

In the world of software development, communication is key. We communicate with machines through code, and with fellow developers through the structure and clarity of that code. **Domain-Specific Languages (DSLs)** are a powerful tool to enhance this communication, allowing us to express solutions in a language that is closely aligned with a particular problem domain. Kotlin, with its expressive syntax and powerful features, stands out as an excellent language for creating elegant and type-safe internal DSLs.

This chapter will guide you through the process of building a DSL in Kotlin. We'll take a practical example that we have already used in previous chapters – defining a `Book` object with its authors and chapters – and construct a DSL that makes the creation of such objects intuitive and readable.

We have learned about lambdas with and without receivers, about extension functions, operator overloading, high-order functions, and type inference. All this knowledge is a prerequisite to address the concept of DSLs, and using a DSL makes your concept more accessible even for non-developers.

In this chapter, we will learn about the following:

- DSLs
- How to build and enhance a DSL
- Benefits and trade-offs of DSLs

Understanding DSLs

A **DSL** is a computer language specialized for a particular application domain. Unlike a **general-purpose language** (**GPL**) such as Kotlin, Java, or Python, which is designed to solve a wide array of problems, a DSL is tailored for a specific set of tasks or a particular domain.

There are generally two types of DSLs:

- **External DSLs:** These are languages parsed independently of the host GPL. They have their own syntax, parser, and often, an interpreter or compiler. Examples include SQL (for database queries), HTML (for web page structure), or regular expressions. Creating external DSLs is a significant undertaking, requiring expertise in language design and parsing technologies. Another example is how a Kotlin DSL is used for writing Gradle configuration scripts.
- **Internal DSLs (or embedded DSLs):** These are created within an existing GPL. An internal DSL is essentially a particular way of using the host language, leveraging its syntax and features to create a more domain-specific API. The result is code that still compiles with the host language's compiler but reads like a specialized language. This is the type of DSL we will focus on in this chapter, using Kotlin as our host language.

Some of the most prominent advantages of using DSLs are as follows:

- **Improved readability and expressiveness**: DSLs allow you to express concepts in a way that is natural to the problem domain, making the code easier to understand, even for non-programmers or domain experts.
- **Increased productivity**: By providing high-level constructs tailored to the domain, DSLs can reduce the amount of boilerplate code needed to perform common tasks.
- **Enhanced communication**: They can serve as a common language between developers and domain experts, fostering better collaboration.
- **Domain focus:** DSLs help keep the focus on the *what* (the problem domain logic) rather than the *how* (the low-level implementation details).
- **Type safety (for internal DSLs)**: When built with a statically-typed language such as Kotlin, internal DSLs benefit from compile-time checks, catching errors early.

Why Kotlin for DSLs?

Kotlin offers a rich set of features that make it exceptionally well-suited for creating internal DSLs. These features allow for a fluent, concise, and type-safe syntax.

- **Lambdas with receivers (this context)**: This is arguably the cornerstone of Kotlin DSLs. A lambda with a receiver is a function literal that can be called as if it were an extension function of a specific "receiver" object. Inside the lambda, you can access members of this receiver object implicitly (without needing to qualify them with `this`). This allows for structured, builder-like syntax.

  ```
  // Example: html { body { h1 { ... } } }
  // Here, 'body' is called on an 'HTML' receiver, 'h1' on a 'Body'
  receiver.
  ```

  We described lambdas with receivers extensively in *Chapter 9*.

- **Extension functions**: Kotlin allows you to extend existing classes with new functionality without inheriting from them. This is useful for adding DSL-specific methods to classes – even those you don't own.

  ```
  fun String.greet(): String {
      return "Hello, $this!"
  }
  // "World".greet() // "Hello, World!"
  ```

  Extension functions were discussed in *Chapter 4*.

- **Infix functions**: Functions marked with the `infix` keyword can be called using `infix` notation (omitting the dot and parentheses for single-parameter functions). This can lead to more natural-looking expressions in a DSL.

  ```
  infix fun Int.plusCustom(other: Int): Int = this + other
  // val sum = 5 plusCustom 3 // sum is 8
  ```

  Infix functions have not been discussed in this book. For more details on them, please look at `https://kotlinlang.org/docs/functions.html#infix-notation`.

- **Operator overloading**: Kotlin allows you to provide custom implementations for a predefined set of operators (such as +, *, `()`, etc.) on your types. This can make DSL expressions more concise and intuitive. For example, you could overload the unary plus operator + to add items to a collection within a DSL.

- **Higher-order functions and function literals**: Kotlin treats functions as first-class citizens. The ability to pass functions as arguments and return them from other functions, combined with concise lambda syntax, is fundamental to building DSLs. We dealt with higher-order functions in great detail in *Chapter 8*.
- **Type inference**: Kotlin's powerful type inference reduces boilerplate, making the DSL cleaner while maintaining static type safety.

These features, when combined, enable the creation of DSLs that are not only readable but also robust and maintainable.

Defining our domain: the book model

Before we build our DSL, let's define the data structures that represent our domain. We have already used the book example in previous chapters. Here, we are going to extend that example a bit. We want to describe a book, which has a title, a number of pages, a list of authors, and a list of chapters.

We'll use Kotlin's `data class` for this, which automatically provides `equals()`, `hashCode()`, `toString()`, `copy()`, and component functions.

Note that while it is possible, and probably better, to split the code into multiple source files, we have opted against it here. For simplicity reasons, all the code is placed into one file, `Main.kt`.

```
data class Author(
    val name: String,
    val country: String
)
data class Chapter(
    val chapterNumber: Int,
    val title: String,
    val pages: Int
)
data class Book(
    val title: String,
    val numberOfPages: Int,
    val authors: List<Author>,
    val chapters: List<Chapter>
)
```

Our goal is to create a DSL that allows us to define instances of these data classes in a structured and readable way, like this (this is what we're aiming for):

```
val myBook = book {
    title = "Kotlin for Pragmatic Programmers"
    numberOfPages = 450
    authors {
        author {
            name = "José Dimas Luján"
            country = "Mexico"
        }
        author {
            name = "Ron Veen"
            country = "The Netherlands"
        }
    }
    chapters {
        chapter {
            chapterNumber = 1
            title = "An introduction to Kotlin and its basic types"
            pages = 30
        }
        chapter {
            chapterNumber = 2
            title = "Interoperability, Gradle and Mave"
            pages = 37
        }
        // ... more chapters
    }
}
```

This syntax is much more declarative and easier to read than manually instantiating objects and adding them to lists.

Building the book DSL – step by step

We'll build our DSL from the inside out, starting with the nested component functions and ending with the top-level book function – the builder classes.

The core idea behind many Kotlin DSLs is the **Type-Safe Builder** pattern. Builders are helper classes that accumulate data and then create the final immutable object. Each builder will expose properties and methods that correspond to the DSL syntax we want to achieve.

We'll need builders for `Book`, `Author` (within a list of authors), and `Chapter` (within a list of chapters).

AuthorBuilder

This builder will help construct an `Author` object.

Add the following code:

```
class AuthorBuilder {
    var name: String = ""
    var country: String = ""
    fun build(): Author {
        if (name.isBlank()) throw IllegalArgumentException("Author name
cannot be blank.")
        if (country.isBlank()) throw IllegalArgumentException("Author
country cannot be blank.")
        return Author(name, country)
    }
}
```

We can see the following in the preceding code:

- It has mutable properties (`name`, `country`) that will be set through the DSL.
- The `build()` method validates the data and creates the immutable `Author` instance.

AuthorsBuilder

This builder will manage a list of authors. It will provide a way to define individual authors within an `author` { ... } block.

Add this below the code from the previous section.

```
class AuthorsBuilder {
    private val authorsList = mutableListOf<Author>()
    // This function will be the entry point for defining an author within
the 'authors' block.
    // It takes a lambda with AuthorBuilder as its receiver.
```

```
    fun author(block: AuthorBuilder.() -> Unit) {
        val builder = AuthorBuilder()
        builder.block() // Apply the user's configuration to the
AuthorBuilder instance
        authorsList.add(builder.build()) // Build the Author and add to
the list
    }
    fun build(): List<Author> = authorsList.toList() // Return an
immutable list
}
```

Let's try to understand the preceding code:

- `authorsList`: A mutable list to temporarily store authors as they are being defined.
- `author(block: AuthorBuilder.() -> Unit)`: This is a key function.
- It takes a lambda (block) which has `AuthorBuilder` as its receiver. This means within the lambda provided by the user (e.g., author { name = "..." }), this refers to an `AuthorBuilder` instance.
- It creates `AuthorBuilder`, applies the configuration from the lambda to it, builds `Author`, and adds it to the list.
- `build()`: Returns an immutable `List<Author>`.

ChapterBuilder

Similar to `AuthorBuilder`, this will construct a `Chapter` object.

Add this code below the code we added in the previous section.

```
class ChapterBuilder {
    var chapterNumber: Int = 0
    var title: String = ""
    var pages: Int = 0
    fun build(): Chapter {
        if (chapterNumber <= 0) throw IllegalArgumentException("Chapter
number must be positive.")
        if (title.isBlank()) throw IllegalArgumentException("Chapter title
cannot be blank.")
        if (pages <= 0) throw IllegalArgumentException("Chapter pages must
be positive.")
        return Chapter(chapterNumber, title, pages)
```

```
    }
}
```

ChaptersBuilder

Similar to `AuthorsBuilder`, this will manage a list of chapters.

Add this code below all the other code.

```
class ChaptersBuilder {
    private val chaptersList = mutableListOf<Chapter>()
    fun chapter(block: ChapterBuilder.() -> Unit) {
        val builder = ChapterBuilder()
        builder.block()
        chaptersList.add(builder.build())
    }
    fun build(): List<Chapter> = chaptersList.toList()
}
```

BookBuilder

This is the main builder for the `Book` object. It will allow setting the title and number of pages, and will host the authors and chapters blocks.

Add this code below the code from the `ChapterBuilders` section.

```
class BookBuilder {
    var title: String = ""
    var numberOfPages: Int = 0
    private var authorsList: List<Author> = emptyList()
    private var chaptersList: List<Chapter> = emptyList()
    // Function to define authors using the AuthorsBuilder
    fun authors(block: AuthorsBuilder.() -> Unit) {
        val builder = AuthorsBuilder()
        builder.block()
        authorsList = builder.build()
    }
    // Function to define chapters using the ChaptersBuilder
    fun chapters(block: ChaptersBuilder.() -> Unit) {
        val builder = ChaptersBuilder()
        builder.block()
```

```
        chaptersList = builder.build()
    }
    fun build(): Book {
        if (title.isBlank()) throw IllegalArgumentException("Book title 
cannot be blank.")
        if (numberOfPages <= 0) throw IllegalArgumentException("Number of 
pages must be positive.")
        // Optionally, add validation for authors and chapters (e.g., must 
not be empty)
        // if (authorsList.isEmpty()) throw IllegalArgumentException("A 
book must have at least one author.")
        // if (chaptersList.isEmpty()) throw IllegalArgumentException("A 
book must have at least one chapter.")
        return Book(title, numberOfPages, authorsList, chaptersList)
    }
}
```

Let's try to understand this code:

- It has mutable properties for `title` and `numberOfPages`.
- `authors(block: AuthorsBuilder.() -> Unit)`: This function enables the `authors` { ... } block. It creates an `AuthorsBuilder`, lets the user configure it via the lambda, and then gets the list of built `Author` objects.
- `chapters(block: ChaptersBuilder.() -> Unit)`: Similarly enables the `chapters` { ... } block.
- `build()`: Validates and constructs the final `Book` object.

The top-level DSL entry point: book function

Now we need a way to start our DSL. A common practice is to define a top-level function that takes a lambda with our main builder (`BookBuilder`) as its receiver.

Add this code below all the other preceding code:

```
// This is the main entry point for our DSL.
// It takes a lambda with BookBuilder as its receiver.
fun book(block: BookBuilder.() -> Unit): Book {
    val builder = BookBuilder() // Create an instance of our main builder
    builder.block()             // Execute the user-provided lambda on 
this builder instance.
```

```
                                    // Inside the lambda, 'this' will refer to
'builder'.
    return builder.build()          // Construct and return the final Book
object.
}
```

Let's break down `fun book(block: BookBuilder.() -> Unit): Book`:

- `fun book(...)`: This defines a function named `book`.
- `block: BookBuilder.() -> Unit`: This is the crucial part. It declares a parameter named `block`.
- The type of block is `BookBuilder.() -> Unit`. This signifies a "lambda with a receiver."
- `BookBuilder.` means that inside this lambda, this will refer to an instance of `BookBuilder`. All public members of `BookBuilder` (such as `title`, `numberOfPages`, `authors {}`, and `chapters {}`) can be accessed directly.
- `-> Unit` means this lambda doesn't need to return any specific value.
- `: Book`: The `book` function itself will return a fully constructed `Book` object.

Here's what happens inside this function:

- `val builder = BookBuilder()`: We create an instance of `BookBuilder`.
- `builder.block()`: We invoke the lambda passed by the user (`block`) *on* our `builder` instance. This is what allows the user to write `title = "..."` directly within the `book { ... }` block, as those assignments are effectively `builder.title = "..."`.
- `return builder.build()`: After the lambda has configured the builder, we call its `build()` method to get the final `Book` object.

Using the DSL

With all the pieces in place (`BookModel.kt`, `BookDslBuilders.kt`, `BookDsl.kt`), we can now use our DSL:

Finally, add this `main` method below all the other code.

```
fun main() {
    val myNovel = book {
        title = "The Adventures of Kotlin DSL"
        numberOfPages = 320
        authors {
            author {
```

```
                name = "Alex Koder"
                country = "Kotlinland"
            }
            author {
                name = "Lexi Syntax"
                country = "TypeSafia"
            }
        }
        chapters {
            chapter {
                chapterNumber = 1
                title = "The Beginning"
                pages = 15
            }
            chapter {
                chapterNumber = 2
                title = "The Lambda with Receiver"
                pages = 25
            }
            chapter {
                chapterNumber = 3
                title = "Building Blocks"
                pages = 40
            }
            // ... more chapters
        }
    }
    println("Book Created: ${myNovel.title}")
    println("Number of Pages: ${myNovel.numberOfPages}")
    myNovel.authors.forEachIndexed { index, author ->
        println("Author ${index + 1}: ${author.name} from ${author.
country}")
    }
    myNovel.chapters.forEach { chapter ->
        println("Chapter ${chapter.chapterNumber}: ${chapter.title}
(${chapter.pages} pages)")
    }
    // Example of trying to create an invalid book (will throw an
exception)
```

```
    try {
        val invalidBook = book {
            // title = "Incomplete Book" // Missing title
            numberOfPages = 100
            authors {
                author {
                    name = "Ron Veen"
                    country = "The Netherlands"
                }
            }
            chapters {
                chapter {
                    chapterNumber = 1
                    title = "Intro"
                    pages = 10
                }
            }
        }
        println(invalidBook)
    } catch (e: IllegalArgumentException) {
        println("Error creating book: ${e.message}")
    }
}
```

Let's take a closer look at the authors block:

When the DSL encounters the following:

```
authors { // This is a call to BookBuilder.authors(lambda)
    author { // This is a call to AuthorsBuilder.author(lambda)
        name = "Ron Veen" // Inside AuthorBuilder's lambda: this.name =
"Ron Veen"
        country = "The Netherlands" // this.country = " he Netherlands "
    }
}
```

The `authors { ... }` block is actually calling the `authors(block: AuthorsBuilder.() -> Unit)` function on the current `BookBuilder` instance.

1. Inside `BookBuilder.authors()`, a new `AuthorsBuilder` instance is created.
2. The `{ author { ... } }` lambda is then executed with this `AuthorsBuilder` instance as its receiver.
3. The `author { ... }` call within that lambda invokes `AuthorsBuilder.author(block: AuthorBuilder.() -> Unit)`.
4. Inside `AuthorsBuilder.author()`, a new `AuthorBuilder` is created.
5. The inner `{ name = "..."; country = "..." }` lambda is executed with this `AuthorBuilder` as its receiver. The `name` and `country` properties are set on it.
6. `AuthorBuilder.build()` is called, creating an `Author` object, which is added to the `AuthorsBuilder` internal list.
7. This process repeats for each `author { ... }` block.
8. Finally, `AuthorsBuilder.build()` is called, returning `List<Author>` to the `BookBuilder`.

The same logic applies to the `chapters { ... }` block. This hierarchical application of lambdas with receivers is what gives Kotlin DSLs their structured and intuitive feel.

Enhancing the DSL (optional features)

Our current DSL is quite functional and readable. However, Kotlin offers more features that could be used to refine or extend DSLs.

Infix functions for property assignment (alternative style)

For some DSLs, using infix functions for assignments can make the syntax feel even more like a natural language. For example, instead of `name = "Alex Koder"`, you might want `name to "Alex Koder"`.

To achieve this, you could define an infix extension function:

```
// A generic infix function for assignment-like operations in builders
infix fun <T> Property<T>.to(value: T) {
    this.set(value)
}
// Helper class to wrap properties, needed for the 'to' infix function
class Property<T>(private val setter: (T) -> Unit) {
    fun set(value: T) = setter(value)
```

```
}
// Modify AuthorBuilder (and others)
class AuthorBuilder {
    private var _name: String = ""
    private var _country: String = ""
    val name: Property<String> = Property { _name = it }
    val country: Property<String> = Property { _country = it }
    fun build(): Author {
        if (_name.isBlank()) throw IllegalArgumentException("Author name
cannot be blank.")
        // ... rest of build
        return Author(_name, _country)
    }
}
```

Then, usage would look like this:

```
author {
    name to "José Dimas Luján"
    country to "Mexico"
}
```

This is a stylistic choice. The standard property assignment (`name = "value"`) is often clearer and more idiomatic Kotlin for simple assignments. Infix functions shine more when they represent a relationship or operation (e.g., key to value for creating map entries). For this book DSL, the standard assignment is likely sufficient and more straightforward.

Using invoke for more concise list additions

If you wanted to make adding authors or chapters slightly more concise, you could potentially use operator overloading with `invoke` on `AuthorsBuilder` or `ChaptersBuilder`.

```
// Example idea for AuthorsBuilder (stylistic choice)
class AuthorsBuilder {
    // ...
    operator fun invoke(block: AuthorBuilder.() -> Unit) {
         author(block) // Delegate to the existing author function
     }
}
```

If you did this, you could write the following:

```
authors {
    invoke {
        name = "..."
        country = "..."
    }
}
```

This might be slightly more concise but could also be less explicit than `author { ... }`. For clarity, especially in a DSL being taught, the explicit `author { ... }` and `chapter { ... }` method names are preferable.

Benefits and trade-offs of our book DSL

The book DSL we created allows us to define a book, its authors, and its chapters. It does so in a way that is very intuitive and concise.

The benefits are as follows:

- **Readability**: The DSL provides a clear, structured way to define book objects. The hierarchical nature mirrors the actual structure of a book.
- **Type safety**: Kotlin's compiler ensures that all parts of the DSL are used correctly (e.g., you can't put a chapter block inside an authors block directly or assign a number to a title).
- **Reduced boilerplate**: Compare the DSL usage to manually creating `Author` objects, adding them to `ArrayLists`, and then passing those to the `Book` constructor. The DSL is significantly more concise.
- **Maintainability**: If the structure of the book or its components changes, the DSL builders can be updated, and the compiler will help identify areas in the client code that need adjustment.
- **Discoverability (with IDE support)**: Kotlin IDEs offer excellent autocompletion. Within a `book { ... }` block, the IDE will suggest `title`, `numberOfPages`, `authors { ... }`, and `chapters { ... }`, guiding the user.

There are certain trade-offs and considerations too:

- **Initial development effort**: Designing and implementing a DSL requires an upfront investment of time and thought. For very simple object creation, it might be overkill.
- **Learning curve**: Users of the DSL need to understand its syntax and structure, though a well-designed internal DSL should be intuitive.

- **Complexity for simple cases**: If you only ever create one or two books with minimal details, the DSL machinery might seem heavy. However, its benefits scale with complexity and frequency of use.
- **Potential for over-engineering**: It's possible to create DSLs that are too complex or try to be too "magical," sacrificing clarity. The key is to find a balance that enhances readability and productivity for the specific domain.

For our Book example, the DSL provides a clear win in terms of organizing complex object creation.

Summary

Kotlin's powerful features, especially lambdas with receivers, make it an ideal language for crafting internal domain-specific languages. By using the type-safe builder pattern, we can create APIs that are not only expressive and readable but also benefit from Kotlin's static typing and excellent IDE support.

In this chapter, we successfully built a DSL for defining `Book` objects. We saw how to structure builders, use lambdas with receivers to create nested configurations, and provide a clean entry point for the DSL. The resulting code for creating book instances is declarative, closely mirrors the domain's structure, and is significantly cleaner than manual object instantiation.

15

Unlock Your Book's Exclusive Benefits

Your copy of this book comes with the following exclusive benefits:

- Next-gen Packt Reader
- AI assistant (beta)
- DRM-free PDF/ePub downloads

Use the following guide to unlock them if you haven't already. The process takes just a few minutes and needs to be done only once.

How to unlock these benefits in three easy steps

Step 1

Have your purchase invoice for this book ready, as you'll need it in *Step 3*. If you received a physical invoice, scan it on your phone and have it ready as either a PDF, JPG, or PNG.

For more help on finding your invoice, visit `https://www.packtpub.com/unlock-benefits/help`.

Note: Did you buy this book directly from Packt? You don't need an invoice. After completing Step 2, you can jump straight to your exclusive content.

Step 2

Scan this QR code or go to `https://packtpub.com/unlock`.

On the page that opens (which will look similar to *Figure 15.1* if you're on desktop), search for this book by name. Make sure you select the correct edition.

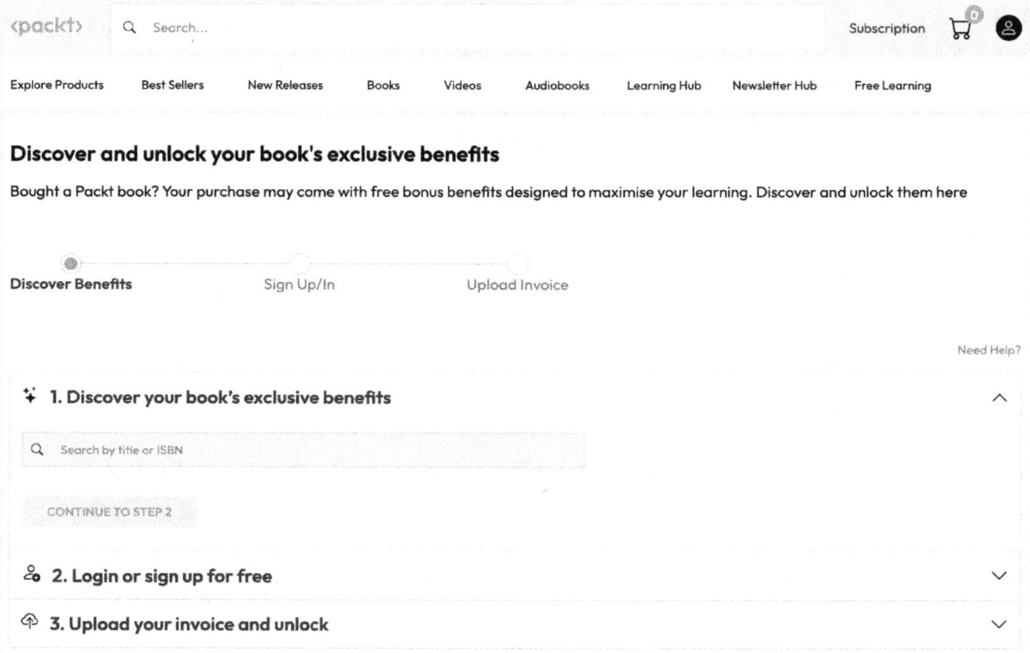

Figure 15.1 – Packt unlock landing page on desktop

Step 3

Once you've selected your book, sign in to your Packt account or create a new one for free. Once you're logged in, upload your invoice. It can be in PDF, PNG, or JPG format and must be no larger than 10 MB. Follow the rest of the instructions on the screen to complete the process.

Need help?

If you get stuck and need help, visit `https://www.packtpub.com/unlock-benefits/help` for a detailed FAQ on how to find your invoices and more. The following QR code will take you to the help page directly:

Note: If you are still facing issues, reach out to `customercare@packt.com`.

Other Books You May Enjoy

If you enjoyed this book, you may be interested in these other books by Packt:

Software Architecture with Kotlin

Jason (Tsz Shun) Chow

ISBN: 978-1-83546-186-0

- Master the fundamental principles of architecture and design
- Explore common architectural styles and their applicable scenarios
- Analyze, break down, compare, and design architectural styles to solve practical problems
- Reason, negotiate, and make difficult choices in the absence of ideal solutions
- Mitigate risks when making compromises and trade-offs
- Create scalable, sustainable, maintainable, and extendable software systems
- Use the Kotlin programming language to achieve your architectural goals

Kotlin Design Patterns and Best Practices

Alexey Soshin

ISBN: 978-1-80512-776-5

- Utilize functional programming and coroutines with the Arrow framework
- Use classical design patterns in the Kotlin programming language
- Scale your applications with reactive and concurrent design patterns
- Discover best practices in Kotlin and explore its new features
- Apply the key principles of functional programming to Kotlin
- Find out how to write idiomatic Kotlin code and learn which patterns to avoid
- Harness the power of Kotlin to design concurrent and reliable systems with ease
- Create an effective microservice with Kotlin and the Ktor framework

Packt is searching for authors like you

If you're interested in becoming an author for Packt, please visit `authors.packt.com` and apply today. We have worked with thousands of developers and tech professionals, just like you, to help them share their insight with the global tech community. You can make a general application, apply for a specific hot topic that we are recruiting an author for, or submit your own idea.

Share your thoughts

Now you've finished *Kotlin for Java Developers*, we'd love to hear your thoughts! Scan the QR code below to go straight to the Amazon review page for this book and share your feedback or leave a review on the site that you purchased it from.

`https://packt.link/r/1835884830`

Your review is important to us and the tech community and will help us make sure we're delivering excellent quality content.

Join us on Discord!

Read this book alongside other users, developers, experts, and the author himself.

Ask questions, provide solutions to other readers, chat with the authors via Ask Me Anything sessions, and much more. Scan the QR or visit the link to join the community.

https://packt.link/deep-engineering-java

Index

G

H

I

J

T

U

V

W

www.ingramcontent.com/pod-product-compliance
Lightning Source LLC
LaVergne TN
LVHW060542061126
851857LV00017B/1874
9781835884829